Diana Jones

# Happy Campers 3

Teacher's Edition

macmillan
education

# Table of Contents

## Contents



## Student Resources

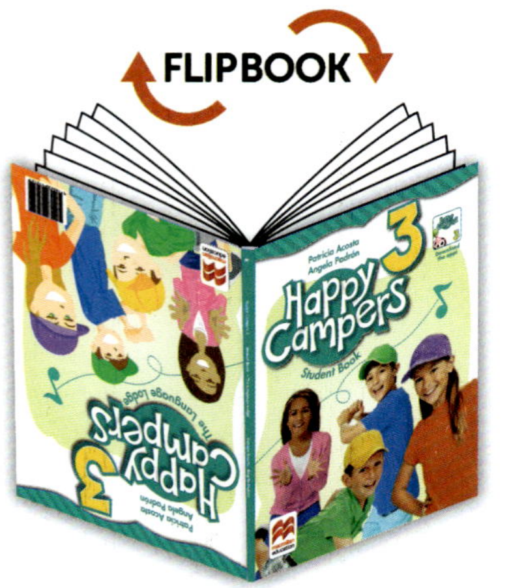


**Student Book** and
**The Language Lodge** Flipbook

**Skills Book**

**Happy Campers app**

# About Happy Campers

***Happy Campers*** is designed to provide a learning environment in which teachers and students feel a continuous sense of **achievement** and **satisfaction**. Lessons and activities are focused on simple, achievable goals that build confidence and encourage a **positive attitude** toward English language learning. By doing the activities in *Happy Campers*, students become part of a **child-centered community**—they work together to meet goals, sing, cheer, and echo while doing tasks and, above all have fun.

Positive Environment
+ Manageable Input
+ Practice

= Learning English

## Teacher Resources

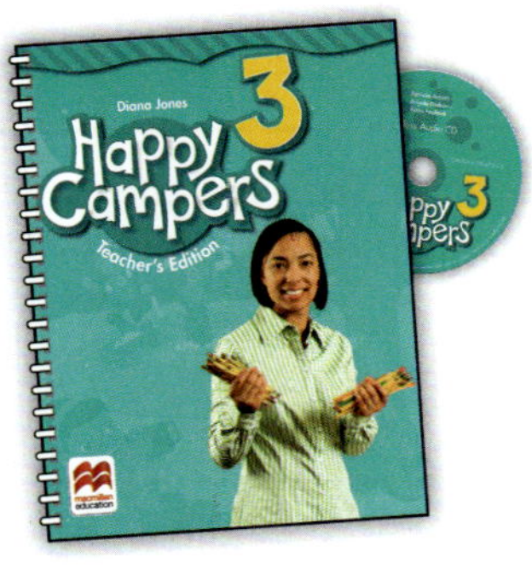


**Teacher's Edition**
**Class Audio CD**
Access code for
**Teacher's Resource Center**

**Teacher's Resource Center**
**www.macmillanyounglearners.com/happycampers**

# Scope and Sequence

| Unit | Pages | Vocabulary | Grammar |
|---|---|---|---|
| 1 | 8–15 | **Numbers:** numbers 10–100<br>**Family:** grandparents, parents, aunt, uncle, cousin, niece, nephew | How old is he? He's ninety-nine.<br>Who is she? She's my aunt. Who are they? They're my grandparents. |
| 2 | 16–23 | **Months of the Year:** January, February, March, April, May, June, July, August, September, October, November, December<br>**Ordinal Numbers:** ordinal numbers 1st–31st | When's your birthday? It's in August.<br>What's the date today? Today is October fifteenth. |
| 3 | 24–31 | **Times of Day / Adverbs of Time:** in the morning, in the afternoon, in the evening, at night, noon, midnight, early, late<br>**Daily Routine:** get up, eat breakfast, go to school, eat lunch, eat dinner, go to bed | What time is it? It's 2 o'clock. It's 2:30. It's noon.<br>What time do you eat breakfast? At 7 o'clock in the morning. |
| 4 | 32–39 | **Sports:** baseball, basketball, football, golf, ping pong, soccer, tennis, volleyball<br>**At Home:** listen to music, talk on the phone, watch TV, take pictures, do homework, work on the computer | I'm (not) playing football. We're (not) playing volleyball.<br>He's listening to music. They're doing homework. |
| 5 | 40–47 | **At the Park:** climb trees, have a picnic, play ball, play on the swings, ride a bike, ride a skateboard, run, take a walk<br>**Chores:** clean, wash the dishes, sweep the floor, feed the pets, take out the trash, set the table, make a snack, wash the car | What are you doing? I'm (not) riding a bike. We're (not) running.<br>What's he doing? He's washing the dishes. What are they doing? They're sweeping. |
| 6 | 48–55 | **Clothes:** T-shirt, pants, cap, shorts, jeans, swimsuit, sandals, sneakers<br>**At the Beach:** swim, sleep, fly a kite, sail a boat, eat ice cream, build a sandcastle | What are you wearing? I'm wearing sneakers. Are you wearing shorts? Yes, I am.<br>Is she swimming? Yes, she is. She isn't sleeping. |
| 7 | 56–63 | **Party Food:** cake, chips, sandwiches, candy, juice, lemonade, popcorn, soda<br>**Party Time:** sing, dance, bake a cake, buy snacks, send invitations, make decorations | Are they eating cake? Yes, they are. Are they drinking soda? No, they aren't.<br>We're making decorations. Are you baking a cake? Yes, we are. |
| 8 | 64–71 | **Abilities:** draw, hop, paint, play the guitar, play the drums, jump rope, speak English, whistle<br>**Vocabulary Review:** Level 3 verbs | I can play the guitar. I can't whistle.<br>Can you whistle? Yes, I can. |

| Extra Practice | Teamwork Activity |
| --- | --- |
| **The Language Lodge:** Pages 1–4<br>**Happy Campers app:** Unit 1 | Family Age Line   |
| **The Language Lodge:** Pages 5–8<br>**Happy Campers app:** Unit 2 | Birthday Calendar   |
| **The Language Lodge:** Pages 9–12<br>**Happy Campers app:** Unit 3 | Daily Activities Poster   |
| **The Language Lodge:** Pages 13–16<br>**Happy Campers app:** Unit 4 | Sing and Act  |
| **The Language Lodge:** Pages 17–20<br>**Happy Campers app:** Unit 5 | Weekly Activities Calendar   |
| **The Language Lodge:** Pages 21–24<br>**Happy Campers app:** Unit 6 | Favorite Activities Chart   |
| **The Language Lodge:** Pages 25–28<br>**Happy Campers app:** Unit 7 | Party Jobs Chart   |
| **The Language Lodge:** Pages 29–32<br>**Happy Campers app:** Unit 8 | Abilities Chart   |

## **Class-building activities** allow students to participate equally.

**Student Book** lessons are organized around a **content centerpiece** used in different ways across **two** lessons, providing plenty of exposure and practice. A **musicalized echo** activity allows students to see, hear, and pronounce new vocabulary in a safe environment. The Grammar Snapshot! provides examples of the new grammar, and **scaffolded activities** help students work out the corresponding grammar rules.

### Lesson 1: Vocabulary

### Lesson 2: Grammar

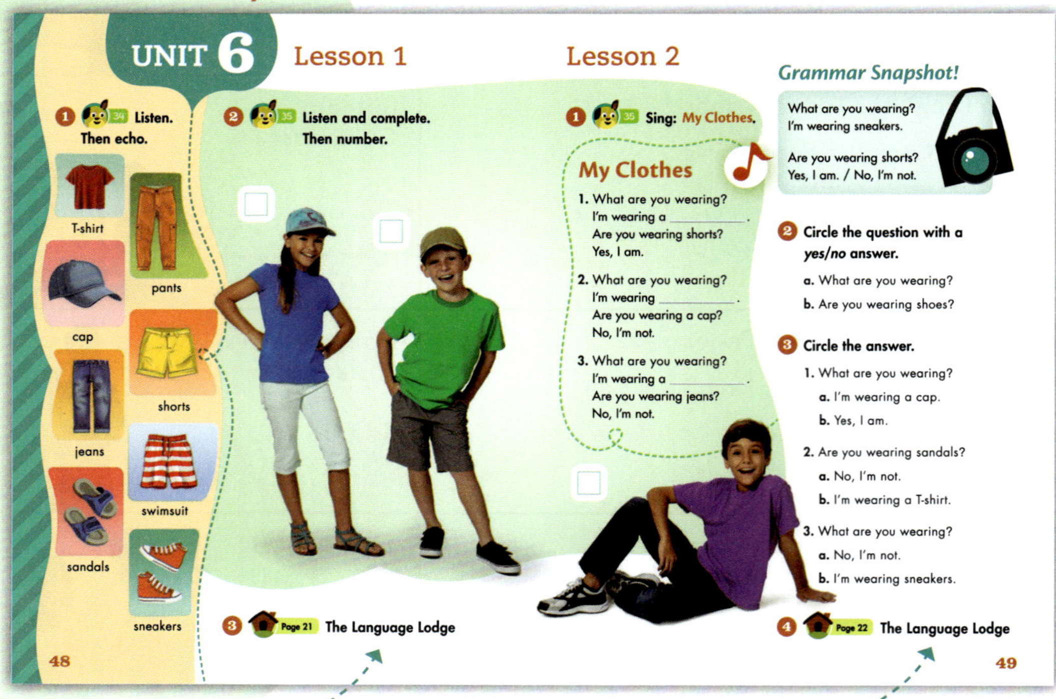
UNIT 6

Lesson 1

1 34 Listen. Then echo.

T-shirt
pants
cap
shorts
jeans
swimsuit
sandals
sneakers

2 35 Listen and complete. Then number.

3 Page 21 The Language Lodge

48

Lesson 2

1 35 Sing: My Clothes.

My Clothes

1. What are you wearing?
I'm wearing a ________.
Are you wearing shorts?
Yes, I am.

2. What are you wearing?
I'm wearing ________.
Are you wearing a cap?
No, I'm not.

3. What are you wearing?
I'm wearing a ________.
Are you wearing jeans?
No, I'm not.

Grammar Snapshot!

What are you wearing?
I'm wearing sneakers.
Are you wearing shorts?
Yes, I am. / No, I'm not.

2 Circle the question with a *yes/no* answer.

a. What are you wearing?
b. Are you wearing shoes?

3 Circle the answer.

1. What are you wearing?
a. I'm wearing a cap.
b. Yes, I am.

2. Are you wearing sandals?
a. No, I'm not.
b. I'm wearing a T-shirt.

3. What are you wearing?
a. No, I'm not.
b. I'm wearing sneakers.

4 Page 22 The Language Lodge

49

### Lesson 1: Vocabulary Practice

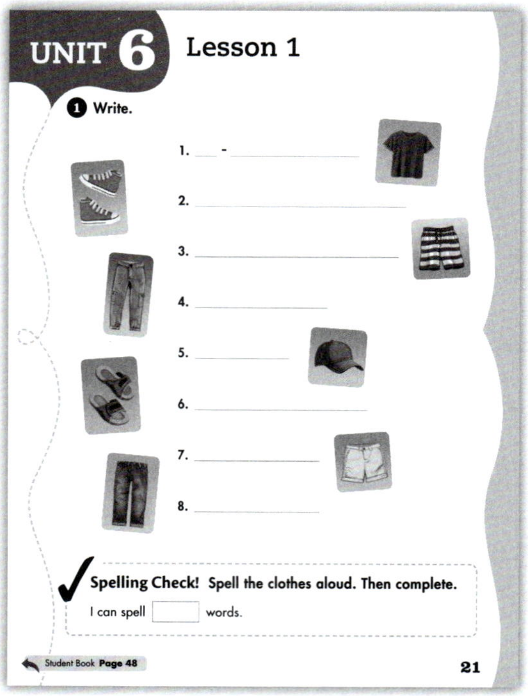
UNIT 6 Lesson 1

1 Write.

1. ___ - ________
2. ________
3. ________
4. ________
5. ________
6. ________
7. ________
8. ________

Spelling Check! Spell the clothes aloud. Then complete.

I can spell [ ] words.

Student Book Page 48

21

### Lesson 2: Grammar Practice

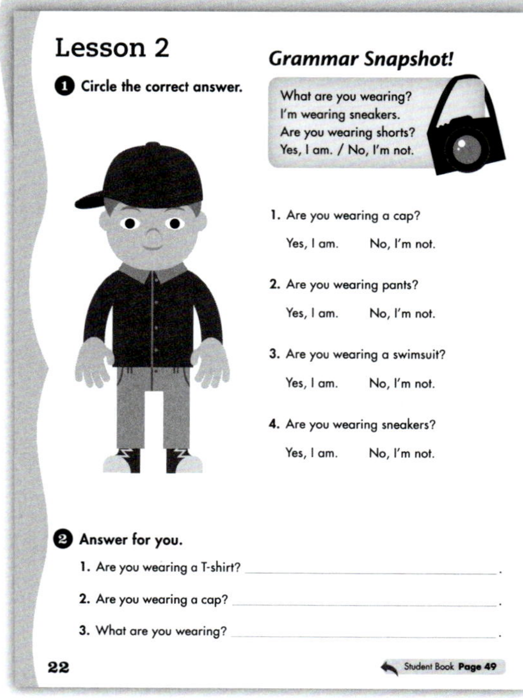
Lesson 2

1 Circle the correct answer.

Grammar Snapshot!

What are you wearing?
I'm wearing sneakers.
Are you wearing shorts?
Yes, I am. / No, I'm not.

1. Are you wearing a cap?
Yes, I am. No, I'm not.

2. Are you wearing pants?
Yes, I am. No, I'm not.

3. Are you wearing a swimsuit?
Yes, I am. No, I'm not.

4. Are you wearing sneakers?
Yes, I am. No, I'm not.

2 Answer for you.

1. Are you wearing a T-shirt? ________.
2. Are you wearing a cap? ________.
3. What are you wearing? ________.

22

Student Book Page 49

Workbook-style pages in The Language Lodge provide **extensive practice** and review activities to help students **remember** and **assimilate** new language. The Spelling Check! self-assessment activity helps students keep track of their progress.

## Lesson 3: Vocabulary in Context

## Lesson 4: Grammar in Context

Lesson 3

Shutterbugs

1 Where are the Shutterbugs?

2 36 Read and listen.



3 37 Dictation! Listen and write. Then say.

1. ______ 2. ______
3. ______ 4. ______
5. ______ 6. ______

4 Page 23 The Language Lodge

50

Lesson 4

1 36 Listen again to Shutterbugs.

2 *Grammar Snapshot!* Write the answers.

1. Is he building a sandcastle? Yes, he is.
2. Is she eating ice cream? ______
3. Is she swimming? ______
4. Is he sleeping? ______

3 38 Listen and cheer!

Is he sailing a boat? Yes, he is! Yes, he is!

Is she eating ice cream? No, she isn't! No, she isn't!

CHEER BOX!

4 Page 24 The Language Lodge

51

"Shutterbugs" is an episodic comic strip story that follows the adventures of a group of children in an after-school camera club. Students will develop reading and listening skills while they learn new vocabulary and grammar structures in context. **Dictation** activities hone receptive and productive skills. The **class-building grammar cheer** provides a memorable example of the new language.

**The Language Lodge** activities can be done in class or at home, and can be quickly checked using the **Presentation Kit**.

## Lesson 3: Vocabulary Practice

Lesson 3

1 Write.

build a sandcastle | eat ice cream | fly a kite
sail a boat | sleep | swim

1. ______ 2. ______
3. ______ 4. ______
5. ______ 6. ______

Spelling Check! Spell the beach activities aloud. Then complete. I can spell ___ words.

Student Book Page 50

23

## Lesson 4: Grammar Practice

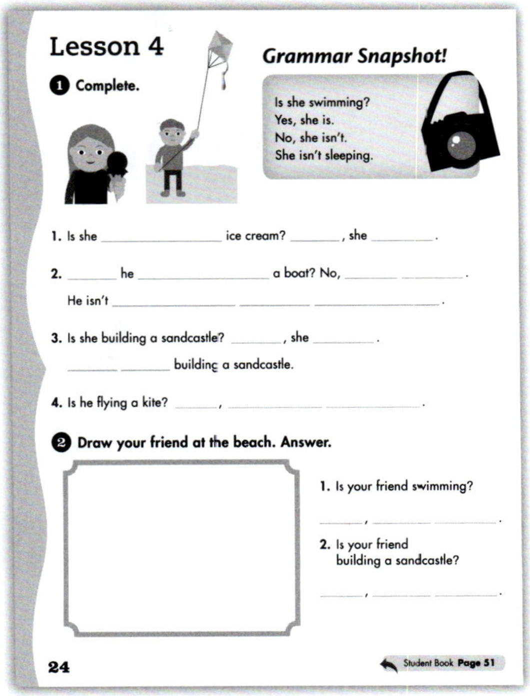
Lesson 4

*Grammar Snapshot!*

Is she swimming?
Yes, she is.
No, she isn't.
She isn't sleeping.

1 Complete.

1. Is she ______ ice cream? ____, she ____.
2. ____ he ______ a boat? No, ____ ____. He isn't ______.
3. Is she building a sandcastle? ____, she ____. ____ ____ building a sandcastle.
4. Is he flying a kite? ____, ____ ____.

2 Draw your friend at the beach. Answer.

1. Is your friend swimming? ____, ____ ____.
2. Is your friend building a sandcastle? ____, ____ ____.

24

Student Book Page 51

Self-assessment develops **critical thinking** skills.

## Lesson 5: Reading

A selection of **fiction** and **nonfiction** texts consolidates and reviews language while developing reading, listening, and fluency skills. Post-reading comprehension activities develop reading skills and comprehension strategies such as identifying details, sequencing events, identifying and describing characters and settings, and comparing and contrasting. Pre-writing and writing activities help students develop skills to write explanatory and descriptive writing pieces.

Lesson 5

1 Circle where the family is.

a. at the park b. at the lake

2 39 Read and listen.

Fun with Grandpa

It's hot and sunny. Eddie, Lily, Mom, and Grandpa are at the lake.
What's Grandpa wearing?
Is he wearing a jacket and pants?
Yes, he is! Oh, Grandpa!

Is Eddie building a sandcastle?
Yes, he is!
Lily isn't building a sandcastle.
She's flying a kite with Mom.

Eddie wants to swim with his sister, Lily.
"Let's swim, Lily! Come on, Grandpa!"

Look! Grandpa is swimming in his clothes!
He's wearing pants and a jacket.
He isn't wearing a swimsuit.
Eddie and Lily are having fun with Grandpa!

52

**Skills-based** practice lessons show **language in context.**

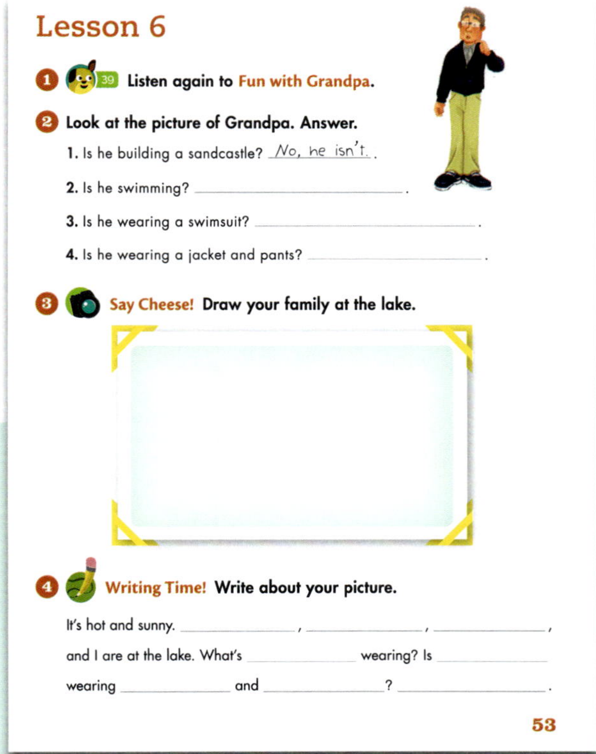
## Lesson 6

1 39 Listen again to Fun with Grandpa.

2 Look at the picture of Grandpa. Answer.

1. Is he building a sandcastle? No, he isn't.
2. Is he swimming? ______.
3. Is he wearing a swimsuit? ______.
4. Is he wearing a jacket and pants? ______.

3 Say Cheese! Draw your family at the lake.

4 Writing Time! Write about your picture.

It's hot and sunny. ______, ______, ______, and I are at the lake. What's ______ wearing? Is ______ wearing ______ and ______? ______.

53

## Lesson 6: Reading Comprehension / Writing

# Think **creatively**, work **collaboratively**!

## Lesson 7: Creative, Collaborative, and Critical Thinking Competencies

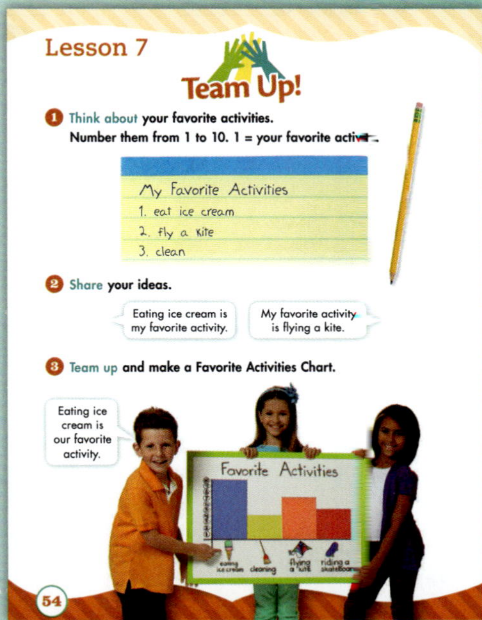
## Lesson 7

Team Up!

1 Think about your favorite activities. Number them from 1 to 10. 1 = your favorite activity.



2 Share your ideas.



3 Team up and make a Favorite Activities Chart.



54

"The Four Cs"—**critical thinking**, **communication**, **collaboration**, and **creativity**—are essential **21st century skills**. Team Up! lessons provide the opportunity for children to create and present a project together while using the target language of the unit in a **child-centered** context.

## Lesson 8: Spelling and Review

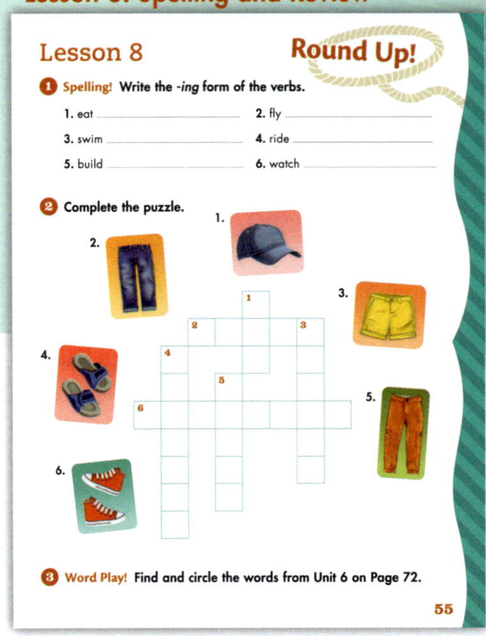
## Lesson 8

Round Up!

1 Spelling! Write the *-ing* form of the verbs.

1. eat ______ 2. fly ______
3. swim ______ 4. ride ______
5. build ______ 6. watch ______

2 Complete the puzzle.

3 Word Play! Find and circle the words from Unit 6 on Page 72.

55

Review and consolidation of new language are essential to learning. Seeing their own progress will make students **happy campers**!

## Skills Book

The *Happy Campers* **Skills Book** is designed to support students in the development of limited, but **specific**, **speaking** and **listening**, **reading**, and **writing** skills.

**Picture Talk** lessons focus on developing simple visual literacy skills to practice vocabulary through speaking and listening.

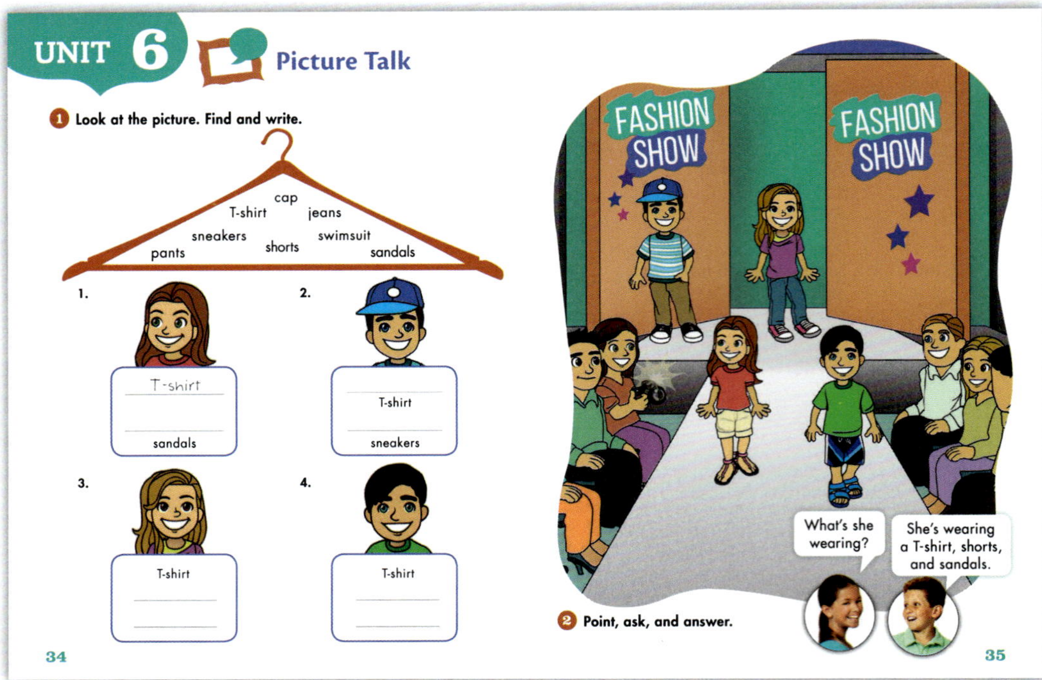


**Real skills.** Really simple.

**Happy Reader** texts include fiction and nonfiction texts. Each reader is supported by a numbered reading guide and a dramatized reading on the **Class Audio CD**. The lesson includes a reading comprehension activity.

Happy Writer

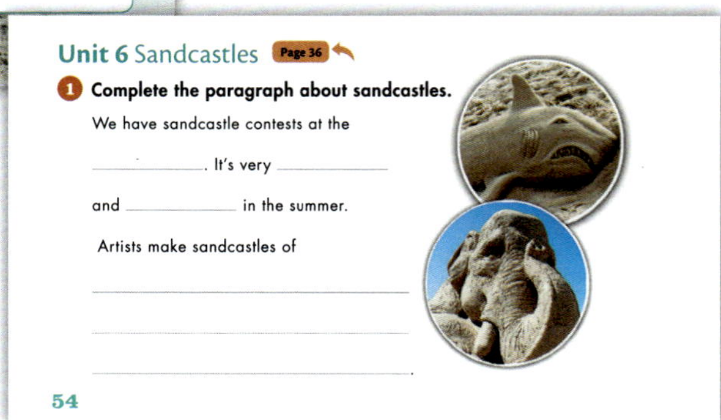


The **Happy Writer** sections at the back of the Skills Book develop specific writing skills such as recalling details, sequencing events, writing an opinion about a text, and personalizing a text.

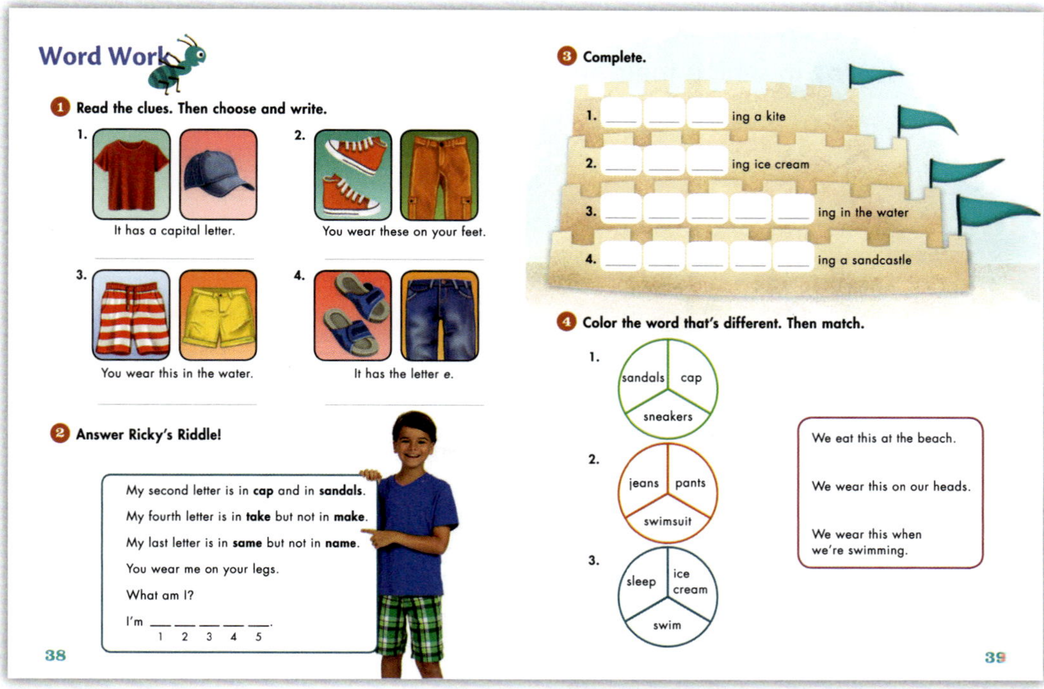

Word Work

1 Read the clues. Then choose and write.

1. It has a capital letter.

2. You wear these on your feet.

3. You wear this in the water.

4. It has the letter *e*.

2 Answer Ricky's Riddle!

My second letter is in **cap** and in **sandals**.
My fourth letter is in **take** but not in **make**.
My last letter is in **same** but not in **name**.
You wear me on your legs.
What am I?
I'm ___ ___ ___ ___ ___.
1 2 3 4 5

38

3 Complete.

1. ___ ___ ___ ing a kite
2. ___ ___ ___ ing ice cream
3. ___ ___ ___ ___ ___ ing in the water
4. ___ ___ ___ ___ ___ ing a sandcastle

4 Color the word that's different. Then match.

1. sandals, cap, sneakers
2. jeans, pants, swimsuit
3. sleep, ice cream, swim

We eat this at the beach.
We wear this on our heads.
We wear this when we're swimming.

39

**Word Work** lessons provide spelling, reading, and thinking activities using the unit vocabulary. Students categorize words, find connections, and recognize spelling patterns.

Ricky's Riddle practices reading comprehension skills and develops **critical thinking** skills such as analyzing information to correctly identify the answer to the riddle.

## Happy Campers app

The **Happy Campers and The Inks 3** is available for download from the App Store[SM] or Google Play™. It provides **game-based learning** to encourage students to practice unit vocabulary, so that learning continues seamlessly from school to home.

Download on the App Store

GET IT ON Google play



**For more information, visit www.macmillanyounglearners.com/happycampers.**

The *Happy Campers* **Teacher's Edition** is designed to help teachers **teach well** and create a **positive environment** in which their **students flourish.**

Each unit opens with a comprehensive overview of the language and skills objectives of the unit, allowing teachers to **prepare** for the lessons ahead.

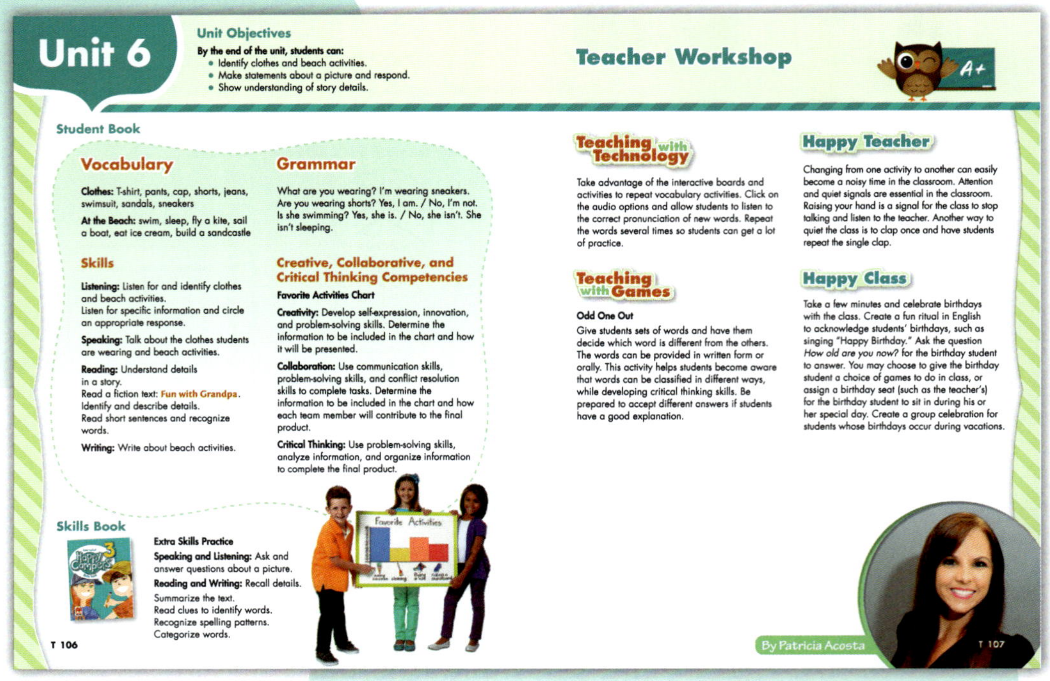

**Unit 6**

**Unit Objectives**

**By the end of the unit, students can:**

- Identify clothes and beach activities.
- Make statements about a picture and respond.
- Show understanding of story details.

**Student Book**

**Vocabulary**

**Clothes:** T-shirt, pants, cap, shorts, jeans, swimsuit, sandals, sneakers

**At the Beach:** swim, sleep, fly a kite, sail a boat, eat ice cream, build a sandcastle

**Grammar**

What are you wearing? I'm wearing sneakers. Are you wearing shorts? Yes, I am. / No, I'm not. Is she swimming? Yes, she is. / No, she isn't. She isn't sleeping.

**Skills**

**Listening:** Listen for and identify clothes and beach activities.
Listen for specific information and circle an appropriate response.

**Speaking:** Talk about the clothes students are wearing and beach activities.

**Reading:** Understand details in a story.
Read a fiction text: Fun with Grandpa.
Identify and describe details.
Read short sentences and recognize words.

**Writing:** Write about beach activities.

**Creative, Collaborative, and Critical Thinking Competencies**

**Favorite Activities Chart**

**Creativity:** Develop self-expression, innovation, and problem-solving skills. Determine the information to be included in the chart and how it will be presented.

**Collaboration:** Use communication skills, problem-solving skills, and conflict resolution skills to complete tasks. Determine the information to be included in the chart and how each team member will contribute to the final product.

**Critical Thinking:** Use problem-solving skills, analyze information, and organize information to complete the final product.

**Skills Book**

**Extra Skills Practice**

**Speaking and Listening:** Ask and answer questions about a picture.

**Reading and Writing:** Recall details.
Summarize the text.
Read clues to identify words.
Recognize spelling patterns.
Categorize words.

T 106

**Teacher Workshop**

**Teaching with Technology**

Take advantage of the interactive boards and activities to repeat vocabulary activities. Click on the audio options and allow students to listen to the correct pronunciation of new words. Repeat the words several times so students can get a lot of practice.

**Teaching with Games**

**Odd One Out**

Give students sets of words and have them decide which word is different from the others. The words can be provided in written form or orally. This activity helps students become aware that words can be classified in different ways, while developing critical thinking skills. Be prepared to accept different answers if students have a good explanation.

**Happy Teacher**

Changing from one activity to another can easily become a noisy time in the classroom. Attention and quiet signals are essential in the classroom. Raising your hand is a signal for the class to stop talking and listen to the teacher. Another way to quiet the class is to clap once and have students repeat the single clap.

**Happy Class**

Take a few minutes and celebrate birthdays with the class. Create a fun ritual in English to acknowledge students' birthdays, such as singing "Happy Birthday." Ask the question *How old are you now?* for the birthday student to answer. You may choose to give the birthday student a choice of games to do in class, or assign a birthday seat (such as the teacher's) for the birthday student to sit in during his or her special day. Create a group celebration for students whose birthdays occur during vacations.

By Patricia Acosta

T 107

A unique program of ideas from **experienced teacher trainers** enhances the classroom experience. Workshops include ideas on how to use technology in the classroom, teaching with games, and classroom management tips to create a happy, learning-rich classroom environment.

## Additional Resources

**Presentation Kit** icon

**Happy Campers app** icon

**The Language Lodge** icon

**Skills Book** icon

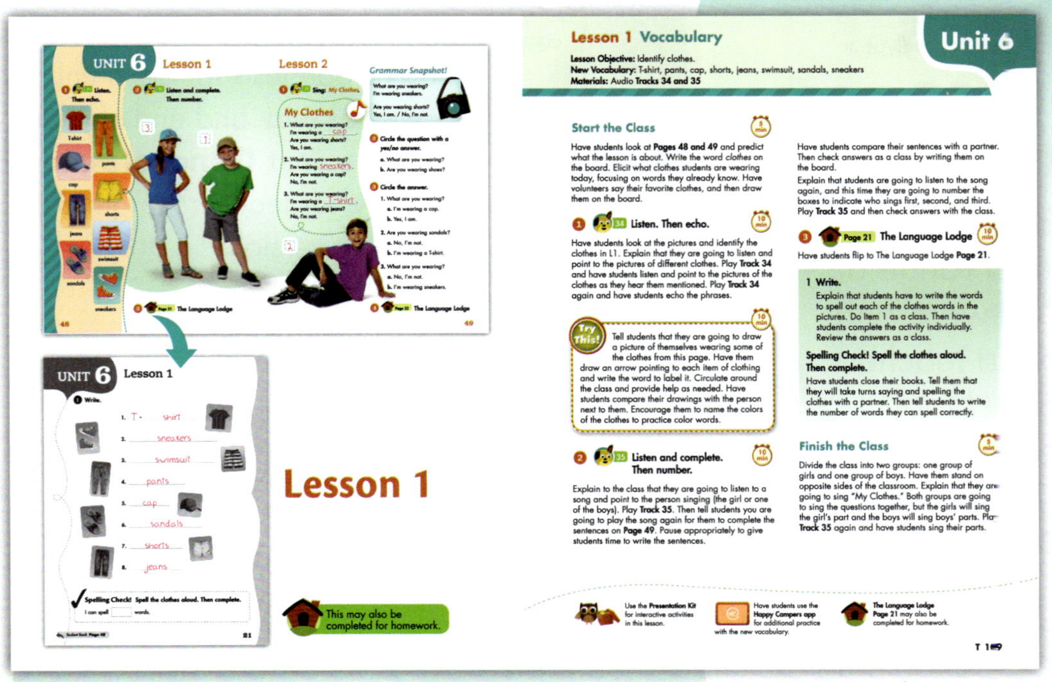


The lesson notes provide a step-by-step guide for teachers to deliver effective, time-efficient classes. Ideas to **start** and **finish** each class, and a **pacing guide** (5 min) are provided to support teachers in keeping students on track.

The interleaved pages provide the Student Book and corresponding pages from The Language Lodge.

Try This! sections in each lesson feature alternative activities to incorporate into everyday teaching practice.

## Continuing professional development, **class by class**.

## Class Audio CD

The **Class Audio CD** contains audio tracks for all listening activities across the Student Book and Skills Book. The *Happy Campers* **vibrant music and vocal program** includes echoes, songs, cheers, comic strip stories, and fiction and nonfiction reading and listening texts.

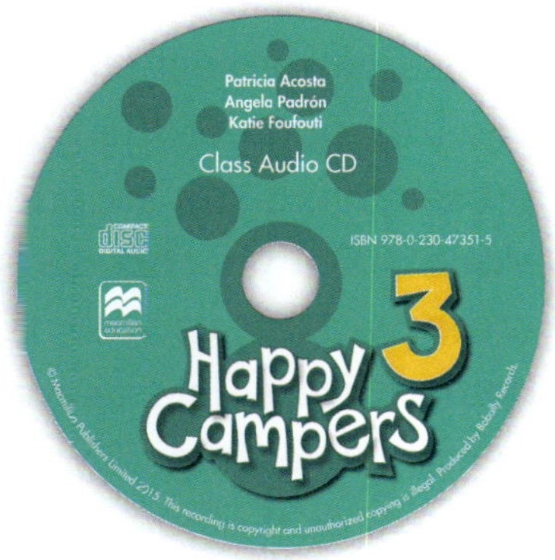

# Teacher's Resource Center

The **Teacher's Resource Center** contains a range of downloadable software and materials to support teachers and enrich the *Happy Campers* program.

## Assessment Pack

The **Assessment Pack** includes ready-made tests for each unit, as well as mid- and end-of-year tests. The **Test Generator** includes software for teachers to generate their own versions.

Students' native language is **digital**!

## Presentation Kit

The **Presentation Kit** is a fully interactive presentation tool that can be used to project all Student Book and The Language Lodge pages. Language presentations are supported by lively **vocabulary echo** and **grammar cheer** videos, as well as **comic strip animations**. Interactive activities can be completed digitally or used to check answers as a whole class.

## Visuals Pack

The Happy Campers **Visuals Pack** provides printable vocabulary flashcards and posters.

## Happy Actors Pack

The **Happy Actors Pack** has plays, poems, and songs that can be used by students for open days and peer-to-peer performances.

## Methodology Handbook

The **Methodology Handbook** is a printable e-book that provides a practical guide to the methodology and thinking behind the *Happy Campers* series.

## Planners

Week-by-week **planners** help teachers organize their lessons and get maximum use out of the *Happy Campers* resources.

Creative teaching tools for today's classroom.

# Unit 1

## Unit Objectives

**By the end of the unit, students can:**

- Use numbers to give ages.
- Ask and answer questions about ages.
- Identify characters in a text.

## Student Book

### Vocabulary

**Numbers:** numbers 10–100

**Family:** grandparents, parents, aunt, uncle, cousin, niece, nephew

### Grammar

How old is he? He's ninety-nine.
Who is she? She's my aunt.
Who are they? They're my grandparents.

### Skills

**Listening:** Listen for and identify numbers.
Listen for specific information.

**Speaking:** Ask and answer questions about age and family relationships.
Respond to questions about age with appropriate answers.
Respond to questions about a character with appropriate information about family relationships.

**Reading:** Read a nonfiction text (social studies): **My Family**.
Identify characters in a text.
Read short sentences and recognize words.

**Writing:** Write information about family members' ages.

### Creative, Collaborative, and Critical Thinking Competencies

**Family Age Line**

**Creativity:** Develop self-expression, innovation, and problem-solving skills. Determine the information to be included in the Family Age Line and how it will be presented.

**Collaboration:** Use communication skills and conflict resolution skills to complete tasks. Determine the information to be included in the Family Age Line and how each team member will contribute to the final product.

**Critical Thinking:** Use problem-solving skills, analyze information, and organize information to complete the final product.

## Skills Book

**Extra Skills Practice**

**Speaking and Listening:** Ask and answer questions about a picture.

**Reading and Writing:** Identify characters.
Summarize the story.
Identify and produce word endings.
Recognize spelling patterns.
Categorize words.

# Teacher Workshop

## Teaching with Technology

Technology can help teachers be more engaged with the class so students become more active learners. Use technology as a way to informally assess students during class to make sure students truly understand what is being taught. Try an activity from the Happy Campers app as a quick way to check comprehension. Students will enjoy interacting with technology without the stress of feeling tested.

## Teaching with Games

**Name Game**

**Materials:** ball

Ask students to sit in a large circle and then join them. Begin by taking the ball and saying your name: *I'm Miss/Mr. (your name).* Pass the ball to the student on your right. The student says *She's/He's Miss/Mr. (your name). I'm (Mary).* Then the student passes the ball to the student on his or her right. This student then says *She's (Mary). I'm (Tom).* This continues until all the names in the circle have been said.

## Happy Teacher

Begin the school year with a number of getting-to-know-you activities. Students may have been involved in different activities over vacation that they would like to share. There may be new students in the group, or you may be their new teacher. This is a great way for everyone to get to know one another. Establish your classroom management style when the school year begins. Explain the classroom rules to students, and teach them the appropriate ways to communicate.

## Happy Class

To energize your class, choose one of these quick break tricks. Have students:

- Listen to music.
- Touch elbows with eight classmates.
- Do neck circles, do arm circles, and stand up and touch their toes.

By Diana Jones

# UNIT 1

## Lesson 1

1 (04) Listen. Then echo.

ten **10**
**20** twenty
thirty **30**
**40** forty
fifty **50**
**60** sixty
seventy **70**
**80** eighty
ninety **90**
**100** one hundred

2 (05) Listen and check (✓).

**Young and Old!**

How old is she?
Thirty? Forty? Fifty?

How old is he?
Thirty? Forty? Fifty?

1.

✓ She's seventy-two.

☐ She's thirty-five.

3 Page 1 The Language Lodge



## Lesson 2

1 (05) Sing: Young and Old!

2.

☐ She's twenty.

✓ She's ten.

3.

☐ He's sixty-seven.

✓ He's ninety-nine.

### Grammar Snapshot!

How old is she?
She's ten.

How old is he?
He's ninety-nine.

2 Read and circle.

1. How old is he?
   He's thirty.
2. How old is she?
   She's seventy.
3. How old is he?
   He's eighty-eight.

3 Point, ask, and answer.

How old is he?

He's ninety-nine.

4 Page 2 The Language Lodge



# UNIT 1

## Lesson 1

1 Write the numbers. Find and circle the number words.

1. fifty-six 56
2. thirty-five 35
3. forty-nine 49
4. twenty-one 21
5. eighty-two 82
6. ninety-eight 98

| | | | | | | | | | | | |
|---|---|---|---|---|---|---|---|---|---|---|---|
| F | O | U | F | O | R | T | Y | N | I | N | E |
| E | I | G | O | N | S | H | S | E | V | E | M |
| I | N | F | R | T | H | R | E | T | F | O | S |
| G | O | W | T | W | E | N | T | Y | O | N | E |
| H | F | N | E | Y | R | E | E | T | W | I | I |
| T | O | I | N | R | S | V | N | W | O | X | G |
| Y | U | N | I | T | X | I | A | Y | F | I | H |
| T | H | I | N | E | Y | T | X | E | I | V | T |
| W | T | H | I | R | T | Y | F | I | V | E | H |
| O | N | I | N | E | T | Y | E | I | G | H | T |

2 Match.

1. seventy-three
2. forty-four
3. ninety-seven
4. eighty

**97**
**73**
**80**
**44**

✓ **Spelling Check!** Spell the number words aloud. **Then complete.** I can spell ☐ words.

Student Book Page 8



# Lesson 1

This may also be completed for homework.

# Lesson 1 Vocabulary



**Lesson Objective:** Identify numbers 10–100.
**New Vocabulary:** ten, twenty, thirty, forty, fifty, sixty, seventy, eighty, ninety, one hundred
**Materials:** Audio **Tracks 04 and 05**

## Start the Class

5 min

Have students guess in L1 about the age of the people in the pictures.

### ① 04 Listen. Then echo.

10 min

Have students look at the numbers and elicit the colors. Explain that they will listen and point to the different numbers. Play **Track 04** and have students listen and point to the numbers as they hear them mentioned. Play **Track 04** again and have students echo the numbers.

Tell students to draw a circle around the words that end in *-ty*. Have students say which two numbers don't have *-ty* at the end (*ten* and *one hundred*). Call out *six*. Have students respond *sixty*. Repeat with different numbers.

**Try This!** 5 min

Explain to students that you will call out the numbers and they will repeat them. Call out the first three numbers (*ten, twenty, thirty*), and have students repeat. Then call out the next three (*forty, fifty, sixty*), and have students repeat. Continue with *seventy, eighty, ninety,* and *one hundred*. Ask three volunteers to come to the board. Have them call out the numbers while the rest of the students repeat.

### ② 05 Listen and check (✓).

15 min

Write the equation *50 + 1 =* on the board and elicit the answer *51*. Write *fifty-one* on the board and point out that some numbers are written with a hyphen. Have a volunteer come to the board and dictate *fifty-two* for him or her to write out.

Write the numbers *1–9* in a row on the board. Then write a large *40* above the row. Point to the numbers in order and have students say them aloud as *41, 42,* etc.

Have a volunteer read the directions and the title of the song. Explain to the class that they will listen to a song. Play **Track 05**.

Have volunteers read the sentences for each picture. Tell students they will listen to the song again and check which pictures are mentioned in the song. Play **Track 05**. Then have volunteers share their answers.

### ③ Page 1 The Language Lodge

10 min

Have students flip to The Language Lodge **Page 1**.

**1 Write the numbers. Find and circle the number words.**

Have a volunteer read the directions. Then have students find the number words in the word search. Circulate among the class and provide help as needed. Have students compare their answers with a partner.

**2 Match.**

Tell students to match the words and the numbers. Have volunteers write the numbers and words on the board.

**Spelling Check! Spell the number words aloud. Then complete.**

Have students close their books. Tell them that they will take turns saying and spelling the numbers with a partner. Then tell students to write the number of words they can spell correctly.

## Finish the Class

5 min

Tell the class that they will say a chain of numbers, starting with *twenty, twenty-one,* etc. Start on one side of the classroom. When the students get to thirty, have the first student on the opposite side of the classroom start a second chain of numbers. The second chain starts with *sixty, sixty-one,* etc. Then have the first side start another chain with *forty, forty-one,* etc.

Use the **Presentation Kit** for interactive activities in this lesson.

Have students use the **Happy Campers app** for additional practice with the new vocabulary.

**The Language Lodge Page 1** may also be completed for homework.

# Lesson 2 Grammar

**Lesson Objective:** Ask and answer questions about ages.
**New Grammar:** How old is she? She's ten. How old is he? He's ninety-nine.
**Vocabulary Review:** numbers 10–100
**Materials:** Audio **Track 05**, strips of paper, ball

## Start the Class

5 min

Explain to students that they will take turns counting aloud. Say *ten* and then throw a ball to a student who says *twenty*; this student then throws the ball to another student to continue the game. When they get to one hundred, start again.

### 1 05 Sing: Young and Old!

5 min

Have students look at the song on **Pages 8 and 9**. Tell students they will listen to the song again and whisper the words as they listen. Play **Track 05**.

Have students practice whispering the lines a few times before singing it. Play **Track 05** again and have the class sing along.

**Try This!**

5 min

Divide the class into three groups. Explain that they are going to sing the song again. This time one group will sing the questions, another group will sing the three options, and the third group will sing the answers. Play the track and sing. Have the groups switch roles.

### 2 Read and circle.

12 min

Have the class read the Grammar Snapshot! together. Explain that we use *she* to talk about a girl or woman and *he* to talk about a boy or man. Divide the class into two groups. Explain that one group asks the question *How old is she*? and the second group responds with *She's ten*. Repeat with *How old is he*? *He's ninety-nine*. Tell students to complete the activity individually, and then compare their answers with a partner. Have volunteers share their answers with the class.

### 3 Point, ask, and answer.

8 min

Have volunteers read the speech bubbles. Tell students they will take turns asking and answering questions with a partner. Explain that they will point to pictures on **Pages 8 and 9**. Have volunteers perform their dialogues for the class.

### 4 Page 2 The Language Lodge

10 min

Have students flip to The Language Lodge **Page 2**. Have volunteers read the questions and answers in the Grammar Snapshot! aloud. Point out the punctuation for the questions and the answers.

**1 Read and circle.**

Explain to the class that they will read the questions and circle the correct answers. Then have pairs of students read the questions and answers aloud.

**2 Look and write.**

Explain that the birthday cakes and candles show how old each person is. Complete Item 1 as a class. Then have students complete the rest of the activity individually. Have volunteers write the answers on the board.

## Finish the Class

5 min

Tell students to write down a random age on a strip of paper. Have each student find out the ages of the people in his or her row. Each student answers according to the age on his or her strip of paper. Have students in each row line up in the order of their ages.

Use the **Presentation Kit** for interactive activities in this lesson.

**The Language Lodge Page 2** may also be completed for homework.

For the next lesson, use **Skills Book Pages 4 and 5** (Picture Talk). Go to Teacher's Edition **Page T 160** for teacher notes.

UNIT 1

1 04 Listen. Then echo.

ten 10
20 twenty
thirty 30
40 forty
fifty 50
60 sixty
seventy 70
80 eighty
ninety 90
100 one hundred

Lesson 1

2 05 Listen and check (✓).

Young and Old!

How old is she?
Thirty? Forty? Fifty?

How old is he?
Thirty? Forty? Fifty?

1.
She's seventy-two.
She's thirty-five.

3 Page 1 The Language Lodge

8

Lesson 2

1 05 Sing: Young and Old!

2.
She's twenty.
She's ten.

3.
He's sixty-seven.
He's ninety-nine.

*Grammar Snapshot!*

How old is she?
She's ten.

How old is he?
He's ninety-nine.

2 Read and circle.

1. How old is he?
He's thirty.

2. How old is she?
She's seventy.

3. How old is he?
He's eighty-eight.

3 Point, ask, and answer.

How old is he?
He's ninety-nine.

4 Page 2 The Language Lodge

9

# Lesson 2

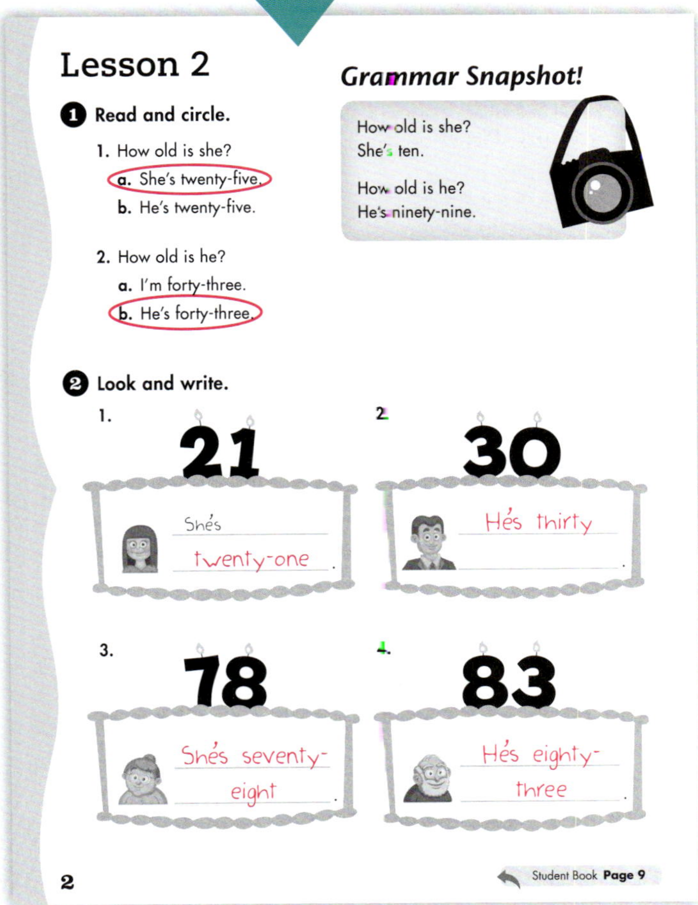

Lesson 2

1 Read and circle.

1. How old is she?
   a. She's twenty-five.
   b. He's twenty-five.
2. How old is he?
   a. I'm forty-three.
   b. He's forty-three.

*Grammar Snapshot!*

How old is she?
She's ten.

How old is he?
He's ninety-nine.

2 Look and write.

1. 21 She's twenty-one.
2. 30 He's thirty.
3. 78 She's seventy-eight.
4. 83 He's eighty-three.

2

Student Book Page 9

This may also be completed for homework.

## Lesson 3

# Shutterbugs

**1** Who are the people in the photos?

**2** 06 Read and listen.

**3** 07 **Dictation!** Listen and write. Then say.

1. grandparents
2. parents
3. aunt and uncle
4. cousin
5. niece
6. nephew

**4** Page 3 The Language Lodge



## Lesson 4

**1** 06 Listen again to **Shutterbugs**.

**2** *Grammar Snapshot!* Read and match.

| | |
|---|---|
| 1. Who is she? | He's my uncle. |
| 2. Who are they? | She's my aunt. |
| 3. Who is he? | They're my parents. |

**3** 08 Listen and cheer!

Who is he? He's my uncle!
Who is she? She's my aunt!
Who are they? They're my cousins!

CHEER BOX!

**4** Page 4 The Language Lodge



## Lesson 3

**1** Choose and label. | aunt cousin grandparents parents uncle |

✓ **Spelling Check!** Spell the family words aloud. **Then complete.** I can spell [ ] words.

Student Book **Page 10**



# Lesson 3

This may also be completed for homework.

# Lesson 3 Vocabulary in Context

**Lesson Objective:** Identify family members.
**New Vocabulary:** grandparents, parents, aunt, uncle, cousin, niece, nephew
**Vocabulary Review:** mom, dad, grandma, grandpa
**Materials:** Audio **Tracks 02, 06, and 07**

## Start the Class

5 min

Have students point to the Shutterbugs title with the picture of the camera on **Page 10**. Tell students to look at the opening spread on **Pages 6 and 7**, and explain that the Shutterbugs are a camera club. Play **Track 02**.

### 1 Who are the people in the photos?

3 min

Point to the characters and ask students to name them: *Tom* and *Lisa*. Have students look at the photos and guess who the people are: *Lisa's parents, grandparents, uncle, aunt, cousins, and friend.*

### 2 06 Read and listen.

12 min

Tell students they will read the comic strip as they listen. Remind them to follow the words with their fingers. Play **Track 06**.

Explain that *parents* are a mom and a dad. Ask students who *grandparents* are, and elicit *grandpa* and *grandma*. Have students circle the family words in the comic strip.

**Try This!** 5 min

Divide the class into pairs. Explain to students that they will each play a part from the story. Have students read their parts aloud.

### 3 07 Dictation! Listen and write. Then say.

10 min

Say the words for the family members in the order they appear in the comic strip and have students point to the correct pictures. Repeat the activity with the words in a different order. Have a volunteer read the directions on **Page 10**. Play **Track 07** and pause for students to write the words. Play the track again.

Have students check their answers with a partner.

Ask volunteers to write the answers on the board. Tell students they will listen to the track again and repeat what they hear aloud. Play **Track 07**.

*Audio script* ***Track 07***
*1. grandparents 2. parents 3. aunt and uncle*
*4. cousin 5. niece 6. nephew*

### 4 Page 3 The Language Lodge

10 min

Have students flip to The Language Lodge **Page 3**.

**1 Choose and label.**

Have a volunteer read the directions and the words in the box aloud. Point out that *me* in the family tree represents the students. Write in *grandparents* as a class. Then have students complete the activity individually. Circulate around the class and provide help as needed. Review the answers as a class.

**Spelling Check! Spell the family words aloud. Then complete.**

Have students close their books. Tell them that they will take turns saying and spelling the family words with a partner. Then tell students to write the number of words they can spell correctly.

## Finish the Class

5 min

Ask students to write the alphabet on a piece of paper. Say family words from this unit. Ask students to point to the letters in the alphabet to spell out the different words.

Use the **Presentation Kit** for interactive activities in this lesson.

Have students use the **Happy Campers app** for additional practice with the new vocabulary.

**The Language Lodge Page 3** may also be completed for homework.

# Lesson 4 Grammar in Context

**Lesson Objective:** Ask and answer questions to identify family members.
**New Grammar:** Who is she? She's my aunt. Who is he? He's my cousin. Who are they? They're my grandparents.
**Vocabulary Review:** grandparents, parents, aunt, uncle, cousin, niece, nephew
**Materials:** Audio **Tracks 06 and 08**

## Start the Class

5 min

Write the family words on the board with scrambled letters. For example, write *n e c u l* for *uncle*. Have students unscramble the words in their notebooks, and then take turns spelling them aloud with a partner. Have volunteers write the words on the board.

### ① 06 Listen again to *Shutterbugs*.

10 min

Tell the class that they will listen again to the comic strip and read along as they listen. Explain that they should listen and raise their hands when they hear questions with *Who*.

Play **Track 06**. Then have students underline the questions with *Who*. Have volunteers read them aloud.

### ② Grammar Snapshot! Read and match.

8 min

Write *he, she,* and *they* on the board. Tell students that you will call out a family word and they have to respond by saying *he, she,* or *they*. For example, *mom*: *she*.

Have a volunteer read the directions for Activity 2 on **Page 11**. Explain to the class that they will match each question with the correct answer. Tell students to work individually, and then have them compare their answers with a partner. Have volunteers share their answers with the class.

**Try This!**

3 min

Divide the class in two groups. Explain that they will take turns asking and answering the questions from the comic strip chorally. One group asks the question, and the other group gives the answer. When one group has asked all the questions, the groups switch roles.

### ③ 08 Listen and cheer!

5 min

Tell the class they are going to listen to a cheer and read the words as they listen. Play **Track 08**. Explain to the class that you are going to play the cheer again and this time they will do the cheer with the track. Play the track again.

### ④ Page 4 The Language Lodge

14 min

Have students flip to The Language Lodge **Page 4**. Direct the class to the Grammar Snapshot! Have volunteers read the Grammar Snapshot! aloud.

**1 Read and circle.**

Explain to the class that they will read the questions and choose the correct answers. Remind them to look at the picture for each question. When they have finished, have students compare their answers with a partner. Have volunteers read their questions and correct answers.

**2 Write questions.**

Have students look at the answers and explain that they have to write the question for each answer. Have volunteers write the questions on the board.

## Finish the Class

5 min

Divide the class into two teams. Draw a line down the center of the board and label the sides *Correct* and *Incorrect*. You will say a sentence such as *She's my aunt* or *He's my grandma*. Students then decide if the sentence is correct or incorrect and stand on a side of the board to show their decisions. The students who make a wrong decision sit down. The team with the last person standing wins.

Use the **Presentation Kit** for interactive activities in this lesson.

**The Language Lodge Page 4** may also be completed for homework.

For the next lesson, use **Skills Book Pages 6 and 7** (Happy Reader). Go to Teacher's Edition **Page T 161** for teacher notes.

## Lesson 3

# Shutterbugs

1 Who are the people in the photos?

2 06 Read and listen.

3 07 **Dictation!** Listen and write. Then say.

1. ______________________
2. ______________________
3. ______________________
4. ______________________
5. ______________________
6. ______________________

4 Page 3 The Language Lodge



## Lesson 4

1 06 Listen again to **Shutterbugs**.

2 ***Grammar Snapshot!*** Read and match.

1. Who is she? — She's my aunt.
2. Who are they? — They're my parents.
3. Who is he? — He's my uncle.

(Options as printed: He's my uncle. / She's my aunt. / They're my parents.)

3 08 **Listen and cheer!**

Who is he? He's my uncle!
Who is she? She's my aunt!
Who are they? They're my cousins!

CHEER BOX!

4 Page 4 The Language Lodge



# Lesson 4

This may also be completed for homework.

## Lesson 4

### *Grammar Snapshot!*

Who is he? He's my cousin.
Who is she? She's my aunt.
Who are they?
They're my grandparents.

1 **Read and circle.**

1. Who is she?
   a. They're my grandparents.
   b. She's my cousin. (circled)

2. Who is he?
   a. He's my uncle. (circled)
   b. She's my niece.

3. Who are they?
   a. He's my nephew.
   b. They're my parents. (circled)

2 **Write questions.**

1. Who is he ? He's my cousin.
2. Who is she ? She's my aunt.
3. Who are they ? They're my parents.



Student Book Page 11

# Lesson 5

## Lesson 5

**1 Look and complete.**

Nick has nine people in his family.

**2 09 Read and listen.**

## My Family

Hi, my name is Nick.
I'm nine. This is my family.
Grandpa is sixty, and Grandma is fifty-five.
I love my grandpa. He's funny!
These are my parents.
My mom is a teacher and my dad is a firefighter.
I have a sister. Her name is Sally. She's twelve.

This is my Uncle Eric and my Aunt Eva.
I also have one cousin, Daniel.
Daniel wants to be a chef.
He's twenty-one.

And who is he?
He's Oscar, my cat.
He's five. That's thirty-six
in human years!

# Lesson 5 Nonfiction Reading

**Lesson Objectives:** Read a nonfiction text to practice unit language. Identify characters.
**Vocabulary Review:** parents, sister, uncle, aunt, cousin
**Grammar Review:** Grandpa is sixty. He's twenty-one.
**Materials:** Audio **Track 09**

## Start the Class

5 min

Divide the class into two teams and have them stand in two lines in front of the board. Have the first student from the front of each line write a number you say: *32*. When students have had their turns, they go to the back of the line. Continue until all the students have participated.

### 1 Look and complete.

5 min

Tell students to open their books to **Page 12** and have a volunteer read the directions for Activity 1. Tell students to look at the pictures. Ask *Is this a nonfiction text?* Elicit *yes*. Have students explain their reasoning. They may do so in L1.

Tell students to look quickly at the photograph of Lisa's grandparents and parents on **Page 10** and elicit how many people are in the photograph. Then have students look at the family photos at the top and bottom of **Page 12,** and point to Nick. Ask *How many people are in Nick's family?* Elicit *nine*.

### 2 09 Read and listen.

20 min

Have a volunteer read the title of the text aloud. Tell students they will listen to the track and follow the words with their fingers as they listen. Play **Track 09**. Then have students underline words for family members in the text (*grandpa, grandma, parents, mom, dad, sister, uncle, aunt,* and *cousin*). Orally review the words they underlined. Ask *How old is his grandpa? How old is his grandma?*

Point out the other member of the family, Oscar, the cat. Have students raise their hands if they have a cat or dog. Ask *How old is Oscar?* Elicit *five*. Explain why cat years are different from human years: cats don't live as long as people do.

Divide the class into groups of three and tell students that they will read the text again in their groups. Explain that each person in the group will read one paragraph of the text. Remind them to read carefully and clearly. Circulate among the groups to check pronunciation and provide help as needed.

**Try This!**

10 min

Divide the class into two teams. Write *Yes* and *No* in large letters on the board. Have one student from each team come to the front of the class. Say a sentence with information from the story: *Grandpa is seventy-five.* The first student to touch the correct answer on the board wins a point for his or her team. Play several times until all students have participated.

## Finish the Class

10 min

Have students draw a chart or family tree showing Nick's family. Have them write the name and the age below each person. Circulate among the groups to provide help as needed.

Use the **Presentation Kit** for interactive activities in this lesson.

# Lesson 6 Reading Comprehension / Writing

**Lesson Objectives:** Recall details from a text. Write about family members.
**Vocabulary Review:** grandpa, parents, sister, uncle, aunt, cousin
**Grammar Review:** She's twelve. She's Nick's sister.
**Materials:** Audio **Track 09**; a blank card for each student; a photo of your family; colored pencils, markers, or crayons

## Start the Class

5 min

Give each student a blank card and have them write one family word on the card, such as *parents*. Explain that you will call out a word and all the students who have that word must stand up and then sit down. Call out *parents* and students with that word stand up. Repeat with other words.

Then have students walk around the classroom with their cards. Say different sets of family members for students to get into groups, such as *grandpa, sister, uncle*.

### 1 09 Listen again to My Family.

10 min

Tell students they will listen to the text again. Remind them to follow the story in their books while they listen. Play **Track 09**.

Tell students they will listen again and whisper along with the text.

### 2 Read and match.

10 min

Explain to students that they will work in pairs. Tell them that you will ask how old one of Nick's family members is, and students will look at the text and find the information. Ask *How old is Daniel*? Elicit *He's twenty-one*. Continue with other family members.

Have a volunteer read the directions and explain that they will work individually to match the sentences about Nick's family. Allow time for students to complete the activity and then have them share their answers with a partner.

### 3 Say Cheese! Draw a picture of your family.

5 min

Show students a photo of your family and tell students about your family members. Explain to students that they will draw pictures of their own families. Circulate around the class to monitor students' work and provide help as needed. Have students show their drawings to a partner. Then have volunteers share their drawings with the class and say who the people are, along with their ages.

### 4 Writing Time! Write about your picture.

10 min

Show students the photo of your family again. Tell students about your family, using the writing outline as a model. Explain to the class that they will write about their own families, so they must write their own names in the first blank. Allow the class time to complete the text. Circulate around the class to monitor students' work and provide help as needed. Then have them exchange their sentences with a partner, checking that they used *he, she,* and *they* correctly. Ask volunteers to share their paragraphs with the class.

**Try This!** 5 min

Put students into groups of four and have them share the paragraphs about their families. Tell them to show their pictures and take turns telling one another about the people in their pictures.

## Finish the Class

5 min

Have students work in pairs to give clues about people in the unit so far. Students take turns giving clues and guessing the people.

Use the **Presentation Kit** for interactive activities in this lesson.

For the next lesson, use **Skills Book Pages 8 and 9** (Word Work). Go to Teacher's Edition **Page T 162** for teacher notes.

# Lesson 6

**1** 09 **Listen again to My Family.**

**2** **Read and match.**

1. She's twelve.
2. They're Eric and Eva.
3. He's twenty-one.
4. She's a teacher and he's a firefighter.
5. He's sixty.

They're Nick's parents.
He's Nick's cousin.
He's Nick's grandpa.
She's Nick's sister.
They're Nick's aunt and uncle.

**3** **Say Cheese! Draw a picture of your family.**

(Students' own answers.)

**4** **Writing Time! Write about your picture.**

Hi, my name is (Students' own answers). I'm ____________.

This is my family. They're my ____________. ____________ is

____________ and ____________ is ____________.

# Lesson 7

Lesson 7

## Team Up!

**1 Think about people in your family. Make notes.**

**2 Share with your team.**

Jim is my brother. He's two.

Katy is my sister. She's thirteen.

**3 Team up and make a team Family Age Line.**

Joe is my grandpa. He's eighty-two.

# Lesson 7 Creative, Collaborative, and Critical Thinking Activity

**Lesson Objective:** Talk about family members.
**Vocabulary Review:** grandparents, parents, aunt, uncle, cousin, niece, nephew, sister, brother, mom, dad
**Grammar Review:** Joe is my grandpa. He's eighty-two.
**Materials:** Audio **Track 05**; paper; colored pencils, markers, or crayons

## Start the Class

4 min

Have students stand and face one another in two rows. Explain that they will do a zigzag quiz. The first student in row A says a family member: *aunt*. The first student in row B responds *she* and says to the second student in row A: *grandpa*. This creates a zigzag between the rows. Repeat until the last student in row B has answered.

**Try This!** 5 min

Tell students you are going to play the song "Young and Old!" again. Divide students into two groups and explain they are going to sing the song again. One group will sing the questions, and the other group will respond with the answers. Write the ages on the board to help students remember. Practice speaking the lines a few times before singing. Then play **Track 05** and sing along. If time allows, have the groups switch roles.

### ① Think about people in your family. Make notes.

6 min

Tell students to look at **Page 14** and have volunteers read the directions and the sample text. Explain that students will work individually to write a list of family members and their ages. Monitor and assist students as necessary.

### ② Share with your team.

5 min

Ask two volunteers to read the sample dialogue on the page.

Tell students that they will work in teams of three and take turns asking and answering questions about their families. Circulate around the classroom, correcting pronunciation and providing help as needed.

### ③ Team up and make a team Family Age Line.

15 min

Have teams look at the Family Age Lines on **Page 14**. Point out that Bill, Lucy, and Sam are on that team, and they each made an age line with two people in their families. Explain that an age line is made up of blocks of 10 years. Ask students to draw a timeline for each person in the group. Have them draw three timelines in 10 square blocks on construction paper, and color them as they appear in the book. Then have each student illustrate two family members on his or her own Family Age Line. Have students label the name, role, and age of each family member next to the appropriate picture. Finally, students write the title on the top of the poster.

## Finish the Class

15 min

Have teams share their Family Age Lines with the class. Remind them to point to the family members and say how old they are. Be sure each member of the team tells the class about his or her family. Display the Family Age Lines in the classroom.

Use the **Presentation Kit** for interactive activities in this lesson.

Use the **Assessment Pack** to carry out the Unit 1 Teamwork Assessment during this lesson.

# Lesson 8 Review

**Lesson Objective:** Review vocabulary and grammar from Unit 1.
**Vocabulary Review:** numbers 10–100, grandparents, parents, aunt, uncle, cousin, niece, nephew, grandpa, grandma, mom, dad, sister, brother
**Grammar Review:** How old is she? She's thirteen. Who is she? She's my grandma.
**Materials:** strips of paper with the beginnings and endings of family words (one per student), music

## Start the Class

2 min

Randomly distribute the strips of paper to students. Explain that each strip has the beginning or ending of a word, and students have to join them, for example, *neph* and *ew* to make *nephew*. Tell them that they each will stand up and find the person with the other half of their word. Play soft music while they are doing this. Then have pairs take turns telling the class their words.

### 1 Spelling! Write the missing letters.

5 min

Have students look at the words on **Page 15** and elicit whether they are numbers or family members. Ask a volunteer to read the directions. Explain to students that they will complete the missing letters. Tell students that they will work individually to complete the words. Check answers by having volunteers go to the board to write the words.

### 2 Write the words.

10 min

Ask different students *How old is your mom (or other family member)?* and have them write the number word for the age on the board. Then have volunteers write the corresponding numerals after each word.

Explain to students that they will write out the words for the numbers. Tell students to compare their answers with a partner. Check answers by having volunteers go to the board to write the words.

**Try This!**

5 min

Have the class form a circle. Explain that students will take turns counting number sequences backward. The first student says *twenty*. The next student says the following number (*nineteen*) and so on. Play the game with different blocks of ten numbers (1–10, 10–20, etc.) that they have been learning in this unit.

### 3 Read and match.

8 min

Point to the questions and answers on **Page 15** and explain that students have to match them. Ask which words can help them decide on the correct answers (*he, she,* and *they*). Students complete the activity individually and then check their answers with a partner. Read the questions aloud and ask students to call out the answers.

### 4 Word Play! Find and circle the words from Unit 1 on Page 72.

15 min

Have students turn to **Page 72** and tell them to find and circle the number and family vocabulary words from Unit 1. Then have students check the words they found with a partner.

## Finish the Class

5 min

Play the Shark Game with the words from this unit. Draw steps leading to an ocean with a shark in it. Draw a stick person at the top of the stairs. Think of a word and write a blank for each letter on the board. Explain to the class that they must guess a letter in the word. If the letter is in the word, write it on the corresponding blank on the board. If the guess is incorrect, move the person down the steps. Tell the class they must guess the word before the shark eats the person. You may choose to have volunteers select the word and write in the letters the class guesses correctly.

Use the **Presentation Kit** for interactive activities in this lesson.

For the next lesson, use Unit 1 Language Assessment from the **Assessment Pack** or create your own test using the **Test Generator** on the **Teacher's Resource Center**.

# Lesson 8

Lesson 8

## Round Up!

**1 Spelling! Write the missing letters.**

1. n e _p_ _h_ e w
2. _u_ n c l _e_
3. _n_ i e _c_ e
4. a _u_ n _t_
5. _c_ o u _s_ i _n_
6. g _r_ _a_ n _d_ _p_ a r _e_ _n_ t s

**2 Write the words.**

1. 35 thirty - five
2. 82 eighty - two
3. 41 forty - one
4. 100 one hundred

**3 Read and match.**

1. How old is she?
2. How old is he?
3. Who are they?
4. Who is he?
5. Who is she?

She's my aunt.
He's thirty-four.
He's my cousin.
They're my parents.
She's fifty-two.

**4 Word Play! Find and circle the words from Unit 1 on Page 72.**

# Unit 2

## Unit Objectives

**By the end of the unit, students can:**

- Ask and answer questions about birthdays.
- Ask and answer questions about the month and date.
- Show understanding of text details.

## Student Book

### Vocabulary

**Months of the Year:** January, February, March, April, May, June, July, August, September, October, November, December

**Ordinal Numbers:** 1st–31st

### Grammar

When's your birthday? It's in August.
What's the date today? Today is October fifteenth.

### Skills

**Listening:** Listen for and identify the date.
Listen for specific information and circle an appropriate response.

**Speaking:** Ask and answer questions about dates.
Respond to questions about dates with appropriate answers.

**Reading:** Read a nonfiction text (social studies): **The Mayan Calendars**.
Identify detailed information in a text.
Read short sentences and recognize words.

**Writing:** Write information about your birthday month.

### Creative, Collaborative, and Critical Thinking Competencies

**Birthday Calendar**

**Creativity:** Develop self-expression, innovation, and problem-solving skills. Determine the information to be included in the Birthday Calendar and how it will be presented.

**Collaboration:** Use communication skills and conflict resolution skills to complete tasks. Determine the information to be included in the Birthday Calendar and how each team member will contribute to the final product.

**Critical Thinking:** Use problem-solving skills, analyze information, and organize information to complete the final product.

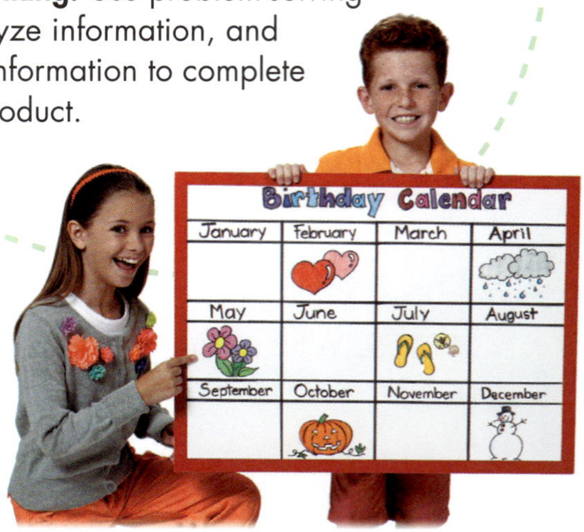


## Skills Book

**Extra Skills Practice**

**Speaking and Listening:** Ask and answer questions about a picture.

**Reading and Writing:** Recall details.
Give opinions.
Identify multi-syllable words.
Identify abbreviations for ordinal numbers.

# Teacher Workshop

## Teaching with Technology

Use the access code in your Teacher's Edition to access the Teacher's Resource Center. There are images of unit vocabulary you can download and photocopy to make flashcards for use in classroom activities.

## Teaching with Games

**Conversation Relay**

Divide students into several teams with equal numbers of students and have them form lines. The last student in line asks the student in front of him or her a question using the grammar structure *When's your birthday*? The other student answers and turns around to ask the next student the same question. When the question and answer reach the front of the line, the first student in the line runs to the back of the line and asks the question again. This continues until the first student is back in his or her original position. The first team to achieve this wins.

## Happy Teacher

Reading aloud is not a technique that promotes reading comprehension. Instead, it helps students see that writing, reading, and speaking are related language processes and a part of everyday life. The objective of reading aloud is for students to work on saying words in connected speech, using the proper intonation and rhythm. When students listen to their classmates read aloud, it helps them identify the spoken form of the words. When students are reading, walk around and take note of the words or phrases that are difficult for students to pronounce. Have the whole class repeat them together so that the words sound natural.

## Happy Class

To energize your class, choose one of these quick break tricks. Have students:

- Play the Shark Game with a friend for three minutes.
- Dance to music and then "freeze" in place when the music stops.
- Do a series of stretches by reaching their arms up to touch the sky, or down to touch their toes.

By Angela Padrón

# UNIT 2

## Lesson 1

1 (10) Listen. Then echo.

2 (11) Listen and complete.

**Birthday Song!**

When's your birthday?
Is it today?
Is it in January, March, or May?

1. It's in April.

3 Page 5 The Language Lodge

## Lesson 2

1 (11) Sing: Birthday Song!

2. It's in June.

3. It's in August.

### Grammar Snapshot!

When's your birthday?
It's in August.

2 Circle the answer.

1. When's your birthday?
   a. It's in school.
   b. It's in July.
2. Use *when* to talk about
   a. times.
   b. places.

3 Ask three friends and complete.

| Name | Birthday Month |
|---|---|
| | |
| | |
| | |

When's your birthday?

It's in January.

4 Page 6 The Language Lodge





# UNIT 2 Lesson 1

1 Complete the calendar.

| | | |
|---|---|---|
| January | February | March |
| April | May | June |
| July | August | September |
| October | November | December |

**Spelling Check!** Spell the months aloud. Then complete.

I can spell ____ words.

Student Book Page 16



# Lesson 1

This may also be completed for homework.

# Lesson 1 Vocabulary



**Lesson Objective:** Identify the months of the year.
**New Vocabulary:** January, February, March, April, May, June, July, August, September, October, November, December
**Materials:** Audio **Tracks 10 and 11**, magazine pictures representing several well-known local and international holidays

## Start the Class

6 min

Put up the holiday pictures on the board and elicit the names of the holidays. Write the name of the holiday under each picture and then ask students to tell you the dates of the holidays. Allow them to use L1 if necessary.

### 1 10 Listen. Then echo.

8 min

Elicit the current year and then write the word *calendar* on the board. Elicit the number of months in a year. Explain that they appear in a calendar. Have students look at the pictures and describe what they can see. Elicit some of the holidays, like *Valentine's Day* and *Christmas*, and the months in which they are celebrated. Explain other illustrations, such as the turkey used to celebrate Thanksgiving.

Play **Track 10** and have students listen and point to the months as they hear them mentioned. Explain that months always begin with a capital letter.

Play **Track 10** again and have students echo the months.

**Try This!** 6 min

Have each student point to his or her birthday month. Explain that you will play **Track 10** again, and students will stand up when they hear their birthday months. Then play the track a second time and have students say their birthday months aloud when they hear them.

### 2 11 Listen and complete.

15 min

Tell students to look at the three children on **Pages 16 and 17**. Explain to the class that they will listen to a song to find out and write the children's birthdays. Play **Track 11** and have students point to the months in Activity 1 as they hear them mentioned. Play **Track 11** again for students to write the months.

Have students compare their answers with the person next to them. Write students' correct responses on the board.

### 3 Page 5 The Language Lodge

10 min

Have students flip to The Language Lodge **Page 5**.

**1 Complete the calendar.**

Tell students to complete the months of the year on the calendar. Remind them to write the first letter of each month with a capital letter. When they have finished, have students compare their answers with a partner. Review the answers as a class.

**Spelling Check! Spell the months aloud. Then complete.**

Have students close their books. Tell them that they will take turns saying and spelling the months with a partner. Then tell students to write the number of words they can spell correctly.

## Finish the Class

5 min

Divide the class into two teams and have students in each team form a line according to the sequence of their birthdays.

Use the **Presentation Kit** for interactive activities in this lesson.

Have students use the **Happy Campers app** for additional practice with the new vocabulary.

**The Language Lodge Page 5** may also be completed for homework.

# Lesson 2 Grammar

**Lesson Objective:** Ask and answer questions about birthday months.
**New Grammar:** When's your birthday? It's in August.
**Vocabulary Review:** January, February, March, April, May, June, July, August, September, October, November, December
**Materials:** Audio **Track 11**

## Start the Class

5 min

Ask *What's the date today*? to elicit the date. Ask *Who has a birthday in (this month)*? and tell students who have birthdays in that month to come to the board. Ask *When's your birthday*? *Is it today*? and students answer *yes* or *no* (or say the correct date). Have the other students sing "Happy Birthday" for the students with birthdays in that month.

### 1 11 Sing: Birthday Song!

5 min

Tell students they will listen to the song from Lesson 1 again. Have them point to each birthday child as they listen. Play **Track 11**.

Practice saying the lines of the song on **Pages 16 and 17**. Play **Track 11** again and have the class sing along.

**Try This!** 5 min

Divide the class into four groups: students with birthdays in April, students with birthdays in June, students with birthdays in August, and everyone else. Explain that the rest of the class is going to sing the verse with the questions, and the students with birthdays in the different months will sing the verses that correspond with their birthday months. Practice speaking the lines a few times before singing the song. Then play the track and sing along.

### 2 Circle the answer.

10 min

Have the class read the Grammar Snapshot! together. Ask several students the question *When's your birthday*? Then have a volunteer ask another student. Repeat several times.

Tell students to complete the activity individually, and then compare their answers with a partner. Have volunteers share their answers with the class.

Remind students that *wh-* words (such as *when, who,* and *what*) are used to ask questions: *When's your birthday? Who is she? What's the date today?*

### 3 Ask three friends and complete.

10 min

Have volunteers read the speech bubbles aloud. Explain that students will ask three classmates about their birthdays, and then use the information to complete the chart. Have volunteers share their answers with the class.

### 4 Page 6 The Language Lodge

10 min

Have students flip to The Language Lodge **Page 6**. Have a volunteer read the Grammar Snapshot! aloud.

**1 Complete.**
Explain to the class that they will complete the questions and answers. Have volunteers share their answers with the class.

**2 Read and answer.**
Have students look at the calendar and read the months aloud in order. Ask a volunteer to read the first question aloud. Then have students find the information about Ben in the box. Review the answers as a class. Have students work in pairs and take turns asking and answering the questions.

## Finish the Class

5 min

Have students draw a scene with a monthly calendar, a birthday cake, and a present. Then ask students to write *My birthday is in (birthday month).*

Use the **Presentation Kit** for interactive activities in this lesson.

**The Language Lodge Page 6** may also be completed for homework.

For the next lesson, use **Skills Book Pages 10 and 11** (Picture Talk). Go to Teacher's Edition **Page T 163** for teacher notes.

# UNIT 2

## Lesson 1

1 Listen. Then echo.

2 Listen and complete.

**Birthday Song!**

When's your birthday?
Is it today?
Is it in January, March, or May?

1. It's in ______.

3 Page 5 The Language Lodge



## Lesson 2

1 Sing: Birthday Song!

2. It's in ______.

3. It's in ______.

***Grammar Snapshot!***

When's your birthday?
It's in August.

2 Circle the answer.

1. When's your birthday?
   a. It's in school.
   b. It's in July.
2. Use *when* to talk about
   a. times.
   b. places.

3 Ask three friends and complete.

| Name | Birthday Month |
|---|---|
| (Students' own | answers.) |
| | |
| | |

When's your birthday?

It's in January.

4 Page 6 The Language Lodge



# Lesson 2

This may also be completed for homework.

## Lesson 2

***Grammar Snapshot!***

When's your birthday?
It's in August.

**1 Complete.**

1. When's your birthday?
   It's in November.
2. When's your birthday?
   It's in May.
3. When's your birthday?
   It's in (Students' own answers).

**2 Read and answer.**

February – Lucy  April – Ben  June – Jack  September – Pat

1. When's Ben's birthday?
   It's in April.
2. When's Jack's birthday?
   It's in June.
3. When's Lucy's birthday?
   It's in February.
4. When's Pat's birthday?
   It's in September.

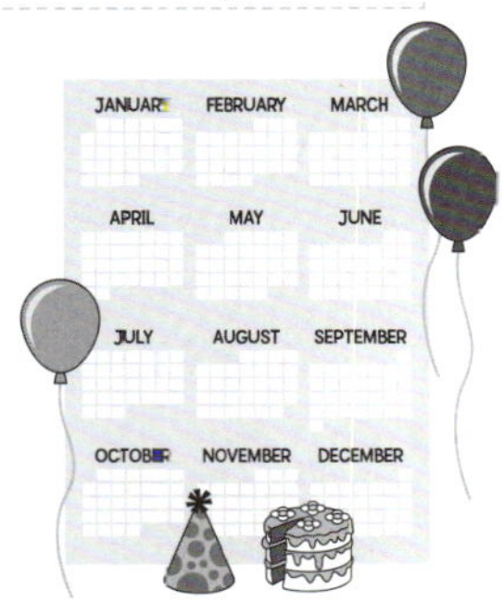




Student Book Page 17

# Lesson 3

## Shutterbugs

1 What month is it?

2 12 Read and listen.

3 13 **Dictation!** Listen and match. Then say.

| | | |
|---|---|---|
| 1. | 1st | fourth |
| 2. | 2nd | first |
| 3. | 3rd | fifth |
| 4. | 4th | second |
| 5. | 5th | third |

4 Page 7 The Language Lodge



# Lesson 4

1 12 Listen again to **Shutterbugs**.

2 *Grammar Snapshot!* Complete.

What's ______ ______ today?

______ twenty-______.

3 14 Listen and cheer!

What's the date today? Hey, hey!
Today is May eighth. Hey, hey!

CHEER BOX!

4 Page 8 The Language Lodge



# Lesson 3

1 Complete the number words in order.

1. first, second, third
2. fourth, fifth, sixth
3. seventh, eighth, ninth
4. tenth, eleventh, twelfth
5. thirteenth, fourteenth, fifteenth
6. sixteenth, seventeenth, eighteenth
7. nineteenth, twentieth, twenty - first
8. twenty-second, twenty - third, twenty - fourth
9. twenty - fifth, twenty-sixth, twenty-seventh
10. twenty - eighth, twenty-ninth, thirtieth, thirty-first

**Spelling Check!** Spell the number words aloud. Then complete. I can spell ______ words.

Student Book Page 18



# Lesson 3

This may also be completed for homework.

# Lesson 3 Vocabulary in Context

**Lesson Objective:** Identify ordinal numbers.
**New Vocabulary:** ordinal numbers
**Review Vocabulary:** months of the year
**Materials:** Audio **Tracks 12 and 13**, flashcards with the months of the year

## Start the Class

5 min

Give 12 students flashcards with the months of the year written on them (one month per card). Have students go to the board and form a line in the correct order. Explain that they will have a parade: one by one, each student marches and holds up his or her flashcard. Then the whole class marches in place and says the months in order as the students hold up the flashcards.

### 1 What month is it?

5 min

Have students point to the calendar in the story. Ask *What month is on the calendar*? Elicit the month from students orally: *February*.

### 2 12 Read and listen.

10 min

Explain that a leap year occurs every four years, and in a leap year February has 29 days instead of 28. Tell students they will read the comic strip as they listen. Play **Track 12**. Pause when Clare says *February thirtieth* and elicit whether that date really exists. Once students have established that it does not exist, continue playing **Track 12.**

**Try This!** 5 min

Divide the class into pairs. Explain to students that they will each read a part from the story. Have students read their parts aloud.

### 3 13 Dictation! Listen and match. Then say.

10 min

Write *March 1st* on the board and have students point to the corresponding phrase in the story. Write *March 1st = March first*. Explain that these are called ordinal numbers and they are often abbreviated.

Explain that we use ordinal numbers for dates.

Play **Track 13** and pause for students to write words. Have students check their answers with a partner. Have students circle the last two letters of each word and the two letters of each abbreviation.

Tell students they are going to listen to **Track 13** again and repeat what they hear. Play **Track 13**.

*Audio script* ***Track 13***
*1. first 2. second 3. third 4. fourth 5. fifth*

### 4 Page 7 The Language Lodge

10 min

Have students flip to The Language Lodge **Page 7**.

**1 Complete the number words in order.**

Have a volunteer read the directions. Explain to the class that they will write out the words. Do Item 1 as a class; then have students complete the activity individually. Review the answers as a class.

**Spelling Check! Spell the number words aloud. Then complete.**

Have students close their books. Tell them that they will take turns saying and spelling the ordinal numbers with a partner. Then tell students to write the number of words they can spell correctly.

## Finish the Class

5 min

Have students line up and, one by one, say the ordinal numbers in sequence. If they say them correctly, they go to their place and sit down. If they do not, they go to the end of the line and get another turn.

Use the **Presentation Kit** for interactive activities in this lesson.

Have students use the **Happy Campers app** for additional practice with the new vocabulary.

**The Language Lodge Page 7** may also be completed for homework.

# Lesson 4 Grammar in Context

**Lesson Objective:** Ask and answer questions about the date.
**New Grammar:** What's the date today? It's February twenty-ninth.
**Vocabulary Review:** months of the year
**Materials:** Audio **Tracks 12 and 14**

## Start the Class

5 min

Have students fold a sheet of paper into nine squares, and tell them to write a number between 1 and 12 on each square. Explain that you will say a sentence about a month: *January is the first month*. They will mark the number *1* if they have it. Say sentences about the months in random order. The first student to mark all his or her numbers wins.

### ① 12 Listen again to Shutterbugs.

5 min

Tell the class that they will listen again to the comic strip and read along as they listen. Tell them to clap once when they hear *Leap Day*. Play **Track 12**.

### ② Grammar Snapshot! Complete.

10 min

Explain to the class that they will find the question and the answer in the comic strip in order to complete them in the activity. Tell students to work individually, and then have them compare their answers with a partner. Have volunteers share their answers with the class.

**Try This!** 5 min

Write the words for the months on the board and ask *How many days does each month have*? Ask volunteers to write the number of days after the name of each month. Divide the class into two teams. Say *It's the (ninth) month. It has (30) days*. The first student to correctly answer wins a point for the team.

### ③ 14 Listen and cheer!

10 min

Tell the class they will listen to a cheer and read the words as they listen. Play **Track 14**. Have students underline the question and circle the answer. Explain to the class that you will play the cheer again and this time they will do the cheer with the track. Play **Track 14** again.

Divide the class into two groups and have them stand and face each other. Explain that one group will say the first part of the cheer and the other group will respond.

### ④ Page 8 The Language Lodge

10 min

Have students flip to The Language Lodge **Page 8**. Direct the class to the Grammar Snapshot! Divide the class into two teams. Have one team read the question aloud and the other team read the answer.

**1 Look and write.**

Have students look at the calendars. Explain that they should write complete sentences to give the month and day for each date. Circulate around the class and provide help as needed. Then have volunteers write the dates on the board.

**2 Complete.**

Explain to the class that they will read the question and write the current date. Then have a volunteer write the answer on the board.

## Finish the Class

5 min

Have students work with a partner. Have them change the words in the grammar cheer for their birthday dates and say a new grammar cheer.

Use the **Presentation Kit** for interactive activities in this lesson.

**The Language Lodge Page 8** may also be completed for homework.

For the next lesson, use **Skills Book Pages 12 and 13** (Happy Reader). Go to Teacher's Edition **Page T 164** for teacher notes.

## Lesson 3

# Shutterbugs

1 What month is it?

2 12 Read and listen.

3 13 **Dictation!** Listen and match. Then say.

1. 1st — fourth
2. 2nd — first
3. 3rd — fifth
4. 4th — second
5. 5th — third

4 Page 7 The Language Lodge



## Lesson 4

1 12 Listen again to Shutterbugs.

2 *Grammar Snapshot!* Complete.

What's __the__ __date__ today?

It's __February__ twenty- __ninth__ .

3 14 Listen and cheer!

What's the date today? Hey, hey!

Today is May eighth. Hey, hey!

CHEER BOX!

4 Page 8 The Language Lodge



# Lesson 4

This may also be completed for homework.

## Lesson 4

### *Grammar Snapshot!*

What's the date today?

It's October fifteenth.

1 Look and write.

1. MAY (31) — It's May thirty-first.
2. JUNE (14) — It's June fourteenth.
3. NOVEMBER (22) — It's November twenty-second.
4. APRIL (3) — It's April third.

2 Complete.

What's the date today?

(Students' own answers).



Student Book Page 19

# Lesson 5

## Lesson 5

**1 Look and circle.**
This Mayan calendar has

**a.** pictures. **b.** numbers.

**2** 15 **Read and listen.**

## The Mayan Calendars

Our calendar has twelve months with twenty-eight, thirty, or thirty-one days. There are many Mayan calendars. One Mayan calendar has nineteen months. Eighteen months have twenty days. But one month has only five days!

The first month in the Mayan calendar is *Pop*.
The nineteenth month is *Wayeb*.

Each month has a picture. The picture for the fourteenth month is a plant under the sun. The sixteenth month has a picture of a different plant.

Some pictures on the Mayan calendar are animals. The picture for the second month is a frog. And the sixth month is a dog.

*Kayab* is the seventeenth month.
What animal is it? It's a turtle.
Both calendars have 365 days.
One of those days is your birthday.
When's your birthday?

# Lesson 5 Nonfiction Reading

**Lesson Objective:** Read a nonfiction text to practice the unit language.
**New Vocabulary:** turtle
**Vocabulary Review:** months, ordinal numbers, frog, dog
**Grammar Review:** Eighteen months have twenty days. *Kayab* is the seventeenth month.
**Materials:** Audio **Track 15**, card stock, music

## Start the Class

10 min

Have each student write his or her birthday date (month and day) on an index card. Divide the class into two groups. Have each group walk around the classroom in opposite directions while you play some music. Tell them to exchange cards with a random student walking in the opposite direction. Students repeat this exchange with several other students. Then have students look for the person with that birthday by asking *When's your birthday?*

### 1 Look and circle.

5 min

Ask students if they have heard of other types of calendars, such as the Aztec calendar. Tell students to open their books to **Page 20** and have a volunteer read the title of the text. Elicit the area where the Mayans lived (southern Mexico and Central American countries). Draw a simple map on the board showing the area they inhabited. Tell students to look at the pictures on the page. Ask *Is this nonfiction or fiction?* Elicit *nonfiction*. Have students explain their reasons. They may do so in L1.

Then ask students to look at the artwork and answer the following question: *Do you think the Mayan calendar has pictures or numbers?* Write the two options on different sides of the board and have students line up on the side of the answer they think is correct. Encourage several students to explain their reasons.

Tell students to return to their seats. Tell them that after they read the text they will see who made the correct prediction.

### 2 15 Read and listen.

20 min

Have a volunteer read the title of the text again. Tell students they are going to listen to the track and follow the words with their fingers as they listen. Play **Track 15**. Students say whose predictions were correct from Activity 1. Elicit *pictures*.

Then have students look for words in the text that show ordinal numbers (*first, nineteenth, fourteenth, sixteenth, second, sixth, seventeenth*) and write them on the board. Ask volunteers to go to the board and number them in sequence.

Divide the class into groups and tell students that they will read the text again in their group. Explain that pairs will take turns reading a part of the text aloud together. Remind them to read clearly so that everyone can understand. Circulate among the groups to check intonation and rhythm, and provide help as needed. Ask simple comprehension questions when they have finished reading to check they have understood: *What is the main idea of the text? What animals appear in the calendar?*

**Try This!** 5 min

Have students think of a new month and draw their own illustrations representing their months, with pictures similar to the frog, dog, and turtle.

## Finish the Class

10 min

Have students write five months as a list on a sheet of paper. Have them stand up and ask their classmates *When's your birthday?* If a classmate has a birthday in one of those five months, students write down the classmate's name next to that month. The first student(s) to get a person's name for all five months is the winner.

Use the **Presentation Kit** for interactive activities in this lesson.

# Lesson 6 Reading Comprehension / Writing

**Lesson Objective:** Identify details in a text.
**Vocabulary Review:** months of the year, ordinal numbers
**Grammar Review:** My birthday is in September. It is the ninth month of the year. There are thirty days in September.
**Materials:** Audio **Track 15**

## Start the Class

5 min

Divide students into pairs and have them take turns asking and answering each other about the months of the year: *What is the ninth month?* Their partner responds *September.*

### ① 15 Listen again to The Mayan Calendars.

5 min

Ask students what they remember about the text they read in the previous lesson. Tell students they will listen to the text again. Remind them to follow the text in their books while they listen. Play **Track 15**.
Ask them to say how well they remembered the information.

### ② Read and check (✓).

5 min

Have different volunteers read the directions and the five sentences in the activity. Explain that they will look at the story again to find the information. Allow time for students to complete the activity, then have them share their answers with a partner.

Copy the chart on the board and have a different student mark the answer for each sentence.

### ③ Say Cheese! Draw a picture for the month of your birthday.

10 min

Write *January* on the board. Tell the class that this is the month when we celebrate the New Year. Draw some party hats and other items that are typically used to celebrate the New Year. Explain to students that they will each draw a picture for the month of their birthday. Circulate around the class to monitor students' work and provide help as needed. Have students show their drawings to a partner.
Then have volunteers share their drawings with the class and say what month it is.

**Try This!** 5 min

Have students with the same birthday month form groups and share the illustrations for their birthday month. Ask them to take a vote on the best picture.

### ④ Writing Time! Write about your birthday month.

15 min

Explain to the class that they will write some sentences about their birthday months. Tell them that they need to know the numbers of their birthday months, for example, *January is the first month of the year.* Elicit the number of other months. Then elicit the number of days for January and two or three other months. Read the first sentence aloud and have students complete it with their birthday months. Allow the class time to complete the sentences. Remind students that months always begin with a capital letter. Ask students to complete the second and third sentences. Circulate around the class to monitor students' work and provide help as needed. Ask volunteers to share their sentences with the class.

## Finish the Class

5 min

Divide the class into two teams and have them line up in front of the board. Tell the class you will say a word or phrase from the text, and a student from each team will go to the board and write it.
If the word or phrase is spelled correctly, the team gets a point. The team with the most points wins. Use words such as *plant, frog, month, turtle, animal,* and *birthday.*

Use the **Presentation Kit** for interactive activities in this lesson.

For the next lesson, use **Skills Book Pages 14 and 15** (Word Work). Go to Teacher's Edition **Page T 165** for teacher notes.

# Lesson 6

## Lesson 6

1 15 Listen again to **The Mayan Calendars.**

2 **Read and check (✓).**

| | Mayan calendar | Our calendar | Both calendars |
|---|---|---|---|
| 1. There are nineteen months. | ✓ | | |
| 2. There are 365 days. | | | ✓ |
| 3. There is a month called May. | | ✓ | |
| 4. There are pictures for each month. | ✓ | | |
| 5. There is a frog, a dog, and a turtle. | ✓ | | |

3 **Say Cheese!** **Draw a picture for the month of your birthday.**

(Student's own answers.)

4 **Writing Time!** **Write about your birthday month.**

My birthday is in (Student's own answers) is the ________ month of the year. There are ________ days in ________.

# Lesson 7

## Lesson 7

## Team Up!

**1** **Think about** how your birthday month is special.

**2** **Share** your ideas.

September is in the fall.

April is rainy.

**3** **Team up** and make a Birthday Calendar.

My birthday is May twenty-second.

# Lesson 7 Creative, Collaborative, and Critical Thinking Activity

**Lesson Objective:** Talk about birthdays, seasons, and weather.
**Vocabulary Review:** months of the year, seasons, weather adjectives
**Grammar Review:** September is in the fall. April is rainy. My birthday is May 22nd.
**Materials:** Audio **Track 11**; colored pencils, markers, or crayons; construction paper

## Start the Class

5 min

Tell students that you will play "Birthday Song!" again. Play **Track 11** again and have students sing along.

**Try This!** 5 min

Draw a grid with four squares on the board; write the four seasons as headings. Ask volunteers to go to the board. Have each volunteer write the month of his or her birthday in the corresponding square.

### ① Think about how your birthday month is special.

5 min

Tell students to look at **Page 22** and have a volunteer read the directions. Explain that each student will work individually to think about a picture that represents his or her birthday month, showing the weather or typical activities in that month.

### ② Share your ideas.

5 min

Ask two volunteers to read the sample dialogue on the page.

Tell students that they will work in groups of four and share their ideas for the different pictures for their birthday months. If possible, students working together should have different birthday months. Circulate around the classroom to correct pronunciation and provide help as needed.

### ③ Team up and make a Birthday Calendar.

15 min

Tell students that each group of four students will make a Birthday Calendar. Each student will work individually to draw a picture for his or her birthday month using colored pencils on white paper. All four students then work to mark the months of the year on construction paper using markers. Then they cut out and glue their pictures onto the corresponding squares of their Birthday Calender.

## Finish the Class

15 min

Have teams share their Birthday Calendars with the class. Remind them to point to the months when they are talking. Be sure each member of the team speaks at least once. After all the teams have presented, have the class vote on the top three Birthday Calendars. Display the calendars in the classroom.

Use the **Presentation Kit** for interactive activities in this lesson.

Use the **Assessment Pack** to carry out the Unit 2 Teamwork Assessment during this lesson.

# Lesson 8 Review

**Lesson Objective:** Review language from Unit 2.
**Vocabulary Review:** months of the year, ordinal numbers
**Materials:** cards with months written on them, 12 safety pins

## Start the Class

5 min

Attach the cards with the months on the backs of 12 students with safety pins so the students cannot see them. Ask students to place themselves in order. Their classmates can give hints, but no one can say the name of the month: *It is the ninth month.*

## ① Spelling! Write the words.

10 min

Draw two columns on the board. In the left column write the numbers *1, 2, 3, 4, 10,* and *14*. In the right column write the endings *-nd, -th, -th, -st, -th,* and *-rd*. Have students match the two columns. Have volunteers go to the board and point to the numbers as they say them aloud (*first, second, third, fourth, tenth, fourteenth*).

Ask a volunteer to read the directions. Explain that they will look at the numbers and write the correct words. Then have volunteers write the correct words on the board, and have students check their answers.

## ② Unscramble.

10 min

Point to the scrambled words and explain to students that they will unscramble them to write the months. Circulate around the class to monitor students and provide help as needed. Encourage them to use the pictures to guide them. Tell students to compare their answers with a partner. Review the answers by having volunteers write the words on the board.

Divide the class into pairs. Tell each student to write three scrambled months and exchange them with his or her partner, who will unscramble them.

**Try This!** 5 min

Tell students to stand in a circle. Say *Change places if your birthday is in (September)*. Students whose birthdays are in September have to change places. Continue with other months.

## ③ Word Play! Find and circle the words from Unit 2 on Page 72.

10 min

Have students turn to **Page 72** and tell them to find and circle the month and ordinal number vocabulary words from Unit 2. Students must find the ordinal numbers from *first* to *tenth,* and all twelve months. Then have students check the words they found with a partner.

## Finish the Class

10 min

Write ordinal number words in random order around the board, with one word for each student in the class. Explain to students that they will go to the board and take turns drawing a line from the highest number to the lowest number.

Use the **Presentation Kit** for interactive activities in this lesson.

For the next lesson, use Unit 2 Language Assessment from the **Assessment Pack** or create your own test using the **Test Generator** on the **Teacher's Resource Center**.

# Lesson 8

Lesson 8

## Round Up!

**1 Spelling! Write the words.**

1. 14th fourteenth
2. 3rd third
3. 22nd twenty - second
4. 31st thirty - first
5. 7th seventh
6. 16th sixteenth

**2 Unscramble.**

1.  rayFberu February
2.  lrpiA April
3.  nuJe June
4.  gutAus August
5.  ovNmerbe November
6.  mebceDer December

**3 Word Play! Find and circle the words from Unit 2 on Page 72.**

# Unit 3

## Unit Objectives

**By the end of the unit, students can:**

- Tell the time.
- Ask and answer questions about the times they do daily activities.
- Show understanding of the main idea and sequence of a text.

## Student Book

### Vocabulary

**Times of Day / Adverbs of Time:** in the morning, in the afternoon, in the evening, at night, noon, midnight, early, late

**Daily Routines:** get up, eat breakfast, eat lunch, eat dinner, go to school, go to bed

### Skills

**Listening:** Listen for and tell the time.
Listen for specific information and circle an appropriate response.

**Speaking:** Ask and answer questions about daily routines.
Respond to questions about time with appropriate answers.

**Reading:** Read a nonfiction text (social studies): **A School Day**.
Identify sequence of events.
Read short sentences and recognize words.

**Writing:** Write a sequence of daily routines and the times.

### Grammar

What time is it? It's noon. / It's 2:30. / It's 2 o'clock in the afternoon.
What time do you eat breakfast? At 7 o'clock in the morning.
What time do they go to bed? At 9 o'clock at night.

### Creative, Collaborative, and Critical Thinking Competencies

**Daily Activities Poster**

**Creativity:** Develop self-expression, innovation, and problem-solving skills. Determine the information to be included in the poster and how it will be presented.

**Collaboration:** Use communication skills and conflict resolution skills to complete tasks. Determine the information to be included in the poster of the team's day and how each team member will contribute to the final product.

**Critical Thinking:** Use problem-solving skills, analyze information, and organize information to complete the final product.

## Skills Book

**Extra Skills Practice**

**Speaking and Listening:** Make statements about a picture and respond.

**Reading and Writing:** Identify the sequence of events.
Summarize the story.
Identify correct prepositions for time phrases.
Categorize words.

# Teacher Workshop

## Teaching with Technology

Use the interactive activities in the Presentation Kit as a way to do a quick review of previous lessons, or instead of having students do the activity in their books during class time. Assign the activity as homework to consolidate what was learned in class. You may choose to use the interactive activity to quickly review homework answers to keep students engaged and focused.

## Teaching with Games

**Circle Game**

Ask students to make a large circle with their chairs. Remove one of the chairs. Ask students to find a chair and sit down. The student who is left stands in the center and says a sentence about daily routines, for example: *I get up at 6:00.* All students who do the routine at the same time stand and switch seats. The student in the center tries to sit in one of the empty seats while everyone is moving around. The student who wasn't able to sit down now says another sentence to repeat the process. Circulate and provide encouragement.

## Happy Teacher

Vary the ways you organize students into pairs or groups. Have them work with the person to the right or left of them, in front of them, or behind them. Have them make a list of six "contacts" (possible partners) and call out *Work with contact number (five)!* You can also prepare two sets of cards and have students pair up with the other student who has the matching card. The cards could have vocabulary words for students to match the pictures to words, or the beginning of a phrase/sentence to the end.

## Happy Class

To energize your class, choose one of these quick break tricks. Have students:

- Take out a blank sheet of paper and doodle for three minutes.
- Play Tic-Tac-Toe with a friend for three minutes.
- Sing a song that has motions.
- Clap their hands in different slow and quick patterns.

By Patricia Acosta

# UNIT 3

## Lesson 1

1 (16) **Listen. Then echo.**

6:00AM – 12:00PM
in the morning

12:00PM – 6:00PM
in the afternoon

6:00PM – 9:00PM
in the evening

9:00PM – 12:00AM
at night

12:00PM noon
12:00AM midnight

early

late

2 (17) **Listen and write the times.**

**Let's Go!**

What time is it? What time is it?
Let's go! Let's go! Let's go!

3 Page 9 **The Language Lodge**



## Lesson 2

1 (17) **Sing: Let's Go!**

1. It's 12 o'clock.
2. It's 7 o'clock.
3. It's 2 o'clock.
4. It's 6 o'clock.
5. It's 10 o'clock.

### Grammar Snapshot!

What time is it?
It's noon.
It's 2:30.
It's 2 o'clock in the afternoon.

2 **Circle the answer.**

1. What time is it?
   a. It's 4 o'clock in the morning.
   b. In the morning.
2. What time is it?
   a. In the evening.
   b. It's 3 o'clock in the afternoon.

3 **Ask and answer.**

What time is it?

It's 10 o'clock at night. It's late!

1. 10:00PM
2. 3:00PM
3. 6:00AM
4. 7:00PM
5. 12:00AM
6. 12:00PM

4 Page 10 **The Language Lodge**



# UNIT 3

## Lesson 1

1 **Circle.**

| | | |
|---|---|---|
| 1. in the afternoon | 7:00AM | (2:00PM) |
| 2. early | (4:00AM) | 6:00PM |
| 3. in the morning | (8:00AM) | 10:00PM |
| 4. at night | (9:00PM) | 5:00AM |
| 5. late | 8:00PM | (11:00PM) |

✓ **Spelling Check! Spell the times of day aloud. Then complete.** I can spell ____ words.

Student Book **Page 24**



# Lesson 1

This may also be completed for homework.

# Lesson 1 Vocabulary



**Lesson Objective:** Identify the times of the day.
**New Vocabulary:** in the morning, in the afternoon, in the evening, at night, noon, midnight, early, late
**Materials:** Audio **Tracks 16 and 17**, a large cardboard clock

## Start the Class

5 min

Write the word *time* on the board and draw a digital clock showing the time. Ask students to give examples in L1 of times of the day, and have them draw clocks on the board showing the times.

### 1 16 Listen. Then echo.

10 min

Have students look at the clocks/pictures and identify the phrases in L1. Explain that *noon* and *midnight* are different ways to say 12:00 p.m. and 12:00 a.m. Make sure students understand *early* and *late*.

Play **Track 16** and have students listen and point to the clocks/pictures as they hear them mentioned.

Play the track again and have students echo the phrases. Tell students to draw a circle around the phrase with *at*, and a square around the phrases with *in*.

**Try This!**

5 min

Play **Track 16** again, pausing after each word for children to repeat the word and clap twice. Then have them chant the words.

### 2 17 Listen and write the times.

15 min

Write the numbers *1–12* on the board and have students say them aloud. Explain that each student is going to say a number in sequence, but that students with even numbers will clap instead of saying their numbers. For example, the first student says *one*, the second student claps, and the third student says *three*. Repeat with claps for odd numbers.

Explain to the class that they are going to listen to a song and write the times they hear. Play **Track 17** and have the students write the times. Play the track again for students to complete any times they missed.

Have students compare their answers with a partner. Play **Track 17** once more, and pause it to check the answers with the class. Have different volunteers come to the front and show the times with a large cardboard clock, or by drawing digital clocks on the board.

### 3 Page 9 The Language Lodge.

10 min

Have students flip to The Language Lodge **Page 9**.

**1 Circle.**

Have a volunteer read the directions. Explain to students that they will look at the word or phrase and circle the correct clock.
Have students compare their answers with a partner. Then review as a class.

**Spelling Check! Spell the times of day aloud. Then complete.**

Have students close their books. Tell them that they will take turns saying and spelling the times of day with a partner. Then tell students to write the number of words they can spell correctly.

## Finish the Class

5 min

Have students decide on gestures for *in the morning, noon, afternoon*, and *evening*.

Play **Track 17** again and pause after each verse for students to stand up and practice the gesture.

Use the **Presentation Kit** for interactive activities in this lesson.

Have students use the **Happy Campers app** for additional practice with the new vocabulary.

**The Language Lodge Page 9** may also be completed for homework.

# Lesson 2 Grammar

**Lesson Objective:** Ask and give the time.
**New Grammar:** What time is it? It's noon. / It's 2:30. / It's 2 o'clock in the afternoon.
**Vocabulary Review:** in the morning, in the afternoon, in the evening, at night, noon, midnight, early, late
**Materials:** Audio **Track 17**, a large cardboard clock

## Start the Class

5 min

Write the words from the previous lesson on the board and ask students to repeat them. Erase the last two letters in each word and ask students to repeat them again. Erase two more letters and ask students to say the words.

### 1 17 Sing: Let's Go!

5 min

Tell students they are going to listen to the song again. Play **Track 17**.

Play the track again and have the class sing along.

**Try This!** 5 min

Divide the class into two groups and have students stand and face one another. Explain that they are going to sing the song again. One group will sing the first two lines of the song and the other group will respond with the time. Practice speaking the lines a few times before singing the song. Then play the track and sing along. If time allows, have the groups switch roles.

### 2 Circle the answer.

10 min

Write the following example on the board: *What _____ is it? It's 7 o'clock in the morning.* Point out that 7 o'clock occurs in the morning *and* in the evening, and that the phrase *in the morning* indicates the part of the day. Elicit other phrases that indicate the part of the day.

Have the class read the Grammar Snapshot! together. Have a volunteer read the directions for Activity 2 on **Page 25**. Then have volunteers share their answers with the class.

### 3 Ask and answer.

10 min

Show students the large cardboard clock with the hands showing 12:00, or draw a clock on the board. Ask students how we know if it is 12:00 noon or 12:00 midnight. Explain that *a.m.* and *p.m.* are used to indicate time before or after noon or midnight. Say different times such as *3 o'clock in the afternoon*, and have students say *a.m.* or *p.m.* Have volunteers read the speech bubbles. Divide students into pairs and tell students they are going to take turns pointing to a clock and asking and answering questions about the time. Encourage students to say if it is early or late. Circulate among the pairs to check understanding and pronunciation. Have volunteers share their dialogues with the class.

### 4 Page 10 The Language Lodge

10 min

Have students flip to The Language Lodge **Page 10**. Have a volunteer read the Grammar Snapshot! aloud.

**1 Match.**

Explain to the class that they will match the clocks and the times. Have volunteers share their answers with the class.

**2 Draw the time. Answer.**

Explain to students that they are going to draw the time on the clock and then write the answer to the question. Then ask the question and have volunteers show their clocks as they answer.

## Finish the Class

5 min

Write *a.m.* and *p.m.* on the board. Say *It's 6 o'clock in the morning.* Have students point to *a.m.* on the board. Repeat with different times of the day.

Use the **Presentation Kit** for interactive activities in this lesson.

**The Language Lodge Page 10** may also be completed for homework.

For the next lesson, use **Skills Book Pages 16 and 17** (Picture Talk). Go to Teacher's Edition **Page T 166** for teacher notes.

UNIT 3

Lesson 1

1 16 Listen. Then echo.

6:00AM – 12:00PM
in the morning

12:00PM – 6:00PM
in the afternoon

6:00PM – 9:00PM
in the evening

9:00PM – 12:00AM
at night

12:00PM noon

12:00AM midnight

early

late

2 17 Listen and write the times.

Let's Go!

What time is it? What time is it?
Let's go! Let's go! Let's go!

3 Page 9 The Language Lodge

24

Lesson 2

1 17 Sing: Let's Go!

1. It's 12 o'clock.
2. It's ______.
3. It's ______.
4. It's ______.
5. It's ______.

*Grammar Snapshot!*

What time is it?
It's noon.
It's 2:30.
It's 2 o'clock in the afternoon.

2 Circle the answer.

1. What time is it?
   a. It's 4 o'clock in the morning.
   b. In the morning
2. What time is it?
   a. In the evening
   b. It's 3 o'clock in the afternoon.

3 Ask and answer.

What time is it?

It's 10 o'clock at night. It's late!

1. 10:00PM 2. 3:00PM
3. 6:00AM 4. 1:00PM
5. 12:00AM 6. 12:00PM

4 Page 10 The Language Lodge

25

# Lesson 2

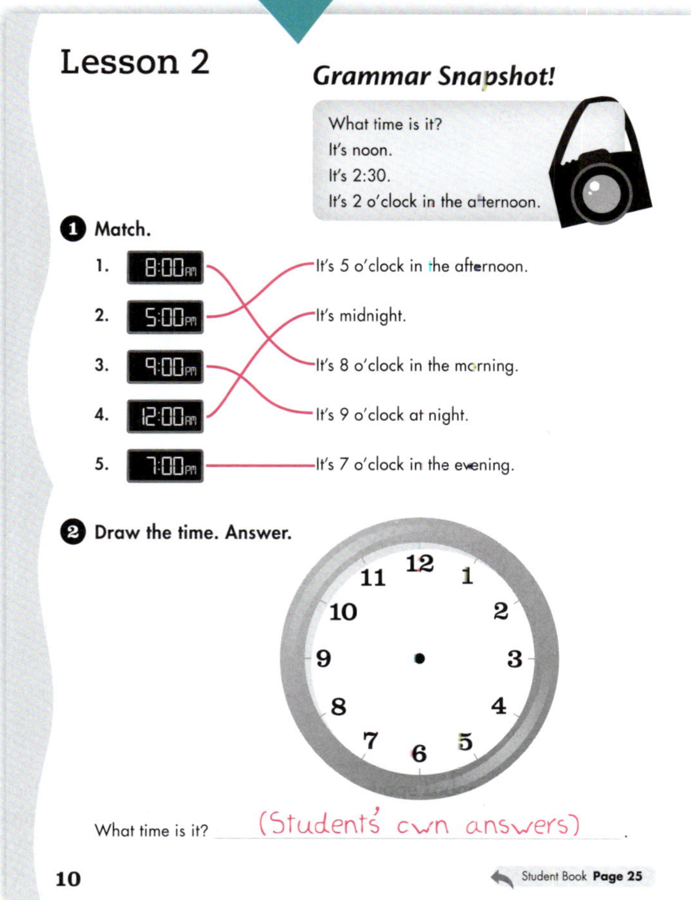

Lesson 2

*Grammar Snapshot!*

What time is it?
It's noon.
It's 2:30.
It's 2 o'clock in the afternoon.

1 Match.

1. 8:00AM — It's 8 o'clock in the morning.
2. 5:00PM — It's 5 o'clock in the afternoon.
3. 9:00PM — It's 9 o'clock at night.
4. 12:00AM — It's midnight.
5. 7:00PM — It's 7 o'clock in the evening.

2 Draw the time. Answer.

What time is it? (Students' own answers).

10

Student Book Page 25

This may also be completed for homework.

## Lesson 3

# Shutterbugs

**1** What is Tom's pet?

**2** 18 Read and listen.

**3** 19 **Dictation!** Listen and write. Then say.

 1. get up
 2. eat breakfast
 3. go to school
 4. eat lunch
 5. eat dinner
 6. go to bed

**4** Page 11 The Language Lodge



## Lesson 4

**1** 18 Listen again to **Shutterbugs**.

**2** ***Grammar Snapshot!*** **Read and match.**

| | |
|---|---|
| 1. What time do they eat lunch? | At 7 o'clock. |
| 2. What time do you get up? | At noon. |
| 3. What time do you eat dinner? | At 6 o'clock. |

**3** 20 **Listen and cheer!**

What time do you go to school?

At 7:00! At 7:00! I go to school at 7 o'clock!

CHEER BOX!

**4** Page 12 The Language Lodge



## Lesson 3

**1** Write.

| | | |
|---|---|---|
| eat breakfast | go to bed | get up |
| go to school | eat lunch | eat dinner |

1.  eat breakfast
2.  eat lunch
3.  go to bed
4.  eat dinner
5.  go to school
6.  get up

✓ **Spelling Check! Spell the daily routines aloud. Then complete.** I can spell ☐ words.

Student Book **Page 26**



# Lesson 3

This may also be completed for homework.

# Lesson 3 Vocabulary in Context

**Lesson Objective:** Identify daily routines.
**New Vocabulary:** get up, eat breakfast, go to school, eat lunch, eat dinner, go to bed
**Vocabulary Review:** noon
**Grammar Review:** It's 9 o'clock.
**Materials:** Audio **Tracks 18 and 19**, strips of paper

## Start the Class

5 min

Demonstrate how to mime the hour and minute hands on a clock face using your arms. For example, put your arms straight up and together to represent 12 o'clock, and your left arm raised and right arm stretched out at shoulder level to represent *3 o'clock*. Practice a few times. Then call out different times and have students show the time with their arms.

### ① What is Tom's pet?

2 min

Have students look at the pictures, find and point to Tom's pet, and answer the question. Elicit *A cat.*

### ② 18 Read and listen.

10 min

Tell students they are going to read the comic strip as they listen. Remind them to follow the words with their fingers. Play **Track 18**.
Say an activity in one of the scenes, for example, *do homework*. Have students point to the correct picture. Repeat the procedure for *eat lunch* and *go to bed*.
Have students circle six daily-routine expressions in the comic strip.

**Try This!**

8 min

Divide the class into groups of four. Have students number off from one to four and form groups with other students with the same number. Explain to students that they will each play a part from the story. Have students read their parts aloud. Remind students to return to their places quickly after the activity.

### ③ 19 Dictation! Listen and write. Then say.

10 min

Have a volunteer read the directions. Play **Track 19** and pause for students to write the phrases. Play the track again. Have students check their answers with a partner. Ask volunteers to write the answers on the board. Tell students they are going to hear the track again and repeat what they hear. Play **Track 19**.

*Audio script **Track 19***
*1. get up 2. eat breakfast 3. go to school*
*4. eat lunch 5. eat dinner 6. go to bed*

### ④ Page 11 The Language Lodge

10 min

Have the students flip to The Language Lodge **Page 11**.

**1 Write.**

Have a volunteer read the directions and the words in the box aloud. Do Item 1 as a class. Then have students complete the activity individually. Circulate around the class and provide help as needed. Review the answers as a class.

**Spelling Check! Spell the daily routines aloud. Then complete.**

Have students close their books. Tell them that they will take turns saying and spelling the daily routines with a partner. Then tell students to write the number of words they can spell correctly.

## Finish the Class

5 min

Write daily routines on six strips of paper. Have a volunteer come to the front of the class, choose a strip of paper, and act it out for the class to guess. Continue the procedure with the other phrases.

Use the **Presentation Kit** for interactive activities in this lesson.

Have students use the **Happy Campers app** for additional practice with the new vocabulary.

**The Language Lodge Page 11** may also be completed for homework.

# Lesson 4 Grammar in Context

**Lesson Objective:** Ask and answer questions about daily routines and times.
**New Grammar:** What time do Lisa and Clare eat lunch? At noon.
What time do you get up? At 7 o'clock.
**Vocabulary Review:** get up, eat breakfast, go to school, eat lunch, eat dinner, go to bed
**Materials:** Audio **Tracks 18 and 20**

## Start the Class
5 min

Write the names of the characters from "Shutterbugs" on the board. Ask students what they remember about the characters' daily routines, and write students' responses after the name of each character.

### 1 18 Listen again to Shutterbugs.
10 min

Tell the class that they are going to listen again to the comic strip and read along as they listen. Explain that they should listen for questions and answers. Play **Track 18**. Then have students underline the questions and circle the answers in the comic strip.

### 2 Grammar Snapshot! Read and match.
10 min

Write *What time do they eat lunch*? on the board. Ask students to read the question aloud. Erase *eat lunch* and ask them to say the whole question again. Erase two more words and have the class repeat the question each time you erase a word.

Have a volunteer read the directions for Activity 2 on **Page 27**. Explain to the class that they will read the story again and match each question with the correct answer and character. Tell students to work individually, and then have them compare their answers with a partner. Have students identify the characters in the activity. Then have volunteers share their answers with the class.

**Try This!** 5 min

Divide the class in two groups. Explain that they will take turns asking and answering the questions from the comic strip chorally. One group asks the question, and the other group gives the answer. When they have asked all the questions, they switch roles.

### 3 20 Listen and cheer!
5 min

Tell the class they are going to listen to a cheer and read the words as they listen. Play **Track 20**. Explain to the class that you are going to play the cheer again and this time they will do the cheer with the track. Play **Track 20**. Have two or three volunteers ask the question in unison for the rest of the class to answer. Repeat several times with different volunteers.

### 4 Page 12 The Language Lodge
10 min

Have the students flip to The Language Lodge **Page 12**. Direct the class to the Grammar Snapshot! Divide the class into two teams. Have one team read the questions aloud and the other team read the answers.

**1 Complete.**
Explain to the class that they will read the questions and complete them. Then have volunteers write the missing words on the board.

**2 Make a daily schedule.**
Have students look at the chart. Explain that they should complete it with the correct times for them. Circulate around the class and provide help as needed.

## Finish the Class
5 min

Have students work with a partner. Have them change the words in the cheer for other activities and times, and then say a new cheer.

Use the **Presentation Kit** for interactive activities in this lesson.

**The Language Lodge Page 12** may also be completed for homework.

For the next lesson, use **Skills Book Pages 18 and 19** (Happy Reader). Go to Teacher's Edition **Page T 167** for teacher notes.

## Lesson 3

# Shutterbugs

1 What is Tom's pet?

2 18 Read and listen.

3 19 **Dictation!** Listen and write. Then say.

1. ______________ 2. ______________
3. ______________ 4. ______________
5. ______________ 6. ______________

4 Page 11 The Language Lodge



## Lesson 4

1 18 Listen again to **Shutterbugs**.

2 ***Grammar Snapshot!*** Read and match.

1. What time do they eat lunch? — At 7 o'clock.
2. What time do you get up? — At noon.
3. What time do you eat dinner? — At 6 o'clock.

3 20 Listen and cheer!

What time do you go to school?
At 7:00! At 7:00! I go to school at 7 o'clock!

CHEER BOX!

4 Page 12 The Language Lodge



# Lesson 4

This may also be completed for homework.

## Lesson 4

### *Grammar Snapshot!*

What time do you eat breakfast?
At 7 o'clock in the morning.
What time do they go to bed?
At 9 o'clock at night.

1 **Complete.**

1. What time __do__ you eat lunch?
2. What __time__ __do__ they get up?
3. What time __do__ you __go__ to school?

2 **Make a daily schedule.**

| Activity | Time |
|---|---|
|  get up | At 6:45 in the morning. |
|  eat breakfast | (Students' own answers.) |
|  go to school | (Students' own answers.) |
|  eat lunch | (Students' own answers.) |
|  eat dinner | (Students' own answers.) |
|  go to bed | (Students' own answers.) |



Student Book Page 27

# Lesson 5

Lesson 5

**1** **Circle what the text is about.**

**a.** school  **b.** daily routines

**2** 21 **Read and listen.**

## A School Day

It's 6:00 in the morning. Time to get up! Children get dressed and eat breakfast. It's almost time to go to school!

At noon many children eat lunch at school. They eat in the cafeteria with their friends. It's a time to relax, eat, and talk.

Children do homework in the evening. Sometimes they have a lot of homework.

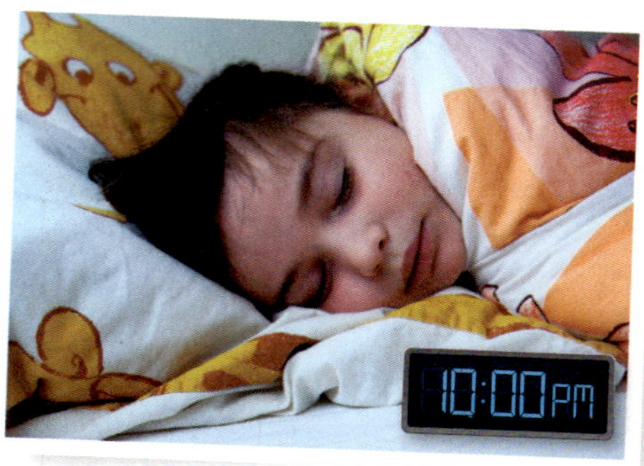


At 9 or 10 o'clock at night, many children go to bed. It's late and it's time to rest. What a long day!

# Lesson 5 Nonfiction Reading

**Lesson Objective:** Read a nonfiction text to practice unit language.
**New Vocabulary:** get dressed
**Vocabulary Review:** eat breakfast, go to school, eat lunch, do homework, go to bed
**Grammar Review:** It's 6:00 in the morning. Children get dressed and eat breakfast.
**Materials:** Audio **Track 21**

## Start the Class

5 min

Write different times on the board and ask *What time is it*? to review times. Point out that times can be written different ways: *7 o'clock*, *7:00*, and *7:00 p.m.*

Pre-teach *time to get up* and *time to rest.*

### ① Circle what the text is about.

10 min

Tell students to open their books to **Page 28**. Tell students to look at the pictures. Ask *Is this a nonfiction text or a story*? Elicit *nonfiction text.* Have students explain their reasons. They may do so in L1. Have a volunteer read the directions for Activity 1. Have students identify the activities in the photos. Then ask *Is the text about school or about daily routines*? Write the two options on different sides of the board and have students line up on the side of the answer they think is correct. Encourage several students to explain their reasons.

Tell students to return to their seats and have a volunteer read the title of the text. Point out that it says "A School Day" (not "School"), and only one of the four pictures is about school. The others are about actions we do every day, or daily routines. Review the answer to Activity 1: *daily routines.*

### ② 21 Read and listen.

20 min

Have a volunteer read the title of the story again. Point to the clocks in each of the pictures and ask *What time is it*?

Tell students they are going to listen to the track and follow the words with their fingers in their books as they listen. Play **Track 21**. Then have students look for words in the text that show what the children are doing (*get dressed, have lunch, do homework, go to bed*). Ask *What time do they get up / eat lunch / do homework / go to bed*?

Divide the class into groups of four and tell students that they are going to read the text again in their groups. Explain that each person in the group will read a part of the text. Remind them to read carefully and clearly. Circulate among the groups to check pronunciation or provide help as needed.

**Try This!**

5 min

Divide the class into two teams. Write *True* and *False* in large letters on the board. Ask one student from each team to the board. Explain that you are going to say a sentence and he or she will decide if the sentence is true or false based on the text. Say *Children get up at 10 o'clock at night.* The first student to touch the correct answer on the board wins a point for his or her team. Play several times until all the children have participated.

## Finish the Class

10 min

Tell students that they will work with a partner to ask and answer questions about the text. Provide the following example: *What time do they get up? They get up at 6 o'clock.*

Use the **Presentation Kit** for interactive activities in this lesson.

# Lesson 6 Reading Comprehension / Writing

**Lesson Objectives:** Recall the sequence of events from a text. Write about daily routines.
**Vocabulary Review:** get up, eat breakfast, go to school, eat lunch in the cafeteria, do homework, go to bed
**Grammar Review:** Children eat lunch in the cafeteria. I get up at 6 o'clock.
**Materials:** Audio **Track 21**, six cards with daily-routine phrases, music

## Start the Class

5 min

Have six volunteers come to the board and give them the six cards with daily-routine phrases written on them. Tell them to stand in order and show the cards with the routines. Once they have come up with a logical order, have the class say the routines aloud.

### 1 21 Listen again to A School Day.

5 min

Tell students they will listen to the text again. Remind them to follow along with the text in their books while they listen. Play **Track 21**.

Tell students they will listen again and whisper along with the text.

### 2 Number the activities in order.

10 min

Have different volunteers read the directions and the six sentences in the activity. Explain that they will work individually to number the sentences in the same order as the text. Allow time for students to complete the activity, and then have them share their answers with a partner.

Tell students they are going to listen to "A School Day" again to check their answers. Play **Track 21** again and pause when appropriate to give students time to check the numbered activities. Read the sentences and have the class say the number.

**Try This!**

5 min

Divide the class into two teams and have them line up. Tell the class you are going to say a word or phrase from the lesson, and a student from each team will go to the board and write it. If the word is spelled correctly, the team gets a point. Use words and phrases such as *morning*, *late*, *go to bed*, and *eat lunch*.

### 3 Say Cheese! Draw an activity from your day. Write the time.

10 min

Write *I get up at 6 o'clock* on the board. Tell the class that it's an activity you do every day. Explain that each student will draw a picture of an activity from his or her daily routine and write the time when it happens. Circulate around the class to monitor students' work and provide help as needed. Have students show their drawings to a partner. Then have volunteers share their drawings with the class, say what activity it is, and say what time it happens.

### 4 Writing Time! Write about your day.

10 min

Explain to the class that they are going to write some sentences about their days. Read the first sentence aloud and have volunteers complete it with the time. Allow the class time to complete the first sentence. Remind students that the sentences should be in the order of their days, and that each sentence starts with a capital letter and ends with a period. Circulate around the class to monitor students' work and provide help as needed. Allow students time to write several sentences, and then have them exchange their sentences with a partner. Check that each sentence has an activity and a time. Ask volunteers to share their sentences with the class.

## Finish the Class

5 min

Have the class form a circle. Give random students the six cards with daily routines. Play some music and have students pass the cards around the circle to the right. Stop the music, and have students with the cards take turns miming the routines on their cards for the class to guess.

Use the **Presentation Kit** for the interactive activities in this lesson.

For the next lesson, use **Skills Book Pages 20 and 21** (Word Work). Go to Teacher's Edition **Page T 168** for teacher notes.

# Lesson 6

## Lesson 6

**1** 21 **Listen again to A School Day.**

**2** **Number the activities in order.**

- 4 They eat lunch in the cafeteria.
- 2 They eat breakfast.
- 3 They go to school.
- 1 Children get up.
- 6 They go to bed.
- 5 They do homework.

**3** **Say Cheese! Draw an activity from your day. Write the time.**

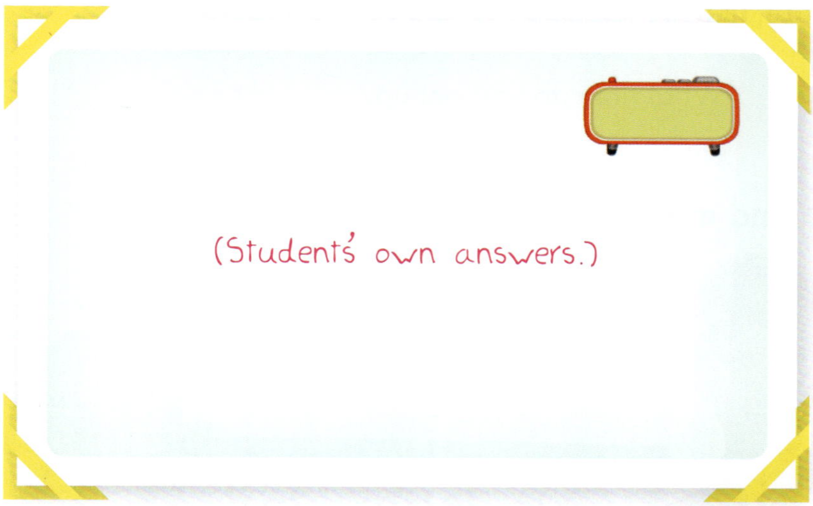


**4** **Writing Time! Write about your day.**

I get up at (Students' own answers). ______________________

______________________________________________

______________________________________________

______________________________________________.

# Lesson 7

Lesson 7

## Team Up!

**1** Think about your day. Make a list of activities and times.

My Day
1. get up: 6:00
2. go to school: 7:00

**2** Share your list.

What time do you get up?

At 6:00.

**3** Team up and make a Daily Activities Poster.

# Lesson 7 Creative, Collaborative, and Critical Thinking Activity

**Lesson Objective:** Talk about daily routines.
**Vocabulary Review:** get up, eat breakfast, go to school, eat lunch, eat dinner, do homework, go to bed
**Grammar Review:** What time do you get up? I get up at 6:00.
**Materials:** Audio **Track 17**; construction paper; pencils, markers, or crayons

## Start the Class

5 min

Ask students at the head of each row *What time do you eat lunch*? Then have that student ask the person seated next to him or her the same question. Repeat until the last student in each row has answered. Ask another daily-routine question such as *What time do you do homework*? Have students ask and answer the question in a chain as they did before.

**Try This!**

5 min

Tell students that you are going to play the song "Let's Go!" again. Divide students into five groups. Assign each group a time from the song, and explain that they will stand up and sing that part. Play **Track 17** again, and have groups stand up and sing their parts of the song.

### ① Think about your day. Make a list of activities and times.

5 min

Tell students to look at **Page 30** and have a volunteer read the directions. Explain that they are going to work individually to write a list of activities and the times they do them.

### ② Share your list.

5 min

Ask two volunteers to read the sample dialogue on **Page 30**.

Tell students that they are going to work with a partner and take turns asking and answering questions about their daily routines. Circulate around the classroom to correct pronunciation and provide help as needed.

### ③ Team up and make a Daily Activities Poster.

15 min

Divide the class into teams of four. Tell them that they will make a poster about their team's day. Explain that they will decide which of their team's activities to include on the poster. Remind students to illustrate the activities, indicate times, and put a title on the poster. Students also must decide which team members will do which tasks to complete the poster for their presentation. Circulate among the teams and provide help as needed.

## Finish the Class

15 min

Have teams share their posters with the class. Remind them to point to the activities and say what time they happen. Be sure each member of the team speaks at least once. After all the teams have presented, have the class vote on the top three posters. Display the posters in the classroom.

Use the **Presentation Kit** for interactive activities in this lesson.

Use the **Assessment Pack** to carry out the Unit 3 Teamwork Assessment during this lesson.

# Lesson 8 Review

**Lesson Objective:** Review vocabulary and grammar from Unit 3.
**Vocabulary Review:** get up, eat breakfast, go to school, eat lunch, do homework, eat dinner, go to bed, in the morning, in the afternoon, in the evening, noon, midnight, at night, early, late
**Grammar Review:** What time is it? It's 5:00 in the morning.
What time do you go to school? At 8:00 in the morning.
**Materials:** six strips of paper with sentences about daily routines

## Start the Class

5 min

Divide the class into several teams. Explain that they are going to take turns saying as many words as they can remember from this unit. A student in each team says the first word, and the rest of the team takes turns adding more words. Circulate around the class and provide help as needed.

### ① Spelling! Write the times of day.

10 min

Have students identify the types of clocks on **Page 31** and elicit the times. Explain to students that you are going to say the times, but in a mixed-up order, so that students have to point to the corresponding clock. Start out slowly at first, and then increase speed while students point to the different times.

Ask a volunteer to read the directions. Explain that they will look at the clocks and write the correct times in sentences. Then have volunteers write the correct times on the board while students check the answers.

### ② Read and match.

10 min

Write the time school starts on the left side of the board, the time students eat lunch in the center of the board, and the time students eat breakfast on the right side of the board. Have four to six volunteers go to the board. Explain that you are going to ask a question and they have to stand under the correct time. Ask *What time do you go to school*? and have them stand under the corresponding time. The students who are sitting down must confirm if the time is correct. Continue with the other times.

Point to the two columns in Activity 2, and explain to students that they are going to match the questions and the times. Circulate around the class to monitor students and provide help as needed. Tell students to compare their answers with a partner. Review the answers by reading the questions and having the class say the answers chorally.

**Try This!**

5 min

Tell students to stand in a circle. Say *Change places if you get up at 6 o'clock*. Students who get up at 6:00 have to change places. Continue with other routines and times.

### ③ Word Play! Find and circle the words from Unit 3 on Page 72.

15 min

Have students turn to **Page 72** and tell them to circle the time-of-day and daily-routine vocabulary words from Unit 3. Then have students check the words they found with a partner.

## Finish the Class

5 min

Write six sentences about the six daily routines on six separate slips of paper. Give them to different students and have the students go to the board and arrange themselves in the order of the activities. Ask them to read the sentences aloud. The class claps three times if they agree with the order of activities. Repeat with different activities.

Use the **Presentation Kit** for interactive activities in this lesson.

For the next lesson, use Unit 3 Language Assessment from the **Assessment Pack** or create your own test using the **Test Generator** on the **Teacher's Resource Center**.

# Lesson 8

## Lesson 8

## Round Up!

**1 Spelling! Write the times of day.**

1.  It's 5:00 in the morning.

2.  It's 2:00 in the afternoon.



3.  It's 7:00 in the evening.

4.  It's 9:00 at night.



**2 Read and match.**

| | |
|---|---|
| 1. What time do you get up? | Late. At 10:00 at night. |
| 2. What time do you go to school? | At noon. |
| 3. What time do you go to bed? | Early. At 6:00 in the morning. |
| 4. What time do you do homework? | At 8:00 in the morning. |
| 5. What time do you eat lunch? | At 7:00 in the evening. |

**3 Word Play! Find and circle the words from Unit 3 on Page 72.**

# Unit 4

## Unit Objectives

**By the end of the unit, students can:**

- Identify sports and home activities.
- Make statements about a picture and respond.
- Personalize a story.

## Student Book

### Vocabulary

**Sports:** baseball, basketball, football, golf, ping pong, soccer, tennis, volleyball

**At Home:** listen to music, talk on the phone, watch TV, take pictures, do homework, work on the computer

### Grammar

I'm playing basketball. I'm not playing football. He's listening to music. They're doing homework.

### Skills

**Listening:** Listen for and identify sports and home activities. Listen for specific information and circle an appropriate response.

**Speaking:** Talk about sports and home activities.

**Reading:** Read a fiction text:
**Fun in the Park**.
Identify details.
Read short sentences and recognize words.

**Writing:** Write about activities.
Personalize a story.
Write about sports and home activities.

### Creative, Collaborative, and Critical Thinking Competencies

**Sing and Act**

**Creativity:** Develop self-expression, innovation, and problem-solving skills. Determine the information to be included in the team song and how it will be presented.

**Collaboration:** Use communication skills and conflict resolution skills to complete tasks. Determine the information to be included in the team song and how each team member will contribute to the final product.

**Critical Thinking:** Use problem-solving skills, analyze information, and organize information to complete the final product.

## Skills Book

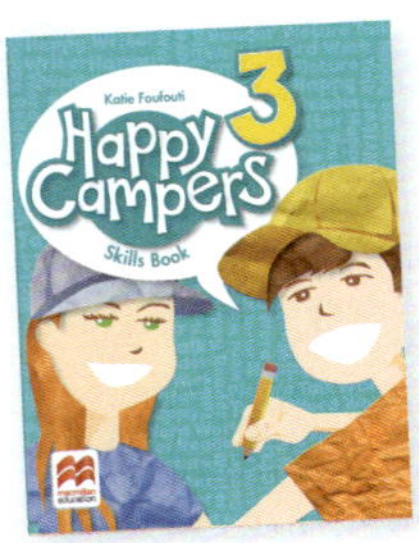


**Extra Skills Practice**

**Speaking and Listening:** Talk about the differences between two pictures.

**Reading and Writing:** Recall details.
Personalize the text.
Identify multi-syllable words.
Read clues to identify words.

# Teacher Workshop

## Teaching with Technology

Use the animated comic strips to get students engaged with the language presented in the comic strip. There are many ways you can use this fun and engaging tool. You may choose to use this as a presentation piece before students read and listen, or at the end of the lesson to review. Students can also provide the voices for the characters as they watch the animation. Show the animated comic strip and have students retell what happened.

## Teaching with Games

**Memory Game**

**Materials:** 8–12 pairs of cards with matching pictures and words

Make a set of 8 to 12 cards with matching pictures and words, or matching word/sentence halves. Randomly write a number on the back of each and put them up on the board so the number side faces the students. Divide the class into two teams and have them take turns choosing two numbers. Turn over the cards; if they are a pair, students claim both cards. The team with the most cards wins.

## Happy Teacher

Cognates are words in two languages that have a common origin, and they can share similar meanings, spelling, and pronunciation. These similarities help students understand and remember new words. Many students need help recognizing these words. This is because cognates have a difference in spelling, sound different, or have different word stress. When you read aloud, ask students to raise their hands when they think they hear a cognate. Then point out the differences between the English word and the word in their native language. Ask students to circle the letters that are different. You can also create a list of cognates for each unit.

## Happy Class

To energize your class, choose one of these quick break tricks. Have students:

- Take out a blank sheet of paper and doodle for three minutes.
- See how many words they can make with the letters of a word in English.
- Do three jumping jacks, hop on one foot two times, and give one classmate a high five.
- Put on some dance music and have students dance for three minutes.

By Diana Jones

## UNIT 4

### Lesson 1

**1** 22 **Listen. Then echo.**

baseball
basketball
football
golf
ping pong
soccer
tennis
volleyball

**2** 23 **Listen and complete.**

**Let's Play!**

1. I'm not playing football.
   I'm playing basketball.
   Basketball is fun!
   Let's play!

2. We're not playing tennis.
   We're playing ping pong.
   Ping pong is fun!
   Let's play!

3. We're not playing volleyball.
   We're playing baseball.
   Baseball is fun!
   Let's play!

**3** Page 13 The Language Lodge



### Lesson 2

**1** 23 **Sing: Let's Play!**

**Grammar Snapshot!**

I'm playing basketball.
I'm not playing football.
We're playing baseball.
We're not playing volleyball.

**2** **Look. Then read and circle.**

1. **a.** I'm playing tennis.
   **b.** We're playing tennis.
2. **a.** I'm not playing golf.
   **b.** We're not playing golf.

**3** **Complete.**

1. We / baseball ✗
   We're not playing baseball.
2. I / golf ✓
   ______.
3. I / soccer ✗
   ______.

**4** Page 14 The Language Lodge



## UNIT 4

### Lesson 1

**1** **Unscramble. Then match.**

1. cceros — soccer
2. kbasbllaet — basketball
3. sealbabl — baseball
4. sitnne — tennis
5. yvlolellab — volleyball
6. gipn pngo — ping pong
7. logf — golf
8. lotfolab — football

**Spelling Check!** Spell the sports aloud. Then complete.

I can spell ____ sports.

Student Book Page 32



# Lesson 1

This may also be completed for homework.

# Lesson 1 Vocabulary



**Lesson Objective:** Identify sports.
**New Vocabulary:** baseball, basketball, football, golf, ping pong, soccer, tennis, volleyball
**Materials:** Audio **Tracks 22 and 23**

## Start the Class

5 min

Have students look at **Pages 32 and 33** and predict what the lesson is about. Write the word *sports* on the board. Ask students to give examples of sports that use balls, and have them draw a ball related to each sport. Then elicit sports that do not use balls. Have students say the sports they like to play and write them on the board. Allow them to use L1 if necessary, but encourage them to use English as much as possible.

### 1 22 Listen. Then echo.

10 min

Explain to the class they are going to listen and point to the different sports. Explain that *football* and *soccer* are two different sports in English. Play **Track 22** and have students listen and point to the pictures as they hear them mentioned. Play **Track 22** again and have students echo the words. Elicit the sports that end in *-ball*.

**Try This!**

5 min

Write dashes on the board for each word from Activity 1, for example, for *soccer*: _ _ _ _ _ _. Then write in the third and fifth letters on each one: _ _ c _ e _. Tell students that they are going to guess the words and spell them. Have students work in pairs and write the missing letters. Review the answers by having some students write in the missing letters on the board.

### 2 23 Listen and complete.

15 min

Explain to the class that they are going to listen to a song and point to the sports as they hear them. Play **Track 23**. Tell students you are going to play the song again for them to complete the sentences. Pause after each line to give students time to write the words. Have students compare their answers with a partner.

Play **Track 23** once more and pause it to check the sports with the class. Write students' correct responses on the board.

### 3 Page 13 The Language Lodge

10 min

Have students flip to The Language Lodge **Page 13**.

**1 Unscramble. Then match.**

Have a volunteer read the directions. Explain to students that they will unscramble the words, write them out correctly, and match them to the corresponding pictures.

When students have finished, have them compare their answers with a partner. Review as a class.

**Spelling Check! Spell the sports aloud. Then complete.**

Have students close their books. Tell them that they will take turns saying and spelling the sports with a partner. Then tell students to write the number of words they can spell correctly.

## Finish the Class

5 min

Name the sports for students to mime. Play **Track 23** again. Students sing along and mime the different sports as they sing about them.

Use the **Presentation Kit** for interactive activities in this lesson.

Have students use the **Happy Campers app** for additional practice with the new vocabulary.

**The Language Lodge Page 13** may also be completed for homework.

# Lesson 2 Grammar

**Lesson Objective:** Talk about sports people are and aren't doing.
**New Grammar:** I'm playing basketball. I'm not playing football. We're playing baseball. We're not playing volleyball.
**Vocabulary Review:** baseball, basketball, football, golf, ping pong, soccer, tennis, volleyball
**Materials:** Audio **Track 23**

## Start the Class

5 min

Have a volunteer go to the board and stand with his or her back to it. On the board, draw a ball (or other piece of equipment) used for a particular sport from Lesson 1. The student at the board makes guesses about the sport; the other students say *yes* or *no* until the student at the board guesses the sport. Repeat with different students.

### ① 23 Sing: Let's Play!

5 min

Have students look at the pictures and elicit what the children are doing. Tell students they are going to listen to the song again and point to the five children playing the sports. Play **Track 23**. Play **Track 23** again and have the class sing along.

**Try This!**

5 min

Divide the class into four groups and ask one student from each group to the board. Explain that each group is going to sing about one of the sports, and the student at the board is going to mime the action for the sport. Play **Track 23** again for students to sing along and mime.

### ② Look. Then read and circle.

10 min

Say *I'm playing basketball* and mime it. Write the sentence on the board. Then write *I'm not playing football.* Mime playing baseball with a student. Say *We're playing baseball* and write it on the board. Say *We're not playing volleyball.*

Have the class read the Grammar Snapshot! together. Then tell students to look at the pictures in Activity 2, circle the correct sentences, and then compare their answers with a partner. Review the answers as a class.

### ③ Complete.

10 min

Explain to students that ✓ indicates *yes* and ✗ indicates *no*. Tell students they are going to write out complete sentences. Circulate among students to check understanding and provide help as needed. Have volunteers write the sentences on the board.

### ④ Page 14 The Language Lodge

10 min

Have students flip to The Language Lodge **Page 14**. Have a volunteer read the Grammar Snapshot! aloud.

**1 Look. Then read and circle.**

Explain to the class that they will look at the pictures, decide which of the two sentences is correct, and circle it. Have students share their answers with the class.

**2 Draw you and a friend playing a sport. Complete the sentences.**

Explain to students that they are going to draw themselves and a friend playing a sport. Then they will write one sentence about what they are doing and another sentence about what they are not doing. Have them share their work with a partner.

## Finish the Class

5 min

Divide the class into two teams. Have one student from each team go to the board. Write *Yes* and *No* on the board. Say *I'm playing soccer,* but mime playing ping pong. The first student to touch the correct answer on the board wins a point for his or her team. Play several times until all students have participated. The team with the most points wins.

Use the **Presentation Kit** for interactive activities in this lesson.

**The Language Lodge Page 14** may also be completed for homework.

For the next lesson, use **Skills Book Pages 22 and 23** (Picture Talk). Go to Teacher's Edition **Page T 169** for teacher notes.

UNIT 4

Lesson 1

1 22 Listen. Then echo.

2 23 Listen and complete.

**Let's Play!**

1. I'm not playing ______.
   I'm playing ______.
   ______ is fun!
   Let's play!

2. We're not playing ______.
   We're playing ______.
   ______ is fun!
   Let's play!

3. We're not playing ______.
   We're playing ______.
   ______ is fun!
   Let's play!

3 Page 13 The Language Lodge



Lesson 2

1 23 Sing: Let's Play!

*Grammar Snapshot!*

I'm playing basketball.
I'm not playing football.
We're playing baseball.
We're not playing volleyball.

2 Look. Then read and circle.

1. a. I'm playing tennis. (circled)
   b. We're playing tennis.

2. a. I'm not playing golf.
   b. We're not playing golf. (circled)

3 Complete.

1. We / baseball ✗
   We're not playing baseball.
2. I / golf ✓
   I'm playing golf.
3. I / soccer ✗
   I'm not playing soccer.

4 Page 14 The Language Lodge



Lesson 2

*Grammar Snapshot!*

I'm playing basketball.
I'm not playing football.
We're playing baseball.
We're not playing volleyball.

1 Look. Then read and circle.

1. a. We're playing basketball. (circled)
   b. We're not playing basketball.

2. a. I'm playing golf.
   b. I'm not playing golf. (circled)

3. a. We're playing ping pong.
   b. We're not playing ping pong. (circled)

2 Draw you and a friend playing a sport. Complete the sentences.

(Students' own answers.)

We're (Students' own answers). We're not (Students' own answers).

 Student Book Page 33

# Lesson 2

This may also be completed for homework.

## Lesson 3

**Shutterbugs**

1 What is Lisa's grandma doing?

2 24 Read and listen.

3 25 **Dictation!** Listen and write. Then say.

1. listen to music
2. talk on the phone
3. watch TV
4. take pictures
5. do homework
6. work on the computer

4 Page 15 The Language Lodge



## Lesson 4

1 24 Listen again to **Shutterbugs**.

2 *Grammar Snapshot!* **Complete.**

1. Jack ____________ his homework.
2. Grandma ____________ on the computer.
3. Suki ____________ TV.

3 26 **Listen and cheer!**

He's reading a book. She's watching TV.
She's talking on the phone.
At home, home, home!

CHEER BOX!

4 Page 16 The Language Lodge



## Lesson 3

**1 Read and look. Then circle *True* or *False*.**

1. I'm working on the computer. — (True) False
2. He's taking a picture. — True (False)
3. I'm doing homework. — True (False)
4. She's listening to music. — (True) False

**2 Read and draw.**

1. He's talking on the phone. — (Students' own answers.)
2. They're watching TV. — (Students' own answers.)

**Spelling Check! Spell the home activities aloud. Then complete.** I can spell ______ words.

Student Book **Page 34**



# Lesson 3

This may also be completed for homework.

# Lesson 3 Vocabulary in Context

**Lesson Objective:** Identify home activities.
**New Vocabulary:** listen to music, talk on the phone, watch TV, take pictures, do homework, work on the computer
**Review Vocabulary:** mom, dad, grandma
**Materials:** Audio **Tracks 24 and 25**, strips of paper with the home activities written on them

## Start the Class

5 min

Draw a simple house on the board. Ask students to say the rooms they know. Write the names of the rooms on the drawing.

### 1 What is Lisa's grandma doing?

5 min

Elicit where they are: *at home*. Have students look at the pictures, find and point to Lisa's grandma, and answer the question. Elicit *She's working on the computer.*

### 2 24 Read and listen.

5 min

Tell students they are going to read the comic strip as they listen. Remind them to follow the words with their fingers. Play **Track 24**.

Say an activity in one of the scenes—*Jack is doing his homework*—and have students point to the correct picture. Repeat for other activities in the frames. Have students underline the six activities in the comic strip.

**Try This!** 10 min

Divide the class into groups of four. Explain to students that they will each read a role from the story: Lisa, Mom, Dad, and Jack. Have students read their parts aloud.

### 3 25 Dictation! Listen and write. Then say.

10 min

Have a volunteer read the directions on **Page 34**. Play **Track 25** and pause for students to write the phrases. Play **Track 25** again. Have students check their answers with a partner, and then have volunteers write the answers on the board.

Tell students they are going to hear the activity again and repeat what they hear. Play **Track 25**.

*Audio script **Track 25***
*1. listen to music 2. talk on the phone 3. watch TV*
*4. take pictures 5. do homework*
*6. work on the computer*

### 4 Page 15 The Language Lodge

10 min

Have the students flip to The Language Lodge **Page 15**.

**1 Read and look. Then circle *True* or *False*.**

Have a volunteer read the directions aloud. Have students complete the activity individually. Review the answers as a class.

**2 Read and draw.**

Explain to students that they are going to read the sentences and draw what they read. Remind them to see if they should draw a boy, a girl, or both. Have them share their drawings and sentences with a partner.

**Spelling Check! Spell the home activities aloud. Then complete.**

Have students close their books. Tell them that they will take turns saying and spelling the home activities with a partner. Then tell students to write the number of words they can spell correctly.

## Finish the Class

5 min

Write home activities on six strips of paper. Have a volunteer come to the board, choose a strip of paper, and act it out for the class to guess. Continue the activity with the other actions.

Use the **Presentation Kit** for interactive activities in this lesson.

Have students use the **Happy Campers app** for additional practice with the new vocabulary.

**The Language Lodge Page 15** may also be completed for homework.

# Lesson 4 Grammar in Context

**Lesson Objective:** Ask and answer questions about home activities.
**New Grammar:** She's working on the computer.
**Vocabulary Review:** listen to music, talk on the phone, watch TV, take pictures, do homework, work on the computer
**Materials:** Audio **Tracks 24 and 26**

## Start the Class

5 min

With the Student Book closed, draw a three-column chart on the board and write the names of the Shutterbugs characters in the first column. Have students copy it into a notebook. Without looking in their books, students should write in the second column what they remember the character doing in Lesson 3.

### 1 24 Listen again to Shutterbugs.

10 min

Tell the class that they are going to listen again to the comic strip and read along as they listen. Explain that when they finish, they will write the activity each character is doing in the third column on the chart from the beginning of class.

Play **Track 24**. Then have students compare the second and third columns to see how well they remembered the story.

### 2 Grammar Snapshot! Complete.

10 min

Have a volunteer read the directions for Activity 2 on **Page 35**. Explain to the class that they will complete each sentence. Tell students to work individually, and then have them compare their answers with a partner. Have students identify the characters in the activity. Then have volunteers share their answers with the class.

**Try This!**

5 min

Divide the class into pairs. Explain that they will take turns saying a sentence about one of the characters; the sentence can be either true (*Lisa is taking a picture*) or false (*Lisa is watching TV*). Their partners will say whether the sentence is true or false and then they switch roles.

### 3 26 Listen and cheer!

5 min

Tell the class they are going to listen to a cheer and read the words as they listen. Play **Track 26**. Explain to the class that you are going to play the cheer again, and this time they will do the cheer with the track. Play **Track 26** again.

### 4 Page 16 The Language Lodge

10 min

Have the students flip to The Language Lodge **Page 16**. Have volunteers read the Grammar Snapshot!

**1 Look and complete.**

Explain to the class that they will look at the pictures and write sentences. Then have volunteers write the missing sentences on the board.

## Finish the Class

5 min

Have students work in groups of three. Have them change the words in the cheer for other activities from this lesson to say a new cheer. Tell them they can include clapping and finger snapping for rhythm. Have several groups go to the board and say their cheer.

Use the **Presentation Kit** for interactive activities in this lesson.

**The Language Lodge Page 16** may also be completed for homework.

For the next lesson, use **Skills Book Pages 24 and 25** (Happy Reader). Go to Teacher's Edition **Page T 170** for teacher notes.

Lesson 3

Shutterbugs

1 What is Lisa's grandma doing?

2 24 Read and listen.



3 25 Dictation! Listen and write. Then say.

1. ______
2. ______
3. ______
4. ______
5. ______
6. ______

4 Page 15 The Language Lodge

34

Lesson 4

1 24 Listen again to Shutterbugs.



2 Grammar Snapshot! Complete.

1. Jack is doing his homework.
2. Grandma is working on the computer.
3. Suki is watching TV.

3 26 Listen and cheer!

He's reading a book. She's watching TV.
She's talking on the phone.
At home, home, home!

CHEER BOX!

4 Page 16 The Language Lodge

35

# Lesson 4

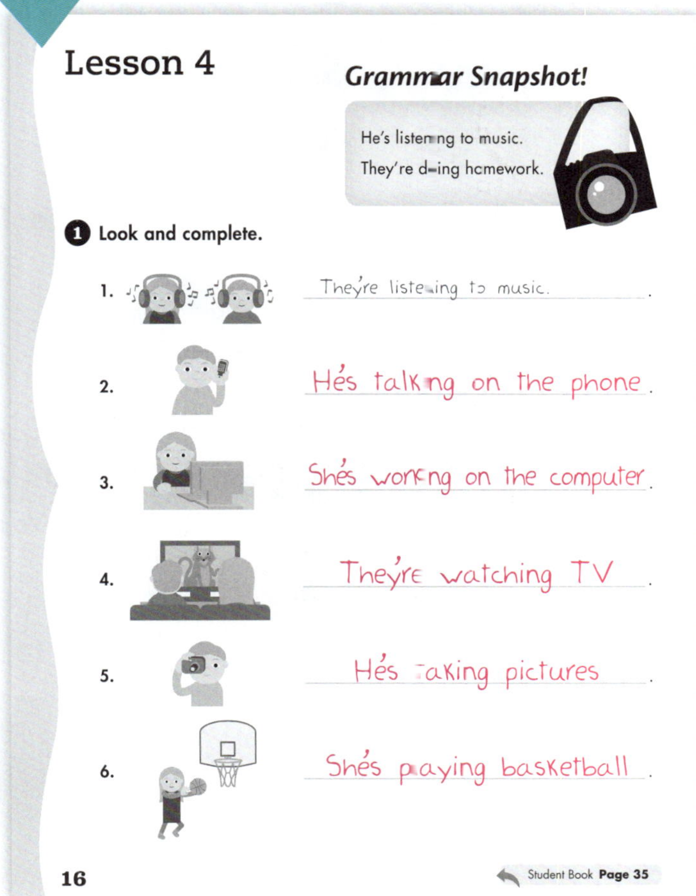

Lesson 4

Grammar Snapshot!

He's listening to music.
They're doing homework.

1 Look and complete.

1. They're listening to music.
2. He's talking on the phone.
3. She's working on the computer.
4. They're watching TV.
5. He's taking pictures.
6. She's playing basketball.

16

Student Book Page 35

This may also be completed for homework.

# Lesson 5

## Lesson 5

**1** **Circle what they're playing in the park.**

**a.** baseball　　**b.** soccer (circled)

**2** 27 **Read and listen.**

## Fun in the Park

Sara is at the park.
Her friend Bella is at home.
"Come to the park, Bella!"

"Paul, Will, and Annie are here.
We're playing soccer and listening to music.
We need you! Please come!"

"Thanks, Sara, but I can't play soccer today.
I'm watching TV."

"Come on!
It's warm and sunny!
We're having fun. You love soccer and … "

"But, Sara, my leg!"
"Oh! That's right. Get well soon!"

# Lesson 5 Fiction Reading

**Lesson Objective:** Read a fiction text to practice unit language.
**Vocabulary Review:** baseball, soccer, home, park, watch TV, sunny, leg
**Grammar Review:** We're playing soccer. We're having fun.
**Materials:** Audio **Track 27**

## Start the Class

5 min

Explain that the first student in each row has to decide on an activity and the last student in the row will act it out. Have the student at the head of each row whisper an activity to the student next to him or her. This student whispers it to the next student, and so on. The last student in the row has to act out the activity.

### 1 Circle what they're playing in the park.

5 min

Tell students to open their books to **Page 36** and have a volunteer read the directions for Activity 1. In pairs, have them name as many things as they can in the pictures. Ask *What are they playing*? and have students circle the correct answer. Check the answer with the class. Elicit *soccer*.

### 2 27 Read and listen.

20 min

Have a volunteer read the title of the story. Elicit what fun things students like to do when they go to the park.

Tell students they are going to listen to the track and follow the words in their books with their fingers as they listen. Play **Track 27**. Then have students look for words in the text that show what Sara and her friends are doing: *playing soccer* and *listening to music*. Next, have students look for words that show what Bella is doing: *talking on the phone* and *watching TV*. Ask students *Why is she watching TV*? Students may give their answers in L1.

Divide the class into groups of three and explain that one student will be the narrator, another Sara, and another Bella. Each will read his or her part. Play **Track 27** so they know when each person speaks. Then they read their parts aloud.

**Try This!** 10 min

Divide the class into several teams. Explain that they are going to take turns saying as many words as they can remember from the story. A student in each team says the first word; the rest of the team takes turns adding more words. Circulate around the class and provide help as needed. See which team can remember the most words.

## Finish the Class

10 min

Tell students that they will do a picture dictation. Explain that you will describe a picture to them and they will draw it. Make sure your description has several items: *Lisa is taking a picture and Suki, the dog, is watching TV*. Repeat the description two or three times, and allow students time to draw. Circulate around the class to monitor comprehension. Have them share and describe their drawing to a classmate.

Use the **Presentation Kit** for interactive activities in this lesson.

# Lesson 6 Reading Comprehension / Writing

**Lesson Objective:** Recall details from a text.
**Vocabulary Review:** listen to music, play basketball, play soccer
**Grammar Review:** She's listening to music. They're playing basketball.
**Materials:** Audio **Tracks 23 and 27**, sets of cut-up sentences

## Start the Class

5 min

Divide the class into groups. Write out four or five sentences from the story on **Page 36**. Give each group a set of cut-up sentences and have them put the sentences together in order.

### 1 27 Listen again to Fun in the Park.

5 min

Tell students they will listen to and read the story again. Remind them to follow the story in their books at the same time as they listen. Play **Track 27**. Have students whisper and read along with the text.

### 2 Circle *True* or *False*.

5 min

Have volunteers read the three sentences in the activity. Explain that they will work individually to decide if the sentences are true or false. Then have them share their answers with a partner.

Tell students they are going to listen to "Fun in the Park" again to check their answers. Play **Track 27** again and pause as appropriate to give students time to check the activities. Read the sentences and have the class say *true* or *false*.

**Try This!**

5 min

Draw a grid on the board with six rows and four columns. In the first column, write the pronouns *I*, *you*, *he*, *she*, *we*, and *they*. In the second column, write *are*, *am*, *is*, *are*, *is*, and *are*. In the third column, write *talking*, *playing*, *watching*, *reading*, *playing*, and *listening*. In the fourth column, write *a book*, *TV*, *volleyball*, *to music*, *tennis*, and *on the phone*. Have students make three sentences in their notebooks from the words in the chart.

### 3 Say Cheese! Draw you and your friends at the park.

10 min

Ask individual students *What do you do at the park?* Have some volunteers go to the board and write their answers. As soon as you have several different examples, explain that students are going to draw a picture of themselves and their friends at the park. Circulate around the class to monitor students' work and provide help as needed. Have students show their drawings to a partner. Then have volunteers share their drawings with the class and say what they and their friends are doing.

### 4 Writing Time! Write about your picture.

15 min

Explain to the class that they are going to write some sentences about the pictures they drew. Read the first sentence aloud and remind students that *Come to the park!* is an invitation, and each student has to describe what everyone in his or her picture is doing. Remind students that each sentence starts with a capital letter and people's names are capitalized. Circulate around the class to monitor students' work and provide help as needed. Allow students time to complete sentences and then have them exchange their sentences with a partner, checking that each sentence has an activity. Ask volunteers to share their sentences with the class.

## Finish the Class

5 min

Tell students that you are going to play the song "Let's Play!" again. Divide students into two groups, and have two volunteers from each group go to the board. Explain that one group will sing the line with *not* and the other group will sing the other line. The volunteers at the board will sing the last two lines of each verse. Play **Track 23** and have groups sing their parts of the song.

Use the **Presentation Kit** for interactive activities in this lesson.

For the next lesson, use **Skills Book Pages 26 and 27** (Word Work). Go to Teacher's Edition **Page T 171** for teacher notes.

# Lesson 6

**1** 27 **Listen again to Fun in the Park.**

**2** **Circle *True* or *False*.**

| | | |
|---|---|---|
| **1.** Sara is listening to music. | (True) | False |
| **2.** Paul, Will, and Annie are playing basketball. | True | (False) |
| **3.** Bella is playing soccer. | True | (False) |

**3** **Say Cheese! Draw you and your friends at the park.**

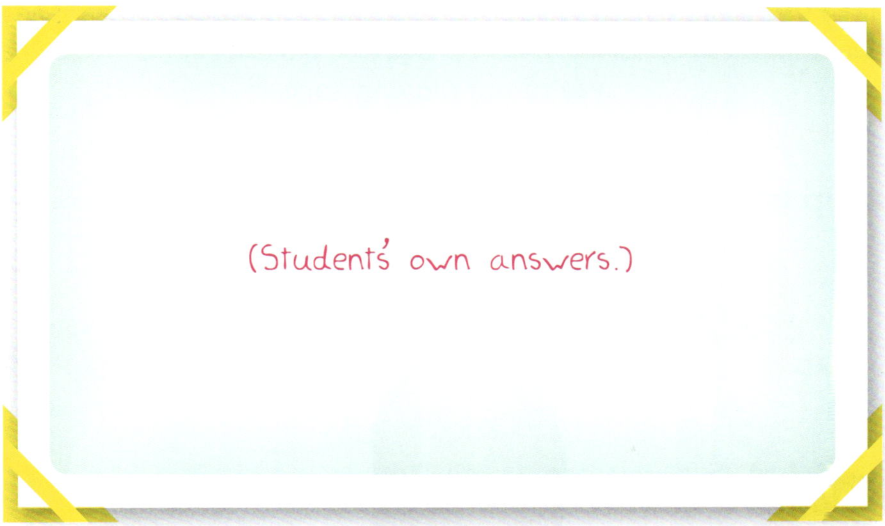


**4** **Writing Time! Write about your picture.**

Come to the park! I'm (Students' own answers) and __________ is playing __________ . __________ is __________ . We're not __________ today.

# Lesson 7

Lesson 7

## Team Up!

**1** **Think about** activities you like. Write a new verse for the song.

Let's Play!

We're not playing soccer.

We're playing baseball.

**2** **Share** your verse.

We're not playing soccer.

**3** **Team up** and sing your team song. Act it out.

# Lesson 7 Creative, Collaborative, and Critical Thinking Activity

**Lesson Objectives:** Talk about activities team members do for fun.
Use communication skills and problem-solving skills to sort information and decide how to present it.
**Vocabulary Review:** baseball, basketball, football, golf, ping pong, soccer, tennis, volleyball
**Grammar Review:** We're not playing soccer. We're playing baseball.
**Materials:** flashcards with sports and home activities, card stock

## Start the Class

5 min

On the board, spread out flashcards with sports and home activities. Divide the class into several teams. Have one student from each team stand up. Explain that you are going to say a sentence about an activity, and the first person in each team should run to the board and touch the corresponding flashcard. If the student touches the correct picture, he or she wins a point for the team. Repeat with different sports and activities. Play several times until all students have participated.

### 1 Think about activities you like. Write a new verse for the song.

10 min

Tell students to look at **Page 38** and have volunteers read the directions and the sentences in the example text. Explain that they are going to work individually to write a new verse for the song about an activity they are *not* doing and an activity that they *are* doing. Make sure there are a variety of activities. Provide help as necessary.

**Try This!** 5 min

Write out five different sentences on cards, then cut the cards in half so that each card has half a sentence. Repeat until you have one card per student. Give them out to students at random. Have each student stand up and look for the student that has the other half of his or her sentence. Ask students to read their sentences aloud.

### 2 Share your verse.

5 min

Put students into pairs. Tell students that they are going to work with a partner and take turns telling each other their new song verses. Circulate around the classroom to correct pronunciation and provide help as needed.

### 3 Team up and sing your team song. Act it out.

10 min

Put two pairs together. Tell them that they will sing their song with all the verses they wrote between them. Explain that they have to decide on appropriate actions to mime each of the activities. Tell them to practice their song in their team. Circulate among the teams and provide help as needed. Encourage students to negotiate to create a plan the whole team is comfortable with.

## Finish the Class

15 min

Have teams share their songs with the class. Remind them to mime the activities while they sing. After all the teams have sung their verses, have the class vote on the top three songs.

Use the **Presentation Kit** for interactive activities in this lesson.

Use the **Assessment Pack** to carry out the Unit 4 Teamwork Assessment during this lesson.

# Lesson 8 Review

**Lesson Objective:** Review vocabulary and grammar from Unit 4.
**Vocabulary Review:** baseball, basketball, football, golf, ping pong, soccer, tennis, volleyball, listen to music, talk on the phone, watch TV, take pictures, do homework, work on the computer
**Grammar Review:** I'm playing football. We're playing soccer. He's listening to music. She's doing homework.

## Start the Class

10 min

Divide the class into two or more teams. Explain that they are going to take turns in their team going to the board to write a word from the unit. Each team wins one point for each correct word. They get double points for any words they wrote that another team didn't. The team with the most points wins.

### 1 Spelling! Write the missing double letters.

5 min

Have students identify the four sports on **Page 39** by looking at the pictures. Explain to students that you are going to say the sports, but in a mixed-up order, and they have to point to the corresponding picture. Start out slowly at first and then increase speed while students point to the different sports.

Ask a volunteer to read the directions. Explain that they will look at the sports and write the missing letters. Then have volunteers write the correct words on the board for students to check their spelling.

### 2 Read and match.

10 min

Point to the two columns and explain to students that they are going to match the sentences to the pictures. Circulate around the class to monitor students and provide help as needed. Tell students to compare their answers with a partner. Review the answers by reading the sentences and having the class point to the matching pictures.

**Try This!** 5 min

Mime playing one of the sports. Have students imitate your actions. Then mime playing another sport; students mime the first and second actions. Mime a third sport; students mime the first, second, and third actions. When you have mimed all six sports, have volunteers come to the board and mime them in the same order while the rest of the class calls out the name of the sports.

### 3 Word Play! Find and circle the words from Unit 4 on Page 72.

15 min

Have students turn to **Page 72** and tell them to find and circle the sport and home activity vocabulary words from Unit 4. Then have students check the words they found with a partner.

## Finish the Class

5 min

Have students write down their three favorite sports. Have them stand up and form two teams. Have each team form a circle, one inside the other. Play some music while they walk around in opposite directions. Stop the music. Have students turn and face a student in the opposite circle and tell them to share their favorite sports. Repeat several times so they tell different classmates.

Use the **Presentation Kit** for interactive activities in this lesson.

For the next lesson, use Unit 4 Language Assessment from the **Assessment Pack** or create your own test using the **Test Generator** on the **Teacher's Resource Center**.

# Lesson 8

## Round Up!

**1 Spelling! Write the missing double letters.**

1. 

so c c er

2. 

te n n is

3. 

basketba l l

4. 

vo l l eyba l l

**2 Read and match.**

1. I'm playing football.
2. We're playing soccer.
3. He's listening to music.
4. She's doing homework.

**3 Word Play! Find and circle the words from Unit 4 on Page 72.**

# Unit 5

## Unit Objectives

**By the end of the unit, students can:**

- Identify park activities and chores.
- Make statements about a picture and respond.
- Personalize a story.

## Student Book

### Vocabulary

**At the Park:** climb trees, have a picnic, play ball, play on the swings, ride a bike, ride a skateboard, run, take a walk

**Chores:** clean, wash the dishes, sweep the floor, feed the pets, take out the trash, set the table, make a snack, wash the car

### Grammar

What are you doing? I'm playing on the swings. I'm not taking a walk. We're riding bikes. We're not running.
What's he doing? He's washing the dishes.
What are they doing? They're sweeping the floor.

### Skills

**Listening:** Listen for and identify park activities and chores. Listen for specific information and circle an appropriate response.

**Speaking:** Talk about park activities and chores.

**Reading:** Read a fiction text:
**Chores Are Fun!**
Identify a sequence of events.
Read short sentences and recognize words.

**Writing:** Write about chores.

### Creative, Collaborative, and Critical Thinking Competencies

**Weekly Activities Calendar**

**Creativity:** Develop self-expression and innovation.

**Collaboration:** Use communication, problem-solving, and conflict resolution skills to complete a weekly calendar for the team. Determine how each team member will contribute to the final product.

**Critical Thinking:** Analyze and organize information. Determine how information will be presented.

## Skills Book

**Extra Skills Practice**

**Speaking and Listening:** Ask and answer questions about a picture.

**Reading and Writing:** Recall details.
Personalize the text.
Recognize spelling patterns.
Identify letter-sound relationships.

# Teacher Workshop

## Teaching with Technology

Use the Presentation Kit to present or review the "Shutterbugs" episodes in Lesson 3.
This animated comic strip is a great way to engage students and is a resource for many different kinds of activities during the class. Show the animated comic strip and follow up with simple comprehension questions before students work with the comic strip in the book. Use the animated comic without sound as a challenging review activity and have students do the voices of the characters.

## Teaching with Games

**Spelling Relay Game**

**Materials:** different-colored board markers

Organize students into teams and have them form a line. Call out a word. The first student has the marker and writes the first letter of the word. He or she then passes the marker to the next student, who writes the next letter of the word, and so on. Students can only write one letter at a time. The first team to correctly spell the word gets a point. If a student writes an incorrect letter, the next student can erase the letter and correct it, but cannot write an additional letter. Variations can be made with vocabulary words or grammar structures.

## Happy Teacher

Sometimes spelling rules in English appear to be inconsistent, but spelling does in fact have numerous rules and patterns. Students need to learn to visually identify words with similar patterns. For example, students can group words with a silent *e* at the end, words with double letters, or words with an *-ing* ending. Have them take notes about similar spelling patterns in words in their notebooks throughout the school year to help them with their spelling.

## Happy Class

To energize your class, choose one of these quick break tricks. Have students:

- Take out a blank sheet of paper and doodle for three minutes.
- Line up as quickly as possible in a variety of orders according to birthdays, first names, and last names.
- Play some music, stop it suddenly, and have students freeze in place.

By Angela Padrón

# UNIT 5

## Lesson 1

1 28 Listen. Then echo.

2 29 Listen and check (✓) or cross (✗). Then circle.

✗ taking a walk

✓ playing on the swings

✗ running

✓ riding bikes

3 Page 17 The Language Lodge



## Lesson 2

1 29 Sing: In the Park.

### In the Park

1. What are you doing
In the park today?
I'm / I'm not taking a walk
In the park today.
I'm / I'm not playing on the swings
In the park today.

2. What are you doing
In the park today?
We're / We're not running
In the park today.
We're / We're not riding bikes
In the park today.

### Grammar Snapshot!

What are you doing?
I'm playing on the swings.
I'm not taking a walk.
We're riding bikes.
We're not running.

2 Circle the answer.

1. What are you doing?
   a. I'm running.
   b. He's playing on the swings.
2. What are you doing?
   a. They're playing ball.
   b. We're climbing trees.
3. We can answer the question *What are you doing?* with
   a. *I* and *We*.
   b. *He* and *They*.

3 Complete.

1. What ______________________?
   I ______________________ picnic.
2. What ______________________?
   We ______________________ skateboards.

4 Page 18 The Language Lodge



# UNIT 5 Lesson 1

1 Write.

| | | |
|---|---|---|
| climb trees | have a picnic | take a walk |
| play on the swings | ride a bike | play ball |

1. ride a bike
2. climb trees
3. take a walk
4. play on the swings
5. have a picnic
6. play ball

✓ **Spelling Check! Spell the park activities aloud. Then complete.** I can spell ____ words.

Student Book Page 40



# Lesson 1

This may also be completed for homework.

# Lesson 1 Vocabulary

Unit 5

**Lesson Objective:** Identify park activities.
**New Vocabulary:** climb trees, have a picnic, play ball, play on the swings, ride a bike, ride a skateboard, run, take a walk
**Materials:** Audio **Tracks 28 and 29**, strips of paper

## Start the Class

5 min

Have students look at **Pages 40 and 41** and predict what the lesson is about. Have them give examples in L1 of activities that they can do at the park.

### 1 28 Listen. Then echo.

10 min

Have students look at the pictures and identify the words of any items they already know the words for. Explain that they are going to listen and point to the different activities. Play **Track 28** and have students listen and point to the pictures as they hear them mentioned. Play **Track 28** again and have students echo the phrases.

**Try This!**

10 min

Tell students that they are going to scramble and unscramble words. Give them strips of paper and have each student write a scrambled word; then have them write their names on the other side. Collect the strips of paper and then give a scrambled word to each student. Have students unscramble the word and return it to the student who scrambled the word to check.

### 2 29 Listen and check (✓) or cross (✗). Then circle.

10 min

Mime one of the activities from Activity 1, such as *take a walk*; elicit the word or phrase from students and say *I'm taking a walk*. Repeat with each of the activities. Point to the pictures and ask students to mime the activities and say what they are chorally.

Explain to the class that they are going to listen to a song and point to the sports. Play **Track 29**. Tell students you are going to play the song again for them to mark the words or phrases. Pause after each line of the song to give them time to mark the phrases with a check or cross. Have students compare their answers with a partner.

Have students look at the words for the song on **Page 41**. Explain that they are going to listen again, and this time they are going to circle the correct words. Play **Track 29**. Then play it once more, pausing it to check answers with the class. Write students' correct responses on the board.

### 3 Page 17 The Language Lodge

10 min

Have students flip to The Language Lodge **Page 17**.

**1 Write.**

Have volunteers read the directions and the words in the box aloud. Tell students to choose and write the correct phrase next to each picture. Do Item 1 as a class; then have students complete the activity individually. Circulate around the class and provide help as needed. Review the answers as a class.

**Spelling Check! Spell the park activities aloud. Then complete.**

Have students close their books. Tell them that they will take turns saying and spelling the park activities with a partner. Then tell students to write the number of words they can spell correctly.

## Finish the Class

5 min

Tell each student to draw a picture of his or her favorite park activity and then label it. Have volunteers share their drawings with the class.

Use the **Presentation Kit** for interactive activities in this lesson.

Have students use the **Happy Campers app** for additional practice with the new vocabulary.

**The Language Lodge Page 17** may also be completed for homework.

# Lesson 2 Grammar

**Lesson Objective:** Ask and answer questions about actions.
**New Grammar:** What are you doing? We're riding bikes. We're not running.
**Vocabulary Review:** climb trees, have a picnic, play ball, play on the swings, ride a bike, ride a skateboard, run, take a walk
**Materials:** Audio **Track 29**

## Start the Class

5 min

Play Simon Says for the actions from Lesson 1. Tell them that if you say *Simon says* before a phrase, they mime the action. If you don't say *Simon says,* they don't do it. Students who mime actions when they shouldn't will sit down. Continue playing until there is only one student standing.

### 1 29 Sing: In the Park.

10 min

Tell students they are going to listen to the song again and point to the four activities as they listen. Explain that when they hear the word *not*, they should wag their fingers to indicate no. Play **Track 29**. Play **Track 29** again and have the class sing along.

### 2 Circle the answer.

10 min

Have the class read the Grammar Snapshot! together. Explain that *you* can address one person (singular) or a group of people (plural). *I* answers for one person, and *We* answers for more than one. Have students complete the activity.

**Try This!**

5 min

Write the base form of the verbs *climb*, *have*, *play*, *ride*, *run*, and *take* in one column on the board. Write *climbing*, *having*, *playing*, *riding*, *running*, and *taking* in random order in another column. Have students copy them in their notebooks, match them, and circle the spelling differences. Review the answers as a class.

### 3 Complete.

5 min

Point to the first question and discuss what could go in the blanks. Have students complete the remaining question and answer. Have volunteers write the complete questions and answers on the board.

### 4 Page 18 The Language Lodge

10 min

Have students flip to The Language Lodge **Page 18**. Have a volunteer read the Grammar Snapshot! aloud.

**1 Look and write questions and answers.**
Explain to the class that they will look at the pictures in the activity and write a question and answer for each one. Have volunteers share their answers with the class.

## Finish the Class

5 min

Divide the class into two teams and have one student from each team come to the board. Write *Yes* and *No* on the board. Say *I'm playing ball,* but mime riding a skateboard. The first student to touch the correct answer on the board wins a point for his or her team. Play several times until all students have participated. The team with the most points wins.

Use the **Presentation Kit** for interactive activities in this lesson.

**The Language Lodge Page 18** may also be completed for homework.

For the next lesson, use **Skills Book Pages 28 and 29** (Picture Talk). Go to Teacher's Edition **Page T 172** for teacher notes.

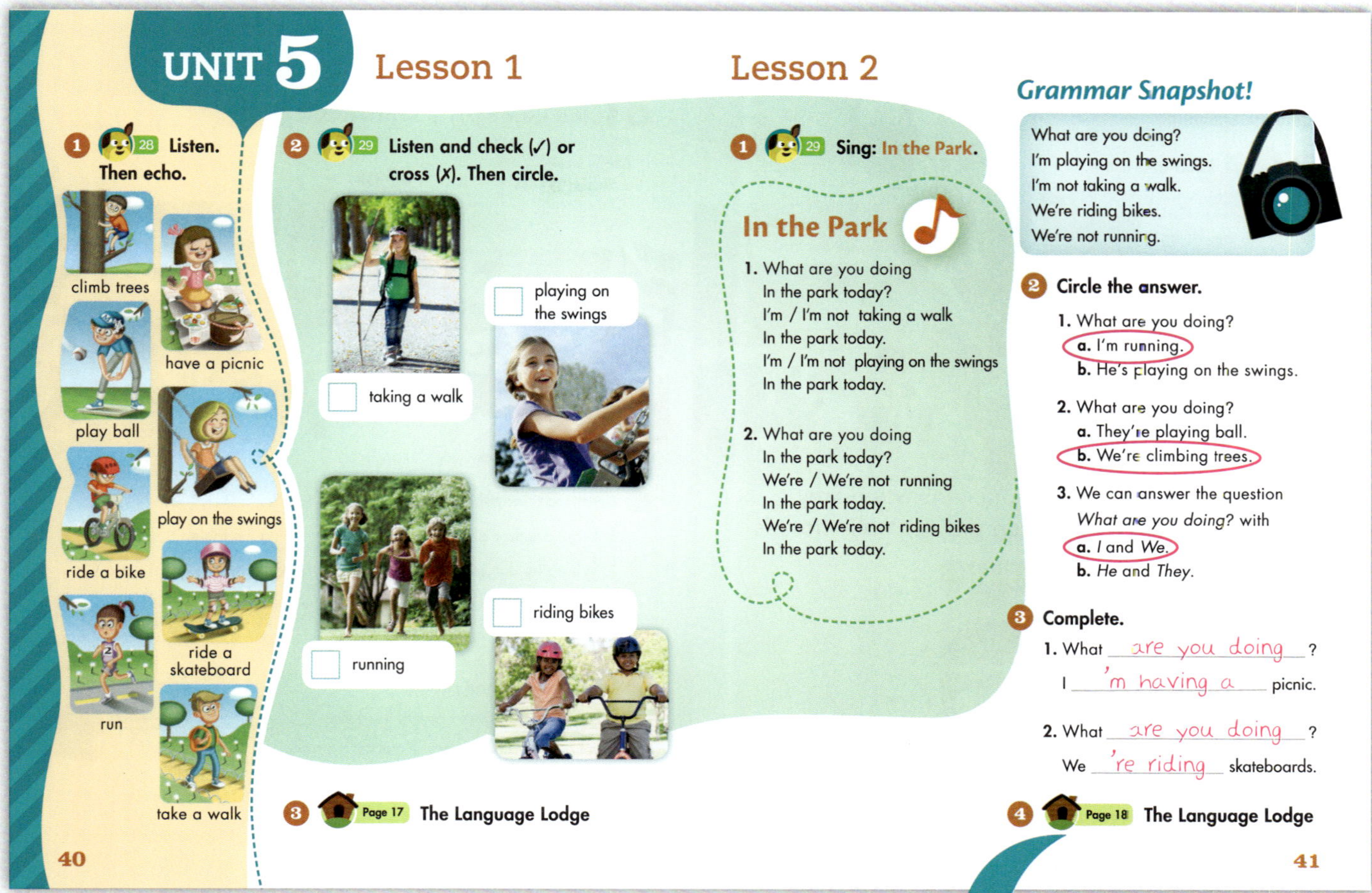

UNIT 5

Lesson 1

1 28 Listen. Then echo.

climb trees
have a picnic
play ball
play on the swings
ride a bike
ride a skateboard
run
take a walk

2 29 Listen and check (✓) or cross (✗). Then circle.

☐ playing on the swings
☐ taking a walk
☐ riding bikes
☐ running

3 Page 17 The Language Lodge

40

Lesson 2

1 29 Sing: In the Park.

In the Park

1. What are you doing
In the park today?
I'm / I'm not taking a walk
In the park today.
I'm / I'm not playing on the swings
In the park today.

2. What are you doing
In the park today?
We're / We're not running
In the park today.
We're / We're not riding bikes
In the park today.

Grammar Snapshot!

What are you doing?
I'm playing on the swings.
I'm not taking a walk.
We're riding bikes.
We're not running.

2 Circle the answer.

1. What are you doing?
a. I'm running.
b. He's playing on the swings.

2. What are you doing?
a. They're playing ball.
b. We're climbing trees.

3. We can answer the question *What are you doing?* with
a. *I* and *We*.
b. *He* and *They*.

3 Complete.

1. What are you doing?
I 'm having a picnic.

2. What are you doing?
We 're riding skateboards.

4 Page 18 The Language Lodge

41

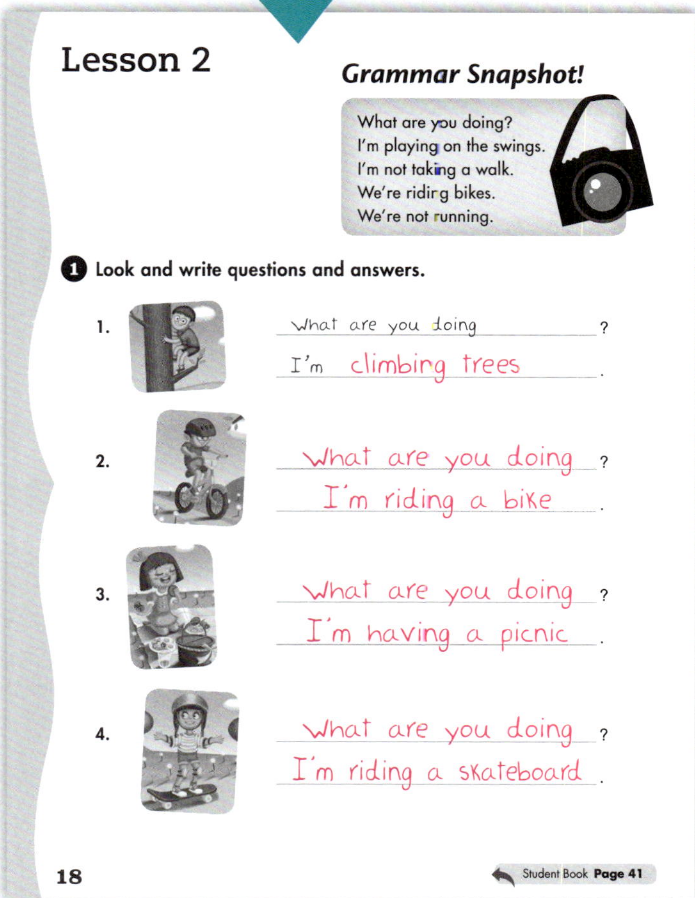

Lesson 2

Grammar Snapshot!

What are you doing?
I'm playing on the swings.
I'm not taking a walk.
We're riding bikes.
We're not running.

1 Look and write questions and answers.

1. What are you doing ?
I'm climbing trees .

2. What are you doing ?
I'm riding a bike .

3. What are you doing ?
I'm having a picnic .

4. What are you doing ?
I'm riding a skateboard .

18

Student Book Page 41

# Lesson 2

This may also be completed for homework.

# Lesson 3

## Shutterbugs

1 Is Tom helping?

2 30 Read and listen.

3 31 **Dictation!** Listen and write. Then say.

 1. clean

 2. wash the dishes

 3. sweep the floor

 4. feed the pets

 5. take out the trash

 6. set the table

 7. make a snack

 8. wash the car

4 Page 19 The Language Lodge

42

# Lesson 4

1 30 Listen again to **Shutterbugs**.

2 ***Grammar Snapshot!*** **Match.**

| | |
|---|---|
| 1. What are they doing? | She's setting the table. |
| 2. What's he doing? | They're washing the car. |
| 3. What's she doing? | He's washing the dishes. |

3 32 **Listen and cheer!**

What's he doing? He's washing the dishes!

What are they doing? They're making a snack!

CHEER BOX!

4 Page 20 The Language Lodge

43

# Lesson 3

1 **Match.**

1. take out the trash
2. feed the pets
3. sweep the floor
4. wash the dishes
5. set the table
6. wash the car

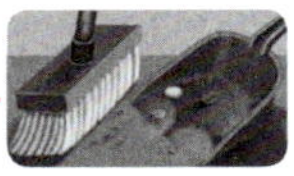

**Spelling Check!** Spell the chores aloud. Then complete.

I can spell ☐ words.

Student Book **Page 42**

19

# Lesson 3

This may also be completed for homework.

# Lesson 3 Vocabulary in Context

**Lesson Objective:** Identify chores.
**New Vocabulary:** clean, wash the dishes, sweep the floor, feed the pets, take out the trash, set the table, make a snack, wash the car
**Materials:** Audio **Tracks 29, 30, and 31**; strips of paper with lines from the song (one set for every four students)

## Start the Class
5 min

Divide students into groups of four and give each group a set of paper strips with lines from the song. Explain that they are going to put the lines in order, and then they are going to listen and check that they are ordered correctly. Play **Track 29** for them to check their answers.

### 1 Is Tom helping?
5 min

Have students look at the pictures and identify if Tom is helping his friends. Elicit *No, he isn't.* Ask students how they help out at home, and write their ideas on the board.

### 2 30 Read and listen.
10 min

Tell students they are going to read the comic strip as they listen. Remind them to follow the words with their fingers. Play **Track 30**.

Describe one of the scenes and have students point to the correct frame. For example, say *Tom is taking out the trash, Clare is setting the table, Sam and Clare are making a snack*, and *Tom is feeding the pets*.

**Try This!**
5 min

Divide the class into groups of four. Explain to students that they will each read a part for a character from the story: Lisa, Clare, Tom, or Sam. Have them choose their roles and then read their parts aloud. If time allows, ask them to change roles and reread the story.

### 3 31 Dictation! Listen and write. Then say.
10 min

Have a volunteer read the directions. Play **Track 31**, pausing for students to write the phrases. Play **Track 31** again. Ask volunteers to write the answers on the board. Tell students they are going to listen again and repeat what they hear. Play **Track 31**.

*Audio script **Track 31***
*1. clean 2. wash the dishes 3. sweep the floor*
*4. feed the pets 5. take out the trash 6. set the table*
*7. make a snack 8. wash the car*

### 4 Page 19 The Language Lodge
10 min

Have students flip to The Language Lodge **Page 19**.

**1 Match.**

Explain to students that they will match the phrases to the pictures. Tell students to compare their answers with a partner. Read the phrases and have students point to the pictures.

**Spelling Check! Spell the chores aloud. Then complete.**

Have students close their books. Tell them that they will take turns saying and spelling the chores with a partner. Then tell students to write the number of words they can spell correctly.

## Finish the Class
5 min

Play Charades using the actions from this unit. Tell a volunteer an action to act out for the class. The first student to guess will act out a new action. Play until several students get to participate in miming.

Use the **Presentation Kit** for interactive activities in this lesson.

Have students use the **Happy Campers app** for additional practice with the new vocabulary.

**The Language Lodge Page 19** may also be completed for homework.

# Lesson 4 Grammar in Context

**Lesson Objective:** Ask and answer questions about chores.
**New Grammar:** What's he doing? He's washing the dishes. What are they doing? They're sweeping the floor.
**Vocabulary Review:** clean, wash the dishes, sweep the floor, feed the pets, take out the trash, set the table, make a snack, wash the car
**Materials:** Audio **Tracks 30 and 32**

## Start the Class

10 min

Distribute sheets of paper. Ask students to fold it twice so there are four rectangles. Dictate the actions for students to do simple stick figure drawings in each square: *He's sweeping the floor. He's feeding the pets. She's setting the table. They're washing the car.* Repeat the description two or three times, giving students time to draw. Have students exchange pictures with a partner to check answers.

### 1 30 Listen again to Shutterbugs.

5 min

Tell the class that they are going to listen again to the comic strip and read along as they listen. Explain that while they listen, they should point to each of the chores when they hear them mentioned. Play **Track 30**.

### 2 *Grammar Snapshot!* Match.

10 min

Draw three columns on the board. At the top of each one write *He*, *She*, and *They*. Elicit where students would put *Sam and Clare*, *Lisa*, and *Sam*.

Explain to the class that they will match the questions and the answers. Tell students to work individually and then compare their answers with a partner. Then have volunteers share their answers with the class.

**Try This!** 5 min

Write the song lyrics on the board, but substitute chores for the park activities. Practice saying the lines of the song. Play **Track 30** at a low volume and have the class sing along, substituting the chores.

### 3 32 Listen and cheer!

5 min

Tell the class they are going to listen to a cheer and read the words as they listen. Play **Track 32**. Explain to the class that you are going to play the cheer again, and they will say the cheer with the track. Play **Track 32** again. Then have them do the cheer in pairs.

### 4 Page 20 The Language Lodge

10 min

Have students flip to The Language Lodge **Page 20**. Have volunteers read the Grammar Snapshot! aloud.

**1 Look. Then read and circle.**

Explain to the class that they will look at the pictures and circle the correct answer to the questions. Tell students to work individually, and then have them compare their answers with a partner. Have volunteers write the answers on the board.

**2 Draw your family doing chores. What are they doing?**

Tell each student to draw a picture of his or her family doing chores. Have students show and explain their drawings to a partner.

## Finish the Class

5 min

Have students work in groups of three. Have them change the words in the grammar cheer for other activities they have learned this unit to say a new grammar cheer. Tell them they can include clapping, stomping, and finger snapping for rhythm. Have volunteers teach their cheer to the class.

Use the **Presentation Kit** for interactive activities in this lesson.

**The Language Lodge Page 20** may also be completed for homework.

For the next lesson, use **Skills Book Pages 30 and 31** (Happy Reader). Go to Teacher's Edition **Page T 173** for teacher notes.

## Lesson 3

# Shutterbugs

1 Is Tom helping?

2 30 Read and listen.

3 31 **Dictation!** Listen and write. Then say.

 1. ____________

 2. ____________

 3. ____________

 4. ____________

 5. ____________

 6. ____________

 7. ____________

 8. ____________

4 Page 19 The Language Lodge



## Lesson 4

1 30 Listen again to Shutterbugs.

2 *Grammar Snapshot!* Match.

1. What are they doing? — They're washing the car.
2. What's he doing? — He's washing the dishes.
3. What's she doing? — She's setting the table.

3 32 Listen and cheer!

What's he doing? He's washing the dishes!
What are they doing? They're making a snack!

CHEER BOX!

4 Page 20 The Language Lodge



## Lesson 4

*Grammar Snapshot!*

What's he doing?
He's washing the dishes.
What are they doing?
They're sweeping the floor.

1 Look. Then read and circle.

1. What's he doing?
   a. He's sweeping the floor. (circled)
   b. He's feeding the pets.

2. What's she doing?
   a. She's cleaning.
   b. She's making a snack. (circled)

3. What are they doing?
   a. They're setting the table. (circled)
   b. They're washing the car.

2 Draw your family doing chores. What are they doing?

(Students' own answers.)

They're (Students' own answers)



Student Book Page 43

# Lesson 4

This may also be completed for homework.

# Lesson 5

**1 Look and circle *True* or *False*.**

The children like to do chores. True (circled) False

**2 33 Read and listen.**

## Chores Are Fun!

Kendra and Seth are riding bikes. Zack is taking out the trash. "Dad is making a snack. Let's do chores and then eat!" Zack says.

"I'm not doing chores. Chores aren't fun!" Seth says.

Kendra and Seth are playing ball. Zack is washing the car. Kendra wants to help Zack. She wants a snack, too. But Seth doesn't like chores.

Kendra is cleaning and Zack is sweeping the floor. Seth smells the cookies. Now he wants to help. He's setting the table.

Zack, Kendra, and Seth are eating the snacks and taking a walk. "See, Seth, chores are fun!" Zack says.

# Lesson 5 Fiction Reading

**Lesson Objective:** Read a text to understand main ideas and details.
**New Vocabulary:** smell, help
**Vocabulary Review:** clean, sweep the floor, take out the trash, set the table, make a snack, wash the car
**Grammar Review:** He's setting the table. Kendra and Seth are playing ball.
**Materials:** Audio **Track 33**, card stock

## Start the Class

5 min

Prepare cards with chores or park activities and cut them in half vertically. Mix up the halves and give them to students. Explain that they have to stand up and walk around to find the other parts of their words. When they find the matching parts, the two students stand together. When everybody has found their match, they read the words aloud. Play the game again if you have time.

### 1 Look and circle *True* or *False*.

5 min

Tell students to open their books to **Page 44**. In pairs, have students name as many chores as they can in the pictures. Then have students say whether the children are happy or not doing the chores. Circulate around the class to monitor students and provide help as needed. Have a volunteer read the directions. In pairs, students read the sentence and decide if it is true or false. Students give reasons for their answers.

### 2 33 Read and listen.

20 min

Elicit what chores students do at home. Have a volunteer read the title of the story. Explain that *fun* means something that you enjoy doing.
Tell students they are going to listen to the track and follow the words in their books with their fingers as they listen. Play **Track 33**.

Then have students look for words in the text that show what chores the children are doing: *taking out the trash, washing the car, sweeping the floor,* and *setting the table.* Next, have students look for activities that are not chores: *riding bikes, playing ball, eating the snacks,* and *taking a walk.*

Divide the class into groups and tell students that they are going to read the text again in their group. Explain that they will each take turns reading a part of the text aloud. Remind them to read clearly so everyone can understand; the rest of the group will follow the words in their books with their fingers as they listen. Circulate among the groups to check intonation and rhythm, and provide help as needed.

**Try This!**

10 min

Divide the class into several teams. Explain that they are going to write as many words as they can remember from the story. Circulate around the class and provide help if needed. Two teams exchange lists, open their books, and mark the answers. The team with the most correct words wins.

## Finish the Class

10 min

Write the following on the board: *take skateboard out car the eat trash.* Explain that there is a hidden phrase. Students have to copy the words and color the ones that make the phrase: *take out the trash.* Write several other hidden phrases on the board for them to find and color.

Use the **Presentation Kit** for interactive activities in this lesson.

# Lesson 6 Reading Comprehension / Writing

**Lesson Objective:** Recall the sequence of events from a text.
**Vocabulary Review:** clean, sweep the floor, take out the trash, set the table, make a snack, wash the car
**Grammar Review:** He's setting the table. Kendra and Seth are playing ball.
**Materials:** Audio **Track 33**; sets of cards with individual words for sentences: *Zack is washing the car. / Zack is taking out the trash. / Zack is sweeping the floor.*; blank cards (one per student)

## Start the Class

5 min

With books closed, write the following chores and fun activities on the board as a list: *setting the table, taking out the trash, sweeping the floor, cleaning, making a snack, playing ball, riding bikes,* and *taking a walk.* Have students copy it. Explain that without looking at their books, they should write the name of the character in the story who did the activity next to it.

### ① 33 Listen again to Chores Are Fun!

5 min

Tell students they will listen to the text again. Remind them to follow the story in their books at the same time as they listen. Play **Track 33**.

Have students check their answers from the beginning of the class.

### ② Number the events in order.

10 min

Put students into pairs. Explain that they will work together to number the events in the order they happen in the story.

Tell students they are going to listen to "Chores Are Fun!" again to check their answers. Play **Track 33** again and pause as appropriate to allow them time to number the events. Check answers as a class.

**Try This!**

5 min

Write words from sentences from this lesson on separate cards. Have students form a circle, and play music while students pass the cards around. When the music stops, the students with the cards go to the center of the circle and stand to form the sentence in order.

### ③ Say Cheese! Draw you and your friends doing chores.

10 min

Ask individual students *What chores do you do?* Have some volunteers go to the board and write their answers. As soon as you have several different examples, explain that students are going to draw a picture of themselves and their friends doing chores. Circulate around the class to monitor students' drawing and provide help as needed. Ask them questions about their drawings while they work: *What are you doing? I'm washing the car.* Have volunteers share their drawings with the class, and say what they are doing with their friends.

### ④ Writing Time! Write about your picture.

10 min

Explain to the class that they are going to write some sentences about the picture they drew in Activity 3. Remind students that each sentence starts with a capital letter and people's names are also capitalized. Circulate around the class to monitor students' work and provide help as needed. Allow students time to complete sentences. Then have them exchange their sentences with a partner to check that each sentence has a chore in it. Correct students' sentences.

## Finish the Class

5 min

Give each student a blank card and have them write a chore on it, for example, *wash the car.* Explain that you are going to call out a chore, such as *wash the car,* and students with that chore stand up and then sit down. Repeat with other chores. Do it slowly at first, then do it faster.

Use the **Presentation Kit** for interactive activities in this lesson.

For the next lesson, use **Skills Book Pages 32 and 33** (Word Work). Go to Teacher's Edition **Page T 174** for teacher notes.

# Lesson 6

## Lesson 6

1 33 Listen again to **Chores Are Fun!**

2 Number the events in order.

4 

1 

2 

3 

3 **Say Cheese!** Draw you and your friends doing chores.

(Students' own answers.)

4 **Writing Time!** Write about your picture.

Today we're (Students' own answers)

______________________________________________

______________________________________________.

# Lesson 7

## Team Up!

**1** Think about your week. Write about four activities.

| Day | Activity |
|---|---|
| Monday | set the table |
| | |
| | |
| | |

**2** Share your chart.

It's Monday. What are you doing?

I'm setting the table.

**3** Team up and make a Weekly Activities Calendar.

# Lesson 7 Creative, Collaborative, and Critical Thinking Activity

**Lesson Objective:** Talk about activities.
**Vocabulary Review:** clean, wash the dishes, sweep the floor, take out the trash, set the table, make a snack, wash the car
**Grammar Review:** What are they doing? They're taking a walk.
**Materials:** construction paper; colored pencils, markers, or crayons

## Start the Class

5 min

Have a Days of the Week March. Line students up, stand at the front of the line, and lead the march around the classroom. Say *Monday* and students repeat; continue with the rest of the days of the week. At some point, say *Stop!* and everyone must stop at the same time. If someone continues marching, or is out of line, he or she goes to the back of the line. Continue, repeating the activity several times.

### ① Think about your week. Write about four activities.

10 min

Tell students to look at **Page 46** and have volunteers read the directions and the sample text. Explain that they are going to work individually to write a chart showing different chores they do on different weekdays. Make sure there are a variety of chores.

### ② Share your chart.

5 min

Ask two volunteers to read the sample dialogue on the page.

Tell students that they are going to work in pairs and share their ideas for the activities on the different days of the week. If possible, students working together should have different chores. Circulate around the classroom, correct pronunciation, and provide help as needed.

### ③ Team up and make a Weekly Activities Calendar.

20 min

Put two pairs together. Have each group of four students put all their information together to make an illustrated weekly calendar. Distribute materials.

Have students draw the chart on construction paper, putting the days in a vertical column on the left, and the names horizontally across the top. Students draw pictures of the activities and label them in the corresponding boxes. Have teams share their weekly calendars with the class. Remind them to point to the days when they are talking. Be sure each member of the team speaks at least once. After all the teams have presented, have the class vote on the top three weekly calendars. Display the calendars in the classroom.

**Try This!**

5 min

Explain to students that they are going to give three different awards to each team's weekly calendar, and they have to decide what the different awards are. Some suggestions are *most helpful* (who does the most chores at home) and *the best illustration*. Write their suggestions on the board and have students vote for the three awards.

## Finish the Class

5 min

Have the class form a circle. Explain that you will say a word (*picnic*), and the first student will say a word beginning with the last letter of that word (*clean*). The next student says a word beginning with the last letter of that word (*night*). Continue with the rest of the class. If a student misses a word, he or she has to sit down, and the next student starts again with a new word.

Use the **Presentation Kit** for interactive activities in this lesson.

Use the **Assessment Pack** to carry out the Unit 5 Teamwork Assessment during this lesson.

# Lesson 8 Review

**Lesson Objective:** Review vocabulary and grammar from Unit 5.
**Vocabulary Review:** climb trees, have a picnic, play ball, play on the swings, ride a bike, ride a skateboard, run, take a walk, clean, wash the dishes, sweep the floor, take out the trash, set the table, make a snack, wash the car
**Grammar Review:** What are they doing? They're taking a walk.
**Materials:** colored pencils

## Start the Class

5 min

Explain to students that they are going to make a word pyramid. They are going to start with the word *skateboard* (10 letters) at the bottom of the pyramid. Then they will write a word with eight letters above it, then one with six letters, four letters, and two letters. The word at the top will be the pronoun *I* (*skateboard, sweeping, taking, have, an, I*). Circulate around the class to monitor students and provide help as needed. Tell students to compare their word pyramids with a partner.

### ① Spelling! Write the *-ing* form of the verbs.

5 min

Ask a volunteer to read the directions. Explain that they will write the complete form of the verb with the *-ing* ending. Then, have volunteers write the correct words on the board. Point out that for both *take* and *make*, you must eliminate the *-e* and add *-ing*. Point out that for *set* and *run*, you must double the last letter before adding *-ing*. Have students check their answers.

### ② Check (✓) the correct place for the activity.

10 min

Point to the two columns and read the titles aloud. Explain to students that they are going to check the places where the activities take place. Circulate around the class to monitor students and provide help as needed. Tell students to compare their answers with a partner. Walk around and check students' answers while they are working.

**Try This!**

10 min

Draw a grid for Tic-Tac-Toe on the board. Write verbs from this unit in the infinitive form in each square. Divide the class into two teams: O and X. Have the teams take turns saying and spelling the verbs with the *-ing* ending. If they spell the verbs correctly, they put their symbol in the square. The first team to win three squares in a row, vertically, horizontally, or diagonally, wins.

### ③ Look and answer.

5 min

Explain to students that they have to look at the pictures and write an answer for the question according to what they can see. Tell students to work individually and then compare their answers with a partner. Then have volunteers write the sentences on the board.

### ④ Word Play! Find and circle the words from Unit 5 on Page 72.

10 min

Have students turn to **Page 72** and tell them to find and circle the park activity and chore vocabulary words from Unit 5. Then have students check the words they found with a partner.

## Finish the Class

5 min

Distribute paper and colored pencils. Have students draw one of the park activities or chores. Tell students to stand in a circle. Say *Change places if your picture is (playing on the swings)*. Students who have that picture have to change places. Continue with other actions.

Use the **Presentation Kit** for interactive activities in this lesson.

For the next lesson, use Unit 5 Language Assessment from the **Assessment Pack** or create your own test using the **Test Generator** on the **Teacher's Resource Center**.

# Lesson 8

## Lesson 8

## Round Up!

**1 Spelling! Write the *-ing* form of the verbs.**

1. take taking
2. make making
3. set setting
4. run running
5. sweep sweeping
6. feed feeding

**2 Check (✓) the correct place for the activity.**

| | At Home | At the Park |
|---|---|---|
| They're taking a walk. | | ✓ |
| He's setting the table. | ✓ | |
| She's sweeping the floor. | ✓ | |
| They're playing on the swings. | | ✓ |
| They're having a picnic. | | ✓ |
| She's washing the car. | ✓ | |

**3 Look and answer.**

1. What's she doing?

She's taking out the trash.

2. What are they doing?

They're washing the car.

**4 Word Play! Find and circle the words from Unit 5 on Page 72.**

# Unit 6

## Unit Objectives

**By the end of the unit, students can:**

- Identify clothes and beach activities.
- Make statements about a picture and respond.
- Show understanding of story details.

## Student Book

### Vocabulary

**Clothes:** T-shirt, pants, cap, shorts, jeans, swimsuit, sandals, sneakers

**At the Beach:** swim, sleep, fly a kite, sail a boat, eat ice cream, build a sandcastle

### Grammar

What are you wearing? I'm wearing sneakers.
Are you wearing shorts? Yes, I am. / No, I'm not.
Is she swimming? Yes, she is. / No, she isn't. She isn't sleeping.

### Skills

**Listening:** Listen for and identify clothes and beach activities.
Listen for specific information and circle an appropriate response.

**Speaking:** Talk about the clothes students are wearing and beach activities.

**Reading:** Understand details in a story.
Read a fiction text: **Fun with Grandpa**.
Identify and describe details.
Read short sentences and recognize words.

**Writing:** Write about beach activities.

### Creative, Collaborative, and Critical Thinking Competencies

**Favorite Activities Chart**

**Creativity:** Develop self-expression, innovation, and problem-solving skills. Determine the information to be included in the chart and how it will be presented.

**Collaboration:** Use communication skills, problem-solving skills, and conflict resolution skills to complete tasks. Determine the information to be included in the chart and how each team member will contribute to the final product.

**Critical Thinking:** Use problem-solving skills, analyze information, and organize information to complete the final product.

## Skills Book

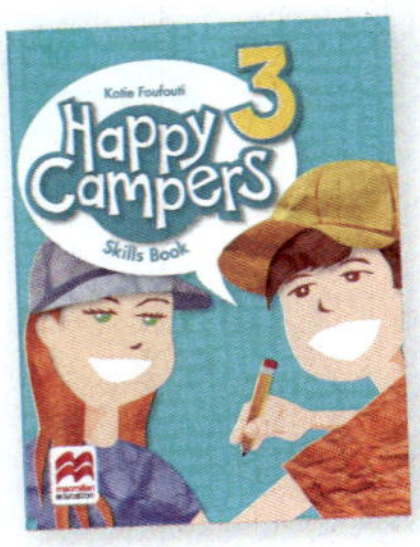


**Extra Skills Practice**

**Speaking and Listening:** Ask and answer questions about a picture.

**Reading and Writing:** Recall details.
Summarize the text.
Read clues to identify words.
Recognize spelling patterns.
Categorize words.

# Teacher Workshop

## Teaching with Technology

Take advantage of the interactive boards and activities to repeat vocabulary activities. Click on the audio options and allow students to listen to the correct pronunciation of new words. Repeat the words several times so students can get a lot of practice.

## Teaching with Games

**Odd One Out**

Give students sets of words and have them decide which word is different from the others. The words can be provided in written form or orally. This activity helps students become aware that words can be classified in different ways, while developing critical thinking skills. Be prepared to accept different answers if students have a good explanation.

## Happy Teacher

Changing from one activity to another can easily become a noisy time in the classroom. Attention and quiet signals are essential in the classroom. Raising your hand is a signal for the class to stop talking and listen to the teacher. Another way to quiet the class is to clap once and have students repeat the single clap.

## Happy Class

Take a few minutes and celebrate birthdays with the class. Create a fun ritual in English to acknowledge students' birthdays, such as singing "Happy Birthday." Ask the question *How old are you now?* for the birthday student to answer. You may choose to give the birthday student a choice of games to do in class, or assign a birthday seat (such as the teacher's) for the birthday student to sit in during his or her special day. Create a group celebration for students whose birthdays occur during vacations.

By Patricia Acosta

# UNIT 6

## Lesson 1

1 34 Listen. Then echo.

2 35 Listen and complete. Then number.

3 Page 21 The Language Lodge



## Lesson 2

1 35 Sing: My Clothes.

### My Clothes

1. What are you wearing?
I'm wearing a cap.
Are you wearing shorts?
Yes, I am.

2. What are you wearing?
I'm wearing sneakers.
Are you wearing a cap?
No, I'm not.

3. What are you wearing?
I'm wearing a T-shirt.
Are you wearing jeans?
No, I'm not.

### Grammar Snapshot!

What are you wearing?
I'm wearing sneakers.

Are you wearing shorts?
Yes, I am. / No, I'm not.

2 Circle the question with a *yes/no* answer.

a. What are you wearing?
b. Are you wearing shoes?

3 Circle the answer.

1. What are you wearing?
   a. I'm wearing a cap.
   b. Yes, I am.
2. Are you wearing sandals?
   a. No, I'm not.
   b. I'm wearing a T-shirt.
3. What are you wearing?
   a. No, I'm not.
   b. I'm wearing sneakers.

4 Page 22 The Language Lodge



# UNIT 6

## Lesson 1

1 Write.

1. T - shirt 
2. sneakers 
3. swimsuit 
4. pants 
5. cap 
6. sandals 
7. shorts 
8. jeans 

✓ **Spelling Check!** Spell the clothes aloud. Then complete.

I can spell ____ words.

Student Book Page 48



# Lesson 1

This may also be completed for homework.

# Lesson 1 Vocabulary



**Lesson Objective:** Identify clothes.
**New Vocabulary:** T-shirt, pants, cap, shorts, jeans, swimsuit, sandals, sneakers
**Materials:** Audio **Tracks 34 and 35**

## Start the Class

5 min

Have students look at **Pages 48 and 49** and predict what the lesson is about. Write the word *clothes* on the board. Elicit what clothes students are wearing today, focusing on words they already know. Have volunteers say their favorite clothes, and then draw them on the board.

### 1 34 Listen. Then echo.

10 min

Have students look at the pictures and identify the clothes in L1. Explain that they are going to listen and point to the pictures of different clothes. Play **Track 34** and have students listen and point to the pictures of the clothes as they hear them mentioned. Play **Track 34** again and have students echo the phrases.

**Try This!** 10 min

Tell students that they are going to draw a picture of themselves wearing some of the clothes from this page. Have them draw an arrow pointing to each item of clothing and write the word to label it. Circulate around the class and provide help as needed. Have students compare their drawings with the person next to them. Encourage them to name the colors of the clothes to practice color words.

### 2 35 Listen and complete. Then number.

10 min

Explain to the class that they are going to listen to a song and point to the person singing (the girl or one of the boys). Play **Track 35**. Then tell students you are going to play the song again for them to complete the sentences on **Page 49**. Pause appropriately to give students time to write the sentences.

Have students compare their sentences with a partner. Then check answers as a class by writing them on the board.

Explain that students are going to listen to the song again, and this time they are going to number the boxes to indicate who sings first, second, and third. Play **Track 35** and then check answers with the class.

### 3 Page 21 The Language Lodge

10 min

Have students flip to The Language Lodge **Page 21**.

**1 Write.**

Explain that students have to write the words to spell out each of the clothes words in the pictures. Do Item 1 as a class. Then have students complete the activity individually. Review the answers as a class.

**Spelling Check! Spell the clothes aloud. Then complete.**

Have students close their books. Tell them that they will take turns saying and spelling the clothes with a partner. Then tell students to write the number of words they can spell correctly.

## Finish the Class

5 min

Divide the class into two groups: one group of girls and one group of boys. Have them stand on opposite sides of the classroom. Explain that they are going to sing "My Clothes." Both groups are going to sing the questions together, but the girls will sing the girl's part and the boys will sing boys' parts. Play **Track 35** again and have students sing their parts.

Use the **Presentation Kit** for interactive activities in this lesson.

Have students use the **Happy Campers app** for additional practice with the new vocabulary.

**The Language Lodge Page 21** may also be completed for homework.

# Lesson 2 Grammar

**Lesson Objective:** Ask and answer questions about clothes.
**New Grammar:** What are you wearing? I'm wearing sneakers. Are you wearing shorts? Yes, I am.
**Vocabulary Review:** T-shirt, pants, cap, shorts, jeans, swimsuit, sandals, sneakers
**Materials:** Audio **Track 35**, Unit 6 clothes flashcards

## Start the Class

5 min

Show the class the clothes vocabulary flashcards. Have volunteers say the names of the clothes. Repeat until each clothing item has been mentioned. Then show the cards faster, having the class respond chorally.

### ① 35 Sing: My Clothes.

5 min

Tell students they are going to listen to the song again and follow the words with their fingers as they listen. Explain that when they hear the word *not*, they should wag their fingers to indicate no. Play **Track 35**.

Play **Track 35** again and have the class sing along.

**Try This!**

5 min

Tell students they are going to listen to the song again, but this time they are going to stand up and say *Yes, I am* each time they hear the words. Play **Track 35**. Then play it a second time for students to stand up on *No, I'm not*.

### ② Circle the question with a *yes/no* answer.

15 min

Remind students of the questions they learned in previous units: *What are you doing? What's the date today? What time is it?* Point out that they all begin with the word *What*. Tell the class that these questions always ask for information—an activity, the date, or the time—and *What are you wearing?* asks for information about clothes.

Have the class read the Grammar Snapshot! together. Tell students to look at the two questions and then circle the question with a *yes/no* answer. Have them compare their answers with a partner before checking as a class.

### ③ Circle the answer.

5 min

Explain to students that they are going to read the questions and check the correct answer for each one. Have volunteers write the questions and answers on the board.

### ④ Page 22 The Language Lodge

10 min

Have students flip to The Language Lodge **Page 22**.

Have two volunteers read the Grammar Snapshot! questions and answers aloud.

**1 Circle the correct answer.**

Explain to the class that they will look at the picture of the boy and circle the correct answer for each question. Then have students share their answers with the class.

**2 Answer for you.**

Read the questions in the activity aloud. Ask students to write answers about themselves. Walk around and check students' answers while they are working.

## Finish the Class

5 min

Form the class into rows. Ask students at the head of each row *Are you wearing (sandals)?* Students answer *Yes, I am* or *No, I'm not*. Then the first student in each row turns around and repeats the question to the student seated next to him or her. Repeat until the last student in each row has answered. Then repeat the activity by starting the question at the other end of the row and having students take turns to ask and answer going back in the opposite direction.

Use the **Presentation Kit** for interactive activities in this lesson.

**The Language Lodge Page 22** may also be completed for homework.

For the next lesson, use **Skills Book Pages 34 and 35** (Picture Talk). Go to Teacher's Edition **Page T 175** for teacher notes.

# UNIT 6

## Lesson 1

1 (34) Listen. Then echo.

2 (35) Listen and complete. Then number.

3 Page 21 The Language Lodge



## Lesson 2

1 (35) Sing: My Clothes.

### My Clothes

1. What are you wearing?
   I'm wearing a ________.
   Are you wearing shorts?
   Yes, I am.
2. What are you wearing?
   I'm wearing ________.
   Are you wearing a cap?
   No, I'm not.
3. What are you wearing?
   I'm wearing a ________.
   Are you wearing jeans?
   No, I'm not.

### Grammar Snapshot!

What are you wearing?
I'm wearing sneakers.

Are you wearing shorts?
Yes, I am. / No, I'm not.

2 Circle the question with a *yes/no* answer.

a. What are you wearing?
b. Are you wearing shoes? (circled)

3 Circle the answer.

1. What are you wearing?
   a. I'm wearing a cap. (circled)
   b. Yes, I am.
2. Are you wearing sandals?
   a. No, I'm not. (circled)
   b. I'm wearing a T-shirt.
3. What are you wearing?
   a. No, I'm not.
   b. I'm wearing sneakers. (circled)

4 Page 22 The Language Lodge



## Lesson 2

1 Circle the correct answer.

### Grammar Snapshot!

What are you wearing?
I'm wearing sneakers.
Are you wearing shorts?
Yes, I am. / No, I'm not.

1. Are you wearing a cap?
   Yes, I am. (circled) No, I'm not.
2. Are you wearing pants?
   Yes, I am. (circled) No, I'm not.
3. Are you wearing a swimsuit?
   Yes, I am. No, I'm not. (circled)
4. Are you wearing sneakers?
   Yes, I am. (circled) No, I'm not.

2 Answer for you.

1. Are you wearing a T-shirt? (Student's own answers).
2. Are you wearing a cap? (Student's own answers).
3. What are you wearing? (Student's own answers).



Student Book Page 49

# Lesson 2

This may also be completed for homework.

## Lesson 3

# Shutterbugs

1 Where are the Shutterbugs?

2 36 Read and listen.

3 37 **Dictation!** Listen and write. Then say.

1. swim

2. sleep

3. fly a kite

4. sail a boat

5. eat ice cream

6. build a sandcastle

4 Page 23 The Language Lodge



## Lesson 4

1 36 Listen again to **Shutterbugs**.

2 ***Grammar Snapshot!*** Write the answers.

1. Is he building a sandcastle? Yes, he is.
2. Is she eating ice cream? ______.
3. Is she swimming? ______.
4. Is he sleeping? ______.

3 38 Listen and cheer!

Is he sailing a boat? Yes, he is! Yes, he is!
Is she eating ice cream? No, she isn't! No, she isn't!

CHEER BOX!

4 Page 24 The Language Lodge



## Lesson 3

1 Write.

| | | |
|---|---|---|
| build a sandcastle | eat ice cream | fly a kite |
| sail a boat | sleep | swim |

1.

build a sandcastle

2.

sleep

3.

swim

4.

eat ice cream

5.

sail a boat

6.
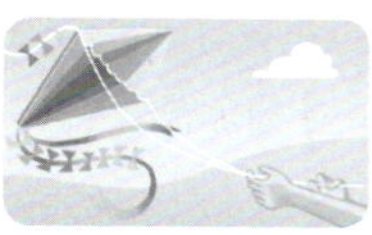
fly a kite

**Spelling Check!** Spell the beach activities aloud.
**Then complete.** I can spell ____ words.

Student Book **Page 50**



# Lesson 3

This may also be completed for homework.

# Lesson 3 Vocabulary in Context

**Lesson Objective:** Identify characters and the activities they are doing at the beach.
**New Vocabulary:** swim, sleep, fly a kite, sail a boat, eat ice cream, build a sandcastle
**Materials:** Audio **Tracks 36 and 37**, strips of paper

## Start the Class

5 min

Have students look at the comic strip on **Pages 50 and 51** and memorize as much as they can about what the characters are wearing. Tell students to close their books. Then have them tell a partner as much as they can remember about what the characters are wearing.

### 1 Where are the Shutterbugs?

5 min

Point out the different characters and elicit their names: *Lisa*, *Clare*, *Tom*, and *Sam*. Have a volunteer read the question and have students say the answer: *At the beach.*

### 2 36 Read and listen.

10 min

Tell students they are going to read the comic strip as they listen. Play **Track 36**.

Draw a vertical line down the board to create two columns. In the right column, write *a kite*, *a sandcastle*, *a boat*, and *ice cream*. Explain to students that they will look at the comic strip and complete the left column with the appropriate verb. For example, *flying* will line up with *a kite*. Have students copy the columns and words in their notebooks.

**Try This!** 5 min

Tell students that they will take turns reading the comic strip with a partner.

### 3 37 Dictation! Listen and write. Then say.

10 min

Have a volunteer read the directions in Activity 3. Mime *swim* and make sure students understand. Play **Track 37** and pause to allow students appropriate time to write the words. Play **Track 37** again. Have students check their answers with a partner.

Then have volunteers write the answers on the board. Tell students they will listen again and then repeat what they hear. Play **Track 37**.

*Audio script **Track 37***
*1. swim 2. sleep 3. fly a kite 4. sail a boat*
*5. eat ice cream 6. build a sandcastle*

### 4 Page 23 The Language Lodge

10 min

Have students flip to The Language Lodge **Page 23**.

**1 Write.**

Have volunteers read the directions and the words in the box aloud. Explain to students that they will label the pictures. Do Item 1 as a class. Then have students complete the activity individually. Have volunteers share their answers with the class.

**Spelling Check! Spell the beach activities aloud. Then complete.**

Have students close their books. Tell them that they will take turns saying and spelling the beach activities with a partner. Then tell students to write the number of words they can spell correctly in the box.

## Finish the Class

5 min

Divide the class into two teams. To review, write the chores from Unit 5 and beach activities from Unit 6 on strips of paper. Have the first person from each team come to the board, choose a strip of paper, and act it out for their team to guess. They must repeat miming the action until a teammate guesses. Continue until students have guessed all the words.

Use the **Presentation Kit** for interactive activities in this lesson.

Have students use the **Happy Campers app** for additional practice with the new vocabulary.

**The Language Lodge Page 23** may also be completed for homework.

# Lesson 4 Grammar in Context

**Lesson Objective:** Ask and answer questions about beach activities.
**New Grammar:** Is she swimming? No, she isn't.
**Vocabulary Review:** swim, sleep, fly a kite, sail a boat, eat ice cream, build a sandcastle
**Materials:** Audio **Tracks 36 and 38**

## Start the Class (5 min)

Write the following words on the board with the first and last letters missing: _ *i t* _, _ *u i l* _, _ *o a* _, _ *l e e* _, and _ *w i* _. Have students complete the words and compare their answers with a partner. Have volunteers write the missing letters on the board to complete the words: *kite, build, boat, sleep,* and *swim*.

### ① 36 Listen again to Shutterbugs. (5 min)

Tell the class that they will listen to the comic strip again and read along in their books. Play **Track 36**.

### ② *Grammar Snapshot!* Write the answers. (10 min)

Ask *Is Clare taking pictures?* Elicit *yes* as an answer and write *Yes, she is* on the board. Then ask *Is she sleeping?* Write the negative short answer *No, she isn't* on the board. Tell students to look at the comic strip and ask *Is Tom flying a kite?* Elicit *No, he isn't.* Ask *What is Tom doing?* to elicit *He's sleeping*. Write the questions and answers on the board.

Have a volunteer read the directions for Activity 2 on **Page 51**. Explain to the class that they will look at the pictures of the characters in the activity and write answers to the questions. Have volunteers share their answers with the class. Finally, have students circle *Is he* or *Is she* in the questions, and *he/she is* or *he/she isn't* in the answers. Point out that to ask about what people are doing, we start *yes/no* questions with *Is he/she*; we use *he/she is* or *he/she isn't* in the answer.

### ③ 38 Listen and cheer! (5 min)

Tell the class they will listen to a cheer and read the words as they listen. Play **Track 38**. Have students underline *Is he* and *Is she* in the questions, and *Yes, he is* and *No, she isn't* in the responses. Explain to the class that you will play the cheer again and this time they will do the cheer along with the audio.

**Try This!** (10 min)

Divide the class into two groups. Explain that one group will say the question parts of the cheer and the other group will say the answers. Do the cheer, then have the groups switch roles and do the cheer again.

### ④ Page 24 The Language Lodge (10 min)

Have students flip to The Language Lodge **Page 24**. Have a volunteer read the Grammar Snapshot!

**1 Complete.**

Tell the class that they will look at the pictures and complete the questions and answers according to what they can see in the pictures. Then have volunteers write the sentences on the board.

**2 Draw your friend at the beach. Answer.**

Tell students they will draw a picture of a friend at the beach, and then answer the questions according to what they drew. Have students show their drawings to a partner and explain what their friend is doing.

## Finish the Class (5 min)

Have students work in groups of three to create a new grammar cheer by adding different activities. Have volunteer groups share their cheers with the class.

Use the **Presentation Kit** for interactive activities in this lesson.

**The Language Lodge Page 24** may also be completed for homework.

For the next lesson, use **Skills Book Pages 36 and 37** (Happy Reader). Go to Teacher's Edition **Page T 176** for teacher notes.

# Lesson 3

## Shutterbugs

1 Where are the Shutterbugs?

2 36 Read and listen.

3 37 **Dictation!** Listen and write. Then say.

1. ____________ 2. ____________

3. ____________ 4. ____________

5. ____________ 6. ____________

____________

4 Page 23 The Language Lodge



# Lesson 4

1 36 Listen again to **Shutterbugs**.

2 *Grammar Snapshot!* Write the answers.

1. Is he building a sandcastle? Yes, he is.
2. Is she eating ice cream? No, she isn't.
3. Is she swimming? No, she isn't.
4. Is he sleeping? Yes, he is.

3 38 Listen and cheer!

Is he sailing a boat? Yes, he is! Yes, he is!

Is she eating ice cream? No, she isn't! No, she isn't!

CHEER BOX!

4 Page 24 The Language Lodge



# Lesson 4

## Lesson 4

## *Grammar Snapshot!*

Is she swimming?
Yes, she is.
No, she isn't.
She isn't sleeping.

1 Complete.

1. Is she eating ice cream? Yes, she is.
2. Is he sailing a boat? No, he isn't. He isn't sailing a boat.
3. Is she building a sandcastle? No, she isn't. She isn't building a sandcastle.
4. Is he flying a kite? Yes, he is.

2 Draw your friend at the beach. Answer.

(Students' own answers.)

1. Is your friend swimming?
(Students' own answers.)
2. Is your friend building a sandcastle?
(Students' own answers.)



Student Book Page 51

This may also be completed for homework.

# Lesson 5

## Lesson 5

**1** **Circle where the family is.**

**a.** at the park **b.** at the lake

**2** 39 **Read and listen.**

## Fun with Grandpa

It's hot and sunny. Eddie, Lily, Mom, and Grandpa are at the lake.
What's Grandpa wearing?
Is he wearing a jacket and pants?
Yes, he is! Oh, Grandpa!

Is Eddie building a sandcastle?
Yes, he is!
Lily isn't building a sandcastle.
She's flying a kite with Mom.

Eddie wants to swim with his sister, Lily.
"Let's swim, Lily! Come on, Grandpa!"

Look! Grandpa is swimming in his clothes!
He's wearing pants and a jacket.
He isn't wearing a swimsuit.
Eddie and Lily are having fun with Grandpa!

# Lesson 5 Fiction Reading

**Lesson Objective:** Read a text to understand main ideas and details.
**Vocabulary Review:** swimsuit, build a sandcastle, swim, fly a kite
**Grammar Review:** Is he building a sandcastle? Yes, he is. She's flying a kite. She isn't building a sandcastle.
**Materials:** Audio **Track 39**

## Start the Class

5 min

Divide the class into two teams. Write *Yes* and *No* on the board. Have a volunteer from each team stand away from the board. Say *I'm swimming*, but mime flying a kite. The first student to touch the correct answer on the board wins a point for his or her team. Vary miming correct and incorrect actions. Play until all students have participated. The team with the most points wins.

### 1 Circle where the family is.

5 min

Tell students to open their books to **Page 52**. Have a volunteer read the directions for Activity 1. Have other volunteers read the answer options. Remind them that they will look at the pictures in the story and circle where the family is. Give a one-minute time limit. Review the answer with the class: *at the lake*. Have students talk about things their families like to do together.

### 2 39 Read and listen.

20 min

In pairs, have students look at the pictures and name as many beach activities as they can. Ask what is unusual or funny in the pictures: *Grandpa is swimming in his clothes*.

Have a volunteer read the title of the story. Tell students they will read the story as they listen. Remind them to follow the words in their books with their fingers as they read and listen. Play **Track 39**. Then have students look for words in the text that say what activities the children are doing: *building a sandcastle*, *flying a kite*, and *swimming*.

Ask students to talk about the activities in the story that they like to do. Have students share their ideas with the class. Ask students to talk about the people in their families who do these activities with them.

Divide the class into groups and tell students that they will read the text again in their group. Explain that they will take turns reading a part of the text aloud. Remind them to read clearly so everyone can understand; the rest of the group will follow the words in their books with their fingers as they listen. Circulate among the groups to check intonation and rhythm, and provide help as needed.

Listen for words that students have difficulty pronouncing correctly. Write these words on the board and have students practice saying them. Then have students read the sentences containing these words aloud. Have them read chorally as a class, and then have volunteers read the sentences aloud.

**Try This!**

10 min

Write the following words and phrases on the board, each one on a line below the previous one, to form a right triangle: *Eddie / Eddie and Lily / Eddie and Lily are / Eddie and Lily are having / Eddie and Lily are having fun / Eddie and Lily are having fun with Grandpa*. Read each line aloud, beginning with the top line, and have students repeat after you until the entire sentence is read out. Divide the class into pairs. Explain that they are going to take turns reading the sentence in the same way. Circulate around the classroom, correcting pronunciation and providing help as needed. Have volunteers read the sentence aloud. Encourage students to speak clearly and naturally. If time allows, choose another sentence from the text and repeat the activity.

## Finish the Class

10 min

Tell students they will each choose one of the scenes from the story and draw their own pictures to illustrate it. Have them write captions that describe their drawings. Have them share their pictures with a partner and describe what the characters are doing. Have volunteers show and describe their drawing to the class. You may choose to display students' drawings in the class.

Use the **Presentation Kit** for interactive activities in this lesson.

# Lesson 6 Reading Comprehension / Writing

**Lesson Objective:** Recall details from a text.
**Vocabulary Review:** build a sandcastle, swim, swimsuit, jacket, pants
**Grammar Review:** Is Grandpa wearing a swimsuit? No, he isn't.
**Materials:** Audio **Track 39**, music

## Start the Class

5 min

Divide the class into two lines. Tell the class you are going to say a word or phrase from the text and a student from each line will go to the board and write it. The first student to spell the word or phrase correctly wins a point for his or her line.

### ① 39 Listen again to Fun with Grandpa.

5 min

Tell students they will read and listen to the text again. Play **Track 39**. Ask questions about the text such as *How many people are at the lake? What is Eddie doing? What is Lily doing? What is Mom doing?* Ask students to say what they like about the story.

### ② Look at the picture of Grandpa. Answer.

10 min

Have students look at the picture and describe what they see. Explain that they will work individually to answer the questions according to what is in the picture. Allow time for students to complete the activity, and then have them share their answers with a partner.

Tell students they will listen to the story again to check their answers. Play **Track 39** again and pause to allow them time to review their answers. Have volunteers read the questions and the class read their answers.

**Try This!** 5 min

Have students write down their favorite beach activities. Have students form two circles, one inside the other. Play some music while they walk in opposite directions. Stop the music and have them share their favorite beach activities with the person across from them.

### ③ Say Cheese! Draw your family at the lake.

10 min

Have students think about activities people do at the lake. On the board, write *Grandpa is swimming.* Explain to students that they will draw pictures of their own families at the lake. Circulate around the class to monitor students and provide help as needed. Have students show their drawings to a partner and say what they are doing and wearing.

### ④ Writing Time! Write about your picture.

10 min

Explain to the class that they are going to write sentences about the picture they drew in Activity 3. Point to the first sentence and have a volunteer read it to the class. Complete the second sentence with the whole class to give them an idea of what to write. Remind students to use the present progressive in their writing.

Circulate around the class to monitor students' work and provide help as needed. Have students share their sentences with a partner. Then have volunteers show their pictures and read their descriptions to the class.

## Finish the Class

5 min

Name a word category such as *clothes*. Call out words at random. If the word fits the category, students clap, for example, *jeans* (clap), *pants* (clap), *sandcastle* (don't clap), *T-shirt* (clap), and *boat* (don't clap). Repeat with different categories, such as activities. You may also choose to have volunteers lead rounds of the game.

Use the **Presentation Kit** for interactive activities in this lesson.

For the next lesson, use **Skills Book Pages 38 and 39** (Word Work). Go to Teacher's Edition **Page T 177** for teacher notes.

# Lesson 6

## Lesson 6

**1** 39 **Listen again to Fun with Grandpa.**

**2** **Look at the picture of Grandpa. Answer.**

1. Is he building a sandcastle? No, he isn't.
2. Is he swimming? No, he isn't.
3. Is he wearing a swimsuit? No, he isn't.
4. Is he wearing a jacket and pants? Yes, he is.

**3** **Say Cheese! Draw your family at the lake.**

(Students' own answers.)

**4** **Writing Time! Write about your picture.**

It's hot and sunny. (Students' own answers) ________, ________, and I are at the lake. What's ________ wearing? Is ________ wearing ________ and ________? ________.

# Lesson 7

Lesson 7

## Team Up!

1 **Think about your favorite activities.**
**Number them from 1 to 10. 1 = your favorite activity.**

2 **Share your ideas.**

Eating ice cream is my favorite activity.

My favorite activity is flying a kite.

3 **Team up and make a Favorite Activities Chart.**

Eating ice cream is our favorite activity.

# Lesson 7 Creative, Collaborative, and Critical Thinking Activity

**Lesson Objectives:** Talk about favorite activities.
Use communication skills and problem-solving skills to sort information and decide how to present it.
**Vocabulary Review:** clean, wash the dishes, sweep the floor, take out the trash, set the table, make a snack, wash the car, play ball, take a walk, ride a skateboard, ride a bike, have a picnic, climb trees, run, play on the swings, swim, sleep, fly a kite, sail a boat, eat ice cream, build a sandcastle
**Grammar Review:** Eating ice cream is my favorite activity. I don't like drawing.
**Materials:** construction paper; colored pencils, markers, or crayons; music

## Start the Class

10 min

Play Bingo. Have students divide a sheet of paper into nine squares. Have them write a chore in the center square, beach activity words in four of the squares, and park activity words in the remaining four squares. Explain that you are going to say a beach activity, park activity, or chore, and they will mark it on their boards if they have it. Say the vocabulary words in a random order. The first student to mark all of his or her squares shouts *Bingo!* Have the student say the words on his or her game card to confirm he or she is the winner.

### ① Think about your favorite activities. Number them from 1 to 10. 1 = your favorite activity.

5 min

Tell students to look at **Page 54** and have volunteers read the directions and the example list. Have some students say their favorite activities. Explain that they will work individually to write a list of their ten favorite activities. Then they will number them. Explain that number 1 will be their favorite activity, number 2 their next favorite, and so on up to ten. Circulate around the classroom and provide help as needed. Encourage students to use vocabulary from this unit when they can, but tell them they may use other words they know.

### ② Share your ideas.

5 min

Have two volunteers read the sample dialogue in the speech bubbles in Activity 2. Tell students that they will work in pairs and share their favorite activities. Circulate around the classroom, correct pronunciation, and provide help as needed.

### ③ Team up and make a Favorite Activities Chart.

20 min

Put two pairs of students from Activity 2 together to form groups of four. Have each group put all their information together to make a Favorite Activities Chart. Students will write the numbers 1–10 in a vertical row, with 1 at the bottom and 10 at the top. At the bottom of the chart, students will draw pictures of the activities and label them in a horizontal row. The bars for each activity reflect how popular they are for each group. Have teams present the information in their charts to the class. Remind them to point to the activities when they are talking. Be sure each member of the team speaks at least once. Display the charts in the classroom.

**Try This!**

5 min

Have students interview another team to get their votes for their favorite activities. Then take a class poll to see what the number one activity is for the class.

## Finish the Class

5 min

Have students stand up with their lists from Activity 1. Play some music and ask them to walk around the classroom. Stop the music and call out a number such as *six*. Students get together in groups of the number you call and share what favorite activity they had in the same position on their lists. *My number six activity is sleeping*. Repeat several times with different numbers, allowing students several opportunities to talk about the different activities on their lists.

Use the **Presentation Kit** for interactive activities in this lesson.

Use the **Assessment Pack** to carry out the Unit 6 Teamwork Assessment during this lesson.

# Lesson 8 Review

**Lesson Objective:** Review vocabulary and grammar from Unit 6.
**Vocabulary Review:** T-shirt, pants, cap, shorts, jeans, swimsuit, sandals, sneakers, swim, sleep, fly a kite, sail a boat, eat ice cream, build a sandcastle
**Grammar Review:** What are they doing? They're taking a walk.
**Materials:** paper, colored pencils

## Start the Class

5 min

Write the six beach activities on the board and number them. Give each student a number from one to six. Distribute sheets of paper and colored pencils. Tell each student to make a drawing of the beach activity that corresponds to his or her number. Have students exchange drawings and check one another's activities. Have students write their names on the pictures. Collect the drawings to use later in the lesson.

### ① Spelling! Write the *-ing* form of the verbs.

5 min

Have a volunteer read the directions. Explain to the class that they will write each verb with the *-ing* ending. Have volunteers write the correct words on the board so students can check their answers. Review which base word doubles the final consonant (*swimming),* and which word drops the final *-e* (*riding*) to form the *-ing* word. Have students think of other examples of words that double the consonant and words that drop the final *-e* to form the *-ing* words.

### ② Complete the puzzle.

10 min

Point to the numbers next to the pictures and explain to students that they have to use them to find where to write the words to complete the crossword puzzle. Elicit Item 1 (*cap*) and have students write the letters in the corresponding squares. Have students complete the puzzle individually. Circulate around the class to monitor students and provide help as needed. Tell students to compare their answers with a partner. Project the interactive activity from the Presentation Kit for students or draw the puzzle on the board. Have volunteers write their answers for the rest of the class to confirm their answers.

**Try This!**

10 min

Have students stand in several small circles. Explain that they are going to spell words from Activity 2. Give them a word to spell; the first student says the first letter, the next says the second letter, and so on. After the last letter, the next student says the whole word. Allow students to play several times in their circles with different words. Circulate around the class while students are playing to monitor spelling and provide help as needed.

### ③ Word Play! Find and circle the words from Unit 6 on Page 72.

15 min

Have students turn to **Page 72** and tell them to find and circle the clothes and beach vocabulary words from Unit 6. Then have students check the words they found with a partner.

## Finish the Class

5 min

Hand out the drawings students made at the beginning of the class. Tell students to stand in a circle. Say *Change places if your picture is sailing a boat.* Students who have that picture have to change places. Continue with other actions. Play several times.

Use the **Presentation Kit** for interactive activities in this lesson.

For the next lesson, use Unit 6 Language Assessment from the **Assessment Pack** or create your own test using the **Test Generator** on the **Teacher's Resource Center**.

# Lesson 8

## Lesson 8

## Round Up!

**1 Spelling!** **Write the *-ing* form of the verbs.**

| | |
|---|---|
| **1.** eat ___eating___ | **2.** fly ___flying___ |
| **3.** swim ___swimming___ | **4.** ride ___riding___ |
| **5.** build ___building___ | **6.** watch ___watching___ |

**2 Complete the puzzle.**

1.

2.

3.

4.

5.

6.

| | | | | | | | |
|---|---|---|---|---|---|---|---|
| | | | | 1 c | | | |
| | | 2 j | e | a | n | 3 s | |
| | 4 s | | | p | | h | |
| | a | | 5 p | | | o | |
| 6 s | n | e | a | k | e | r | s |
| | d | | n | | | t | |
| | a | | t | | | s | |
| | l | | s | | | | |
| | s | | | | | | |

**3 Word Play!** **Find and circle the words from Unit 6 on Page 72.**

# Unit 7

## Unit Objectives

**By the end of the unit, students can:**

- Identify party food and party-time activities.
- Ask and answer questions about a picture.
- Identify the main ideas and details in text.

## Student Book

### Vocabulary

**Party Food:** cake, chips, sandwiches, candy, juice, lemonade, popcorn, soda

**Party Time:** sing, dance, bake a cake, buy snacks, send invitations, make decorations

### Grammar

Are they eating cake? Yes, they are.
Are they drinking soda? No, they aren't.
We're making decorations.
Are you baking a cake? Yes, we are. / No, we aren't.

### Skills

**Listening:** Listen for and identify party food and celebrations. Listen for specific information and choose an appropriate response.

**Speaking:** Talk about party food and party-time activities.

**Reading:** Read a nonfiction text (social studies): **Party Time!**
Identify the main idea and details in a text.

**Writing:** Write about party-time activities.

### Creative, Collaborative, and Critical Thinking Competencies

**Party Jobs Chart**

**Creativity:** Develop self-expression, innovation, and problem-solving skills. Determine the information to be included in the poster and how it will be presented.

**Collaboration:** Use communication and conflict resolution skills. Determine how each team member will contribute to the final product.

**Critical Thinking:** Analyze and organize the information to be included in the poster. Use problem-solving skills to complete the final product.

## Skills Book

**Extra Skills Practice**

**Speaking and Listening:** Ask and answer questions about a picture.

**Reading and Writing:** Identify the sequence of events.
Draw conclusions.
Recognize spelling patterns.
Identify multi-syllable words.

# Teacher Workshop

## Teaching with Technology

Technology can help students become independent learners who take responsibility for improving. If you have access to computers in school, try out extra activities to practice the vocabulary and language in a unit. Alternatively, you can suggest links for students to do extra practice at home.

## Teaching with Games

**Chain Game**

Divide students into several teams and have each team form a line. Explain that the first student is going to say a vocabulary word from this unit. The next student will repeat the word and then say another one. The third student will repeat the first two words and add another one, and so on. The objective is to see which team can say the most words in a row in the correct order. Start a new chain when a student makes a mistake or can't remember. The team that says the longest chain of words wins.

## Happy Teacher

Your class board should look clear and well-organized. Divide the board into sections so you always know where to write the date and other important information. Think about what you will need to write in other sections so you don't run out of space. Make sure your writing is large enough to be seen for students farthest from the board. Check if students can see the bottom part of the board without standing up. Write clearly; if possible, use different colors to highlight words. If you have trouble organizing your board, take photographs of it and use the picture to plan your next lesson.

## Happy Class

To increase concentration in class, give students opportunities to move around the classroom. Change seating plans at the beginning of each new unit, making sure students sit in different places in the classroom throughout the year. Use pair work and group activities, creating simple ways for students to move around. Students can work in rows or with people in front of them, behind them, or next to them. This provides students with the opportunity to move in class, as well as work with different people.

By Diana Jones

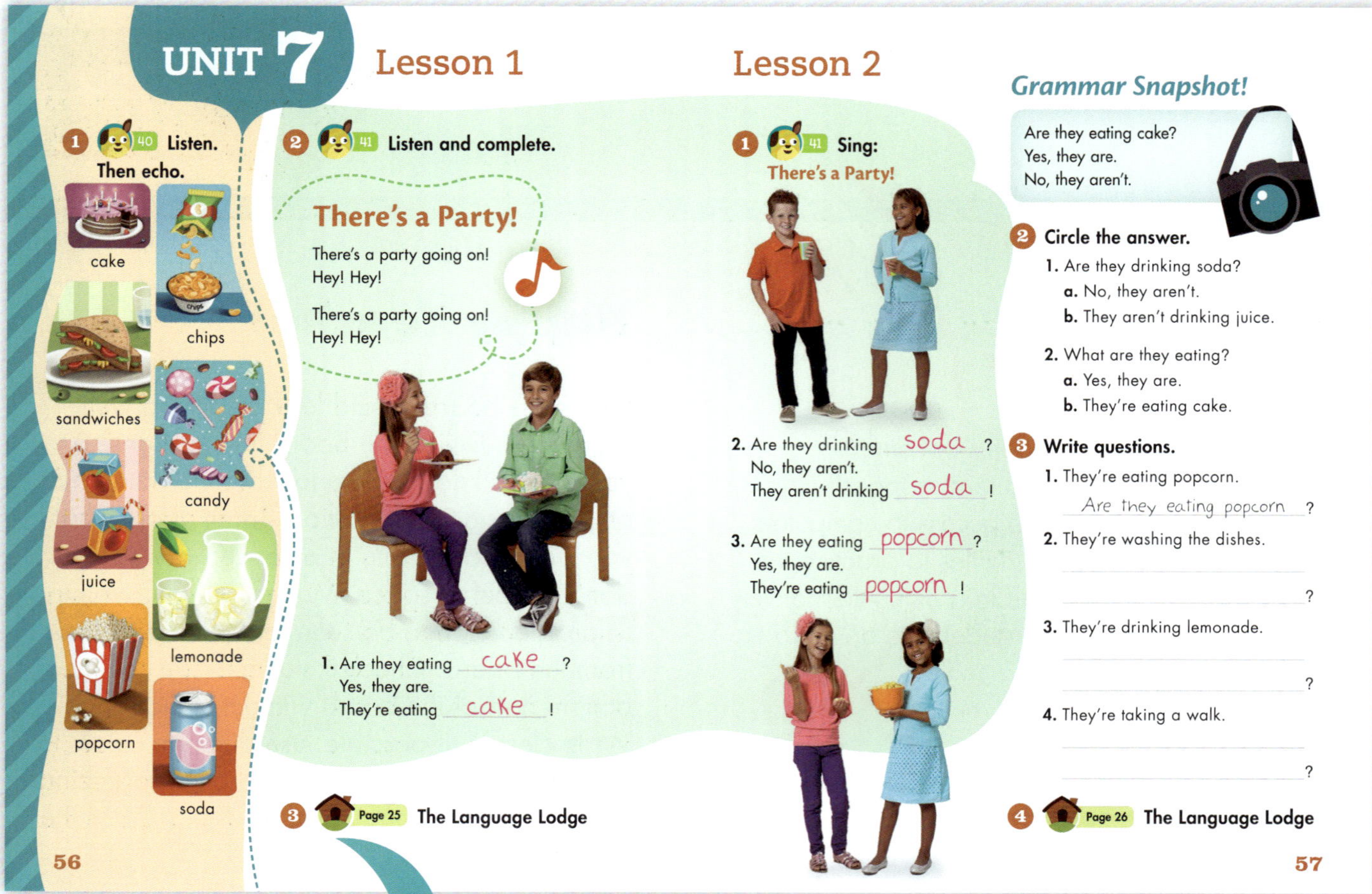

# UNIT 7

## Lesson 1

1 40 Listen. Then echo.

cake, chips, sandwiches, candy, juice, lemonade, popcorn, soda

2 41 Listen and complete.

**There's a Party!**

There's a party going on!
Hey! Hey!

There's a party going on!
Hey! Hey!

1. Are they eating cake ?
   Yes, they are.
   They're eating cake !

3 Page 25 The Language Lodge

56

## Lesson 2

1 41 Sing: There's a Party!

2. Are they drinking soda ?
   No, they aren't.
   They aren't drinking soda !

3. Are they eating popcorn ?
   Yes, they are.
   They're eating popcorn !

*Grammar Snapshot!*

Are they eating cake?
Yes, they are.
No, they aren't.

2 Circle the answer.

1. Are they drinking soda?
   **a.** No, they aren't.
   **b.** They aren't drinking juice.
2. What are they eating?
   **a.** Yes, they are.
   **b.** They're eating cake.

3 Write questions.

1. They're eating popcorn.
   Are they eating popcorn ?
2. They're washing the dishes.
   ?
3. They're drinking lemonade.
   ?
4. They're taking a walk.
   ?

4 Page 26 The Language Lodge

57

# UNIT 7 Lesson 1

1 Unscramble. Then match.

1. acke cake
2. daschnwies sandwiches
3. scihp chips
4. eomdalen lemonade
5. cuije juice
6. ropcopn popcorn
7. daso soda
8. cdyan candy

Spelling Check! Spell the party foods aloud.
Then complete. I can spell ___ words.

Student Book Page 56

25

# Lesson 1

This may also be completed for homework.

# Lesson 1 Vocabulary



**Lesson Objective:** Identify food at a party.
**New Vocabulary:** cake, chips, sandwiches, candy, juice, lemonade, popcorn, soda
**Materials:** Audio **Tracks 40 and 41**, music

## Start the Class

5 min

Have students look at **Pages 56 and 57** and describe what they can see in the pictures. Ask them to predict what the lesson is about. Elicit local customs and traditions for birthday parties. Allow students to share their ideas freely.

### 1 40 Listen. Then echo.

10 min

Have students look at the pictures and identify the party foods. Explain that they are going to listen and point to the different party foods. Play **Track 40**. Elicit the things we eat (*cake, chips, sandwiches, candy,* and *popcorn*) and the things we drink (*juice, lemonade,* and *soda*).

Play **Track 40** again and have students echo the words.

### 2 41 Listen and complete.

15 min

Have students look at the photos on **Pages 56 and 57** and elicit what they think is happening. Point to the children, and elicit the clothes they are wearing and what colors the clothes are. Explain to the class that they are going to listen to a song. Play **Track 41**. Tell students you are going to play the song again for them to complete the sentences.

Have students compare their answers with a partner. Check answers as a class.

**Try This!**

5 min

Tell students to write their favorite party food on a small piece of paper. Play some music. Have students stand up and walk around the classroom. Explain that you will stop the music and they must get together in groups based on their words for their favorite party food. Ask groups to say the word they chose.

### 3 Page 25 The Language Lodge

10 min

Have students flip to The Language Lodge **Page 25**.

**1 Unscramble. Then match.**

Have a volunteer read the directions. Explain to students that they will unscramble the words to write them out correctly, and then match each word to the correct picture. Have students check their answers in pairs.

**Spelling Check! Spell the party foods aloud. Then complete.**

Have students close their books. Tell them that they will take turns saying and spelling the party foods with a partner. Then tell students to write the number of words they can spell correctly.

## Finish the Class

5 min

Have students study the words and the pictures in Activity 1. Ask them to close their books. Divide the class into pairs. Name the party foods one by one. In pairs, students say as many details as they can remember about the food from the picture, for example, for *cake*: *It's chocolate cake. It has pink frosting. It has six candles.*

Use the **Presentation Kit** for interactive activities in this lesson.

Have students use the **Happy Campers app** for additional practice with the new vocabulary.

**The Language Lodge Page 25** may also be completed for homework.

# Lesson 2 Grammar

**Lesson Objective:** Ask and answer questions about party food.
**New Grammar:** Are they eating cake? Yes, they are. Are they drinking soda? No, they aren't.
**Vocabulary Review:** cake, chips, sandwiches, candy, juice, lemonade, popcorn, soda
**Materials:** Audio **Track 41**, Unit 7 flashcards with pictures of party food

## Start the Class

5 min

Have a volunteer go to the board and stand with his or her back to the board. Draw a party food on the board. The student at the board makes guesses about the party food; the other students say *yes* or *no* until the student at the board guesses the party food. Repeat with different students and party foods.

### 1 41 Sing: There's a Party!

5 min

Tell students they are going to listen to the song again and follow the words in their books as they listen. Explain that when they hear *No, they aren't*, they should wag their fingers to indicate no; when they hear *Yes, they are*, they should nod their heads. Play **Track 41**. Play **Track 41** again and have the class sing along and do the actions at the same time.

### 2 Circle the answer.

15 min

Have the class read the Grammar Snapshot! together. Tell students to look at the question and the two answers. Remind students that we begin *yes/no* questions with *Are they*, and we answer these questions with *Yes, they are* or *No, they aren't*.

Tell students to look at the two questions, think about the correct answer to each one individually, and then circle it. Have them compare their answers with a partner before checking as a class.

**Try This!**

5 min

Have pairs or small groups go to the board and give them a flashcard with a party food on it. Ask their classmates *Are they (eating cake)?* to elicit *Yes, they are. / No, they aren't.* Ask *What are they (drinking)?* to elicit food or drink words. Repeat the activity several times.

### 3 Write questions.

5 min

Write *They're eating popcorn* on the board. Elicit from students what the *yes/no* question is: *Are they eating popcorn?* Explain to students that they will write questions for the remaining statements. Circulate among students and provide help as needed. Have volunteers write the questions on the board for the class to check their answers.

### 4 Page 26 The Language Lodge

10 min

Have students flip to The Language Lodge **Page 26**. Have volunteers read the Grammar Snapshot! questions and answers aloud.

**1 Complete.**

Explain to the class that they will look at the pictures and write questions and answers for each one. Remind them that the check mark or cross indicates whether the answer is affirmative or negative. Have volunteers read the questions and answers aloud.

## Finish the Class

5 min

Divide the board into four sections and the students into four teams. Have a volunteer from each team stand in front of a section. Write a long word at the top of the board, such as *sandwiches*. Explain that each team must write a word beginning with each letter in *sandwiches*. Explain they are not allowed to repeat any words in any single round. Repeat with different words.

Use the **Presentation Kit** for interactive activities in this lesson.

**The Language Lodge Page 26** may also be completed for homework.

For the next lesson, use **Skills Book Pages 40 and 41** (Picture Talk). Go to Teacher's Edition **Page T 178** for teacher notes.

# UNIT 7

1 Listen. Then echo.

## Lesson 1

2 Listen and complete.

**There's a Party!**

There's a party going on!
Hey! Hey!

There's a party going on!
Hey! Hey!

1. Are they eating ___________?
Yes, they are.
They're eating ___________!

3 Page 25 The Language Lodge

## Lesson 2

1 Sing: There's a Party!

2. Are they drinking ___________?
No, they aren't.
They aren't drinking ___________!

3. Are they eating ___________?
Yes, they are.
They're eating ___________!

**Grammar Snapshot!**

Are they eating cake?
Yes, they are.
No, they aren't.

2 Circle the answer.

1. Are they drinking soda?
   a. No, they aren't. (circled)
   b. They aren't drinking juice.
2. What are they eating?
   a. Yes, they are.
   b. They're eating cake. (circled)

3 Write questions.

1. They're eating popcorn.
   Are they eating popcorn ?
2. They're washing the dishes.
   Are they washing the dishes ?
3. They're drinking lemonade.
   Are they drinking lemonade ?
4. They're taking a walk.
   Are they taking a walk ?

4 Page 26 The Language Lodge



## Lesson 2

**Grammar Snapshot!**

Are they eating cake?
Yes, they are.
No, they aren't.

1 Complete.

1. 
Are they eating cake?
✓ Yes, they are.

2. 
Are they drinking juice?
✗ No, they aren't.

3. 
Are they eating candy?
✗ No, they aren't.

4. 
Are they drinking lemonade?
✓ Yes, they are.

5. 
Are they eating popcorn ?
✓ Yes, they are.

6. 
Are they eating chips ?
✗ No, they aren't.



Student Book Page 57

# Lesson 2

This may also be completed for homework.

# Lesson 3

## Shutterbugs

1 Are they preparing for a celebration?

2 42 Read and listen.

3 43 **Dictation!** Listen and write. Then say.

 1. sing
 2. dance
 3. bake a cake
 4. buy snacks
 5. send invitations
 6. make decorations

4 Page 27 The Language Lodge



# Lesson 4

1 42 Listen again to **Shutterbugs**.

2 ***Grammar Snapshot!*** Circle.

1. We're sending invitations.  Yes, we are. / No, we aren't.

2. Are you running?  Yes, we are. / No, we aren't.

3 44 **Listen and cheer!**

Are you buying snacks? Yes, we are!
Are you baking a cake? No, we aren't.
We're dancing and singing. It's party time!

CHEER BOX!

4 Page 28 The Language Lodge



# Lesson 3

1 Complete the party to-do list.

**Party To-Do List**

- ✓ send invitations
- ✓ make decorations
- ✓ bake a cake
- ✓ buy snacks

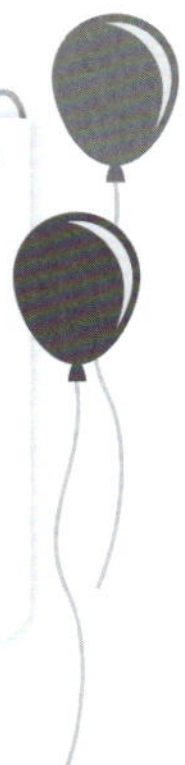

2 Read and circle. Then complete.

1. You and your friend are in the supermarket. Are you dancing?
   Yes, we are. (No, we aren't.) We're buying snacks.
2. There are candles on a birthday cake. Are you singing?
   (Yes, we are.) No, we aren't. We're singing.
3. You and your friend are drawing. Are you making decorations?
   (Yes, we are.) No, we aren't. We're making decorations.
4. You and your friend are in the kitchen. Are you buying snacks?
   Yes, we are. (No, we aren't.) We're baking a cake.

✓ **Spelling Check!** Spell the party words aloud. **Then complete.** I can spell ____ words.

Student Book Page 58



# Lesson 3

This may also be completed for homework.

# Lesson 3 Vocabulary in Context

**Lesson Objective:** Identify party preparation activities.
**New Vocabulary:** sing, dance, bake a cake, buy snacks, send invitations, make decorations
**Vocabulary Review:** cake, snacks
**Materials:** Audio **Tracks 41, 42, and 43**; strips of paper

## Start the Class

5 min

Divide the class into three groups. Explain that they are going to sing "There's a Party!" from Lesson 1. Each group will sing one verse. Have each group stand together in three different parts of the classroom. Play **Track 41** again and have students sing their assigned parts.

### 1 Are they preparing for a celebration?

5 min

Have a volunteer read the question aloud and elicit the answer: *Yes, they are.*

### 2 42 Read and listen.

10 min

Tell students they will read the comic strip as they listen. Play **Track 42**. Point to the picture in the circle in the last scene of the comic strip and ask *Are Tom and Sam dancing?* Elicit *Yes, they are.*

Play **Track 42** again and have students quietly read aloud with the audio.

### 3 43 Dictation! Listen and write. Then say.

10 min

Have a volunteer read the directions. Play **Track 43**, and pause for students to write the phrases. Play **Track 43** again. Then have students check their answers with a partner.

Tell students they will listen again and repeat what they hear. Play **Track 43** again.

*Audio script* ***Track 43***
*1. sing 2. dance 3. bake a cake 4. buy snacks 5. send invitations 6. make decorations*

**Try This!** 5 min

Write *prepare for a party* on one side of the board and *do at a party* on the other side. Elicit which things you do to prepare for a party (*send invitations, make decorations, bake a cake, buy snacks*) and which things you do at a party (*sing, dance*).

### 4 Page 27 The Language Lodge

10 min

Have students flip to The Language Lodge **Page 27**.

**1 Complete the party to-do list.**

Explain to students that they will complete the checklist. Have students complete the activity individually. Then have volunteers read their answers.

**2 Read and circle. Then complete.**

Explain to the class that they will read the question, circle the answer, and then complete the sentence. Do Item 1 as a class. Have volunteers share their answers with the class.

**Spelling Check! Spell the party words aloud. Then complete.**

Have students close their books. Tell them that they will take turns saying and spelling the party words with a partner. Then tell students to write the number of words they can spell correctly.

## Finish the Class

5 min

Write party foods and party-time activities on strips of paper. Divide the class into two teams. Have the first person in each team come to the board, choose a strip of paper, and act it out for their team to guess. Continue the activity until all students on both teams have participated.

Use the **Presentation Kit** for interactive activities in this lesson.

Have students use the **Happy Campers app** for additional practice with the new vocabulary.

**The Language Lodge Page 27** may also be completed for homework.

# Lesson 4 Grammar in Context

**Lesson Objective:** Ask and answer questions about party-time activities.
**New Grammar:** We're making decorations. Are you baking a cake? Yes, we are.
**Vocabulary Review:** sing, dance, bake a cake, buy snacks, send invitations, make decorations
**Materials:** Audio **Tracks 42 and 44**, colored paper

## Start the Class

5 min

Have students say as much as they can remember about the comic strip from Lesson 3 without looking at their books. Encourage them to name the characters and their activities, using the present continuous to make full sentences.

### 1 42 Listen again to Shutterbugs.

10 min

Tell the class that they will read and listen again to the comic strip. Play **Track 42**. Divide the class into groups of four. Explain to students that they will each read a character's role from the comic strip. The first group will be Lisa's part, the second group will be Clare's part, the third group will be Sam's part, and the fourth group will be Tom's part. Have groups read their parts aloud.

### 2 *Grammar Snapshot!* Circle.

10 min

Have a volunteer read the directions for Activity 2 on **Page 59**. Explain to the class that they will circle the correct answers to the questions. Then have volunteers share the answers with the class. Finally, have students underline *Are you* in the questions and *we are* or *we aren't* in the answers.

**Try This!** 5 min

Write the following on the board: *you buying snacks? What you doing? We sending invitations. We're singing dancing. Are baking a cake? We not singing.* Tell students that each question and sentence has one word missing. Explain that they will write the complete questions and sentences in their notebooks. Have volunteers complete the questions and answers on the board.

### 3 44 Listen and cheer!

5 min

Tell the class they are going to listen to a cheer and read the words as they listen. Play **Track 44**. Tell students to say the cheer along with the audio, exaggerating the pronunciation. Play **Track 44** again.

### 4 Page 28 The Language Lodge

10 min

Have students flip to The Language Lodge **Page 28**. Have a volunteer read the Grammar Snapshot! Review when to use *you* and when to use *we*.

**1 Look. Then read and circle.**

Tell students to circle the statements that correctly describe the pictures. Do the first item together. Check answers as a class.

**2 You and your friends are having a party. Answer.**

Tell students they will answer some questions. Have students work individually to answer the questions. Then have volunteers read the questions and other volunteers answer them.

## Finish the Class

5 min

Have students look at the invitation in the first scene of the comic strip. Distribute colored paper and have each student make an invitation for his or her own party. Tell students to decorate the invitations with activities they want to do at their parties. Then have them ask and answer information about their parties with a partner by asking *Are you dancing? Yes, we are. Are you eating cake? No, we aren't.* Walk around and monitor the activity. Display students' invitations in the classroom.

Use the **Presentation Kit** for interactive activities in this lesson.

**The Language Lodge Page 28** may also be completed for homework.

For the next lesson, use **Skills Book Pages 42 and 43** (Happy Reader). Go to Teacher's Edition **Page T 179** for teacher notes.

## Lesson 3

# Shutterbugs

1 Are they preparing for a celebration?

2 42 Read and listen.

3 43 **Dictation!** Listen and write. Then say.

 1. ____________  2. ____________

 3. ____________  4. ____________

 5. ____________  6. ____________

4 Page 27 The Language Lodge



## Lesson 4

1 42 Listen again to Shutterbugs.

2 *Grammar Snapshot!* Circle.

1. We're sending invitations.  (Yes, we are.) No, we aren't.

2. Are you running?  Yes, we are. (No, we aren't.)

3 44 Listen and cheer!

Are you buying snacks? Yes, we are!
Are you baking a cake? No, we aren't.
We're dancing and singing. It's party time!

CHEER BOX!

4 Page 28 The Language Lodge



# Lesson 4

This may also be completed for homework.

## Lesson 4

### *Grammar Snapshot!*

We're making decorations.
Are you baking a cake?
Yes, we are.
No, we aren't.

1 Look. Then read and circle.

1. 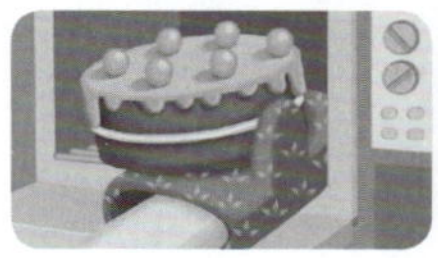

a. We're making decorations.
b. (We're baking a cake.)

2. 

a. (We're buying snacks.)
b. We're sending invitations.

3. 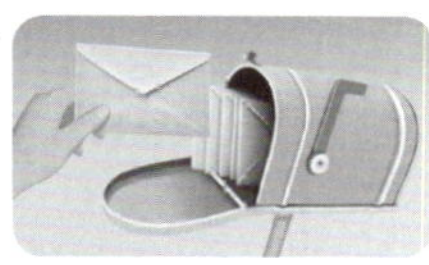

a. We're drinking soda.
b. (We're sending invitations.)

2 You and your friends are having a party. Answer.

1. Are you baking a cake? (Students' own answers).
2. Are you making decorations? (Students' own answers).
3. Are you sending invitations? (Students' own answers).
4. Are you buying snacks? (Students' own answers).



Student Book Page 59

# Lesson 5

## Lesson 5

**1** **Look and circle *True* or *False*.**

The children are sad. True (False)

**2** 45 **Read and listen.**

## Party Time!

All children love parties!
What's she doing?
She's making decorations.
Look at all the fun colors.

They're playing party games.
They're happy.
What are your favorite party games?

The children are eating a lot of party food.
They're eating salad, and fruit, too.
It looks delicious!

Now they're dancing and singing.
They're listening to music and having fun!
It's party time!

# Lesson 5 Nonfiction Reading

**Lesson Objective:** Read a nonfiction text.
**Vocabulary Review:** make decorations, eat party food, dance, sing
**Grammar Review:** She's making decorations. They're playing party games.
**Materials:** Audio **Track 45**; cards with vocabulary words from Unit 7, Lesson 1

## Start the Class

5 min

Have the class form a circle. Show them the flashcards with the Lesson 1 party foods and have them say the words aloud. Explain that you are going to pass the cards around the circle. Students have to read the word on the card aloud and pass it on to the next student. Ask them to begin passing the cards slowly. Then ask students to pass them around faster, or in alternating directions, to make the game more challenging and fun.

### 1 Look and circle *True* or *False*.

5 min

Tell students to open their books to **Page 60**. Have a volunteer read the title of the text in Activity 2. Then have another volunteer read the sentence. Tell the class to circle the answer. Then review with the class and elicit *False*. Have students explain the reasons for their answers.

### 2 45 Read and listen.

20 min

Have students form pairs, look at the pictures, and name as many things as they can to activate previous ideas and knowledge. Circulate around the class to monitor students and provide help as needed. Remind students that *fiction* means the text isn't true and *nonfiction* means the text is true or factual. Have students provide examples of fiction and nonfiction texts they know. Then ask *Is this nonfiction or fiction?* Elicit *nonfiction*. Have students explain their reasons.

Tell students that they will read the text as they listen. Encourage students to follow the words with their fingers as they read and listen. Play **Track 45**. Then have students underline words in the text that show what activities the children are doing, such as *making decorations, playing party games, eating a lot of party food, eating salad, dancing,* and *singing*.

Divide the class into groups and tell students that they will read the text again in their groups. Explain that they will take turns reading a part of the text aloud. Remind them to read clearly so everyone can understand; the rest of the group will follow the words in their books with their fingers as they listen. Circulate among the groups to check intonation and rhythm, and provide help as needed. Ensure that all students are participating.

**Try This!**

10 min

Divide the class into teams and have the teams form lines. Whisper a sentence or question with the present continuous to the first student in each line. Tell each student to whisper the sentence or question to the student behind him or her, forming a chain. The last student in each line says the sentence or question aloud. The teams then mime the action. Award a point if the sentence/question and the miming are correct. Send the first student in each line to the end of the line and repeat with a different sentence or question. The team with the most points wins.

## Finish the Class

10 min

Divide the class in half and have them line up in pairs. The first pair will go to the board. You will say a word from the story, and the students in each pair take turns writing the word. The first student writes the first letter. Then the second student writes the second letter. The first student writes the third letter, and so on. If the word is spelled correctly, the pair gets a point. Try words such as *party, parties, decorations, fun, games, cake, dancing, singing, listening,* and *having*.

Use the **Presentation Kit** for interactive activities in this lesson.

# Lesson 6 Reading Comprehension / Writing

**Lesson Objective:** Recall details from a text.
**Vocabulary Review:** sing, dance, bake a cake, buy snacks, send invitations, make decorations
**Grammar Review:** What's she doing? She's making decorations. They're dancing and singing.
**Materials:** Audio **Track 45**

## Start the Class

5 min

Divide the class into teams. Have students turn to **Page 61**. Read an action from the text on **Page 60** and have students look for it in the text. The first team to find the action will stand up with their fingers on the words in the text. Give the team a point and continue the game. The team with the most points wins.

### ① 45 Listen again to Party Time!

5 min

Tell students they will listen to the text again. Remind them to follow the story in their books as they listen. Play **Track 45**. Have students identify the kind of party they see in the photos, and have them explain their answers.

### ② Circle *True* or *False*.

10 min

Have volunteers read the four sentences aloud. Answer Item 1 with the whole class and ask them to say where the answer is in the text. Explain that they will work individually to decide if the sentences are true or false. Remind them that they can look at the story on **Page 60**. Allow time for students to complete the activity, and then have them share their answers with a partner. Have volunteers read the sentences, and have the class say *True* or *False*.

**Try This!**

5 min

Have students write down their three favorite party activities. Tell students to walk around the classroom and find someone with exactly the same activities as them. Once students have found someone with the same activities, allow them to sit down. Students who don't find a partner must read their lists to the class. Then have all students share their lists with the class. Write the activities on the board and determine the class's favorite party activities.

### ③ Say Cheese! Draw your friends at a party.

10 min

On the board, write *She's making decorations. They're singing.* Explain to students that they will each draw a picture of their friends at a party. Tell students that they can draw any kind of party. Circulate around the class to monitor students' drawings and provide help as needed. Ask them questions about their pictures, such as *What are they doing? Are they dancing? What are they eating?* Have students show their drawings to a partner and describe the scene.

### ④ Writing Time! Write about your picture.

10 min

Explain to the class that they are going to write some sentences about the picture they drew in Activity 3. Have a volunteer read the question. Then brainstorm ideas for the answer with the class. Tell students they will work individually to complete the activity. Remind them that they're writing about their pictures. Circulate around the class to monitor students' work and provide help as needed. Then tell students to share their writings with a partner. Have volunteers read their writing to the class.

## Finish the Class

5 min

Tell students that they will look at **Pages 60 and 61**, find words with double letters, and write them down in a list in their notebooks. Circulate around the class to monitor students' work and provide help as needed. Have volunteers write the words on the board for the class to confirm their answers: *look*, *all*, *happy*, *food*, *too*, *looks*, *Lesson*, and *cheese*. Have them think about other words with double letters. Ask volunteers to write them on the board. Then have students add them to their lists.

Use the **Presentation Kit** for interactive activities in this lesson.

For the next lesson, use **Skills Book Pages 44 and 45** (Word Work). Go to Teacher's Edition **Page T 180** for teacher notes.

# Lesson 6

## Lesson 6

**1** 45 **Listen again to Party Time!**

**2** **Circle *True* or *False*.**

1. She's making decorations. (True) False
2. They're sending invitations. True (False)
3. They're eating breakfast. True (False)
4. They're dancing and singing. (True) False

**3** **Say Cheese! Draw your friends at a party.**

(Students' own answers.)

**4** **Writing Time! Write about your picture.**

What are they doing? They're (Students' own answers) .

They're eating a lot of ________ and ________ .

They're ________ . It's party time!

# Lesson 7

Lesson 7

## Team Up!

**1** Think about party preparations. Make a list of things to do.

Party Preparations
bake a cake
make decorations

**2** Share your list. Act out the party preparations.

Are you baking a cake?

Yes, I am.

**3** Team up and make a Party Jobs Chart.

# Lesson 7 Creative, Collaborative, and Critical Thinking Activity

**Lesson Objective:** Talk about favorite party jobs.
**Vocabulary Review:** clean, wash the dishes, sweep the floor, take out the trash, set the table, make a snack, wash the car, sing, dance, bake a cake, buy snacks, send invitations, make decorations
**Grammar Review:** Are you washing the dishes? Yes, I am. I'm washing the dishes.
**Materials:** construction paper; colored pencils, markers, or crayons; music

## Start the Class

10 min

Play Bingo. Have students divide a sheet of paper so it has nine squares. Have them write a chore word in the center square, words for party activities in three of the squares, and five party foods in the rest of the squares. Remind students that you are going to say a chore, a party food, or a party-time activity, and they will mark it if they have it. Say the words in random order. The first student to mark all of his or her squares and say *Bingo!* wins. Have the student say the words to confirm that he or she is the winner.

### 1 Think about party preparations. Make a list of things to do.

5 min

Tell students to look at **Page 62** and have volunteers read the directions and the example list. Explain that they will work individually to write a list of things to do to prepare for a party. Remind students that sometimes it is necessary to clean before the party, so chores can also be part of planning for a party. Circulate around the classroom and provide help as needed.

### 2 Share your list. Act out the party preparations.

5 min

Ask a volunteer to read the directions. Have two volunteers read the sample dialogue in Activity 2. Remind them that if the guess is incorrect, they will answer *No, I'm not.*

Have students work with a partner. Explain that they will take turns acting out the preparations on their to-do list and guessing what they are. Circulate around the classroom, correct pronunciation, and provide help as needed.

### 3 Team up and make a Party Jobs Chart.

20 min

Put two pairs together. Have students choose four different party preparation activities and decide who will do each one. Distribute materials. Tell them to make an illustrated Party Jobs Chart similar to the one in the book.

Have teams share their charts with the class. Remind them to act out the activities as they present the information to their classmates. Be sure each member of the team speaks at least once. Display the charts in the classroom.

**Try This!**

5 min

Explain that students are going to stand up and do a *This is the way we ...* demonstration. Call out an activity for a party preparation, such as *send invitations.* All students respond *This is the way we send invitations* while miming the activity at the same time. Repeat with different party preparation activities they have studied in this unit.

## Finish the Class

5 min

Play some music. Have students walk around the classroom. When you stop the music, you will say a party activity such as *dancing.* Students will gather in groups according to the number of letters in the word. For example, *dancing* has seven letters, so there will be seven students in each group. Repeat the game several times with different words from this unit. Try to vary the number of letters in the words you call out.

Use the **Presentation Kit** for interactive activities in this lesson.

Use the **Assessment Pack** to carry out the Unit 7 Teamwork Assessment during this lesson.

# Lesson 8 Review

**Lesson Objective:** Review language from Unit 7.
**Vocabulary Review:** cake, chips, sandwiches, candy, juice, lemonade, popcorn, soda, sing, dance, bake a cake, buy snacks, send invitations, make decorations
**Grammar Review:** Are they eating cake? Yes, they are. Are you sending invitations? Yes, we are.
**Materials:** 12–16 pairs of cards with matching pictures for party activities

## Start the Class

5 min

Create a set of game cards for Memory that illustrate six to eight words from Unit 7. Draw the image on one side and a number on the other. There will be two of each of the images, and one of each number. Put the cards on the board with images facing the board. Students should only see the numbers. Divide the class into two teams and have them take turns choosing two numbers. Turn over the cards. If a team finds a pair, students will say the activity to claim both cards. The team with the most cards wins.

### 1 Spelling! Complete the words.

10 min

Tell students that the words are written in code, and the code is in the yellow box at the top of the page. Have them look at the code and explain that each number represents a letter. Elicit the number of letters in the English alphabet (*26*) and whether it is the same in their own language. Explain that they will write out the words according to the code. Circulate around the class to monitor students and provide help as needed. Tell students to compare their answers with a partner. Then have volunteers write the correct words on the board for the rest of the class to confirm their answers.

**Try This!**

5 min

Have students write three different words from Unit 7, using the code in Activity 1 on a sheet of paper. Tell students to exchange papers with a partner. Explain that the partner will decode the words. Have the partners confirm the answers.

### 2 Complete.

10 min

Read and complete the first question and answer with the class. Tell students to complete the questions and answers individually. Circulate around the class to monitor students and provide help as needed. Review the answers by asking volunteers to read the complete questions and answers aloud. You may use the Presentation Kit to project **Page 63** on the board. You may also write the sentence frames on the board and have volunteers complete them for the class to confirm their answers. Then have volunteers read the completed questions and answers.

### 3 Word Play! Find and circle the words from Unit 7 on Page 72.

15 min

Have students turn to **Page 72** and tell them to find and circle the party food and party-time vocabulary words from Unit 7. Then have students check the words they found with a partner.

## Finish the Class

5 min

Divide the class into pairs. Ask one student in the pair to choose a party food from this unit. Explain that the other student will ask questions to guess the food, such as *Are you eating sandwiches? No, I'm not. Are you eating cake? Yes, I am.* Have students take turns asking and answering at least twice.

Use the **Presentation Kit** for interactive activities in this lesson.

For the next lesson, use Unit 7 Language Assessment from the **Assessment Pack** or create your own test using the **Test Generator** on the **Teacher's Resource Center**.

# Lesson 8

## Lesson 8

## Round Up!

**1 Spelling! Complete the words.**

| | | | | | | |
|---|---|---|---|---|---|---|
| 1 = a | 2 = b | 3 = c | 4 = d | 5 = e | 6 = f | 7 = g |
| 8 = h | 9 = i | 10 = j | 11 = k | 12 = l | 13 = m | 14 = n |
| 15 = o | 16 = p | 17 = q | 18 = r | 19 = s | 20 = t | 21 = u |
| 22 = v | 23 = w | 24 = x | 25 = y | 26 = z | | |

1.

| | | | | | | | |
|---|---|---|---|---|---|---|---|
| l | e | m | o | n | a | d | e |
| 12 | | 13 | | 14 | 1 | | 5 |

2.

| | | | | |
|---|---|---|---|---|
| c | h | i | p | s |
| 3 | | 9 | 16 | |

3.

| | | | | |
|---|---|---|---|---|
| j | u | i | c | e |
| 10 | 21 | | | 5 |

4.

| | | | | | |
|---|---|---|---|---|---|
| s | n | a | c | k | s |
| 19 | | | | 11 | 19 |

5.

| | | | | | | | | | | |
|---|---|---|---|---|---|---|---|---|---|---|
| d | e | c | o | r | a | t | i | o | n | s |
| 4 | | 3 | 15 | 18 | | | | | 14 | |

**2 Complete.**

1. Are you baking a cake? Yes, we are.
2. Are they making decorations? No, they aren't.
3. Are you sending invitations? No, we aren't.
4. Are they buying snacks? Yes, they are.

**3 Word Play! Find and circle the words from Unit 7 on Page 72.**

# Unit 8

## Unit Objectives

**By the end of the unit, students can:**

- Identify abilities.
- Make statements about a picture and respond.
- Show understanding of story details.

## Student Book

### Vocabulary

**Abilities:** draw, hop, paint, play the guitar, play the drums, jump rope, speak English, whistle

**Vocabulary Review:** Level 3 verbs

### Grammar

I can play the guitar. I can't whistle.
Can you whistle? Yes, I can.

### Skills

**Listening:** Listen for and identify abilities. Listen for specific information.

**Speaking:** Talk about abilities.

**Reading:** Read a fiction text:
**I Can Help, Too!**
Identify the main idea and details.
Read short sentences and recognize words.

**Writing:** Write about abilities.

### Creative, Collaborative, and Critical Thinking Competencies

**Abilities Chart**

**Creativity:** Develop self-expression and innovation. Determine how to present information.

**Collaboration:** Use communication skills and conflict resolution skills to complete tasks. Determine how each team member will contribute to the final product.

**Critical Thinking:** Analyze and organize information. Use problem-solving skills to complete the final product.

## Skills Book

**Extra Skills Practice**

**Speaking and Listening:** Talk about the differences between two pictures.

**Reading and Writing:** Compare and contrast information.
Write a descriptive text.
Categorize words.
Identify letter-sound relationships.
Read clues to identify words.

# Teacher Workshop

## Teaching with Technology

Interactive whiteboards provide teachers and students with a wide range of resources. They can be used for providing word and language presentations, playing music and chants, listening to native speakers reading texts, and doing interactive activities. They help create cohesion and focus in class. Consider what your strong and weak points have been with the course and technology in general, and take note on how you can improve for the coming year.

## Teaching with Games

**Word Tennis**

Divide the class into two teams. Pretend that there is a ball that bounces back and forth between the two teams. Say a category, for example, *activities*. The first student in Team A will say an activity, and then pass the "ball" to Team B. The first student on Team B must also say a word for another activity, and then pass the "ball" to the second student on Team A. Teams get a point each time they say a word.
If a student repeats a word or cannot answer, the opposing team gets a point. Repeat the whole process for different word sets.

## Happy Teacher

Create your own flashcards using cutouts from magazines, your own drawings, or ready-made flashcards. Make them visually attractive and, if possible, laminate them so you can use them over and over. You can choose to have the word on the reverse side, or prepare separate sets of flashcards for words and pictures. Make sure the images can be clearly seen by all students.

Flashcards are a great way to introduce new vocabulary, and they can be posted around the classroom for reference. Use them so students practice saying the words, and then have students say them in a funny voice.

## Happy Class

Encourage your class to remember the skills they have learned throughout the school year. Ask them to share how they keep their work organized and tidy. Ask them to say or write about how punctual they have been, and how persistent and disciplined they have been about learning throughout the year. Praise students for all their efforts throughout the school year.

By Diana Jones

UNIT 8 Lesson 1

1 46 Listen. Then echo.

draw

hop

paint

play the guitar

play the drums

jump rope

speak English

whistle

2 47 Listen and complete. Then number.

2 play the guitar

3 play the drums

3 Page 29 The Language Lodge

64

Lesson 2

1 47 Sing: All Day Long!

All Day Long!

I can jump

All day long!

I can jump rope

And sing this song.

But I can't whistle

All day long.

I can't whistle and sing

this song.

1 jump rope

Grammar Snapshot!

I can play the guitar.

I can't whistle.

2 Match.

1. I can draw.

2. I can't draw.

3 Talk to a friend.

I can't play the drums.

I can speak English.

4 Page 30 The Language Lodge

65

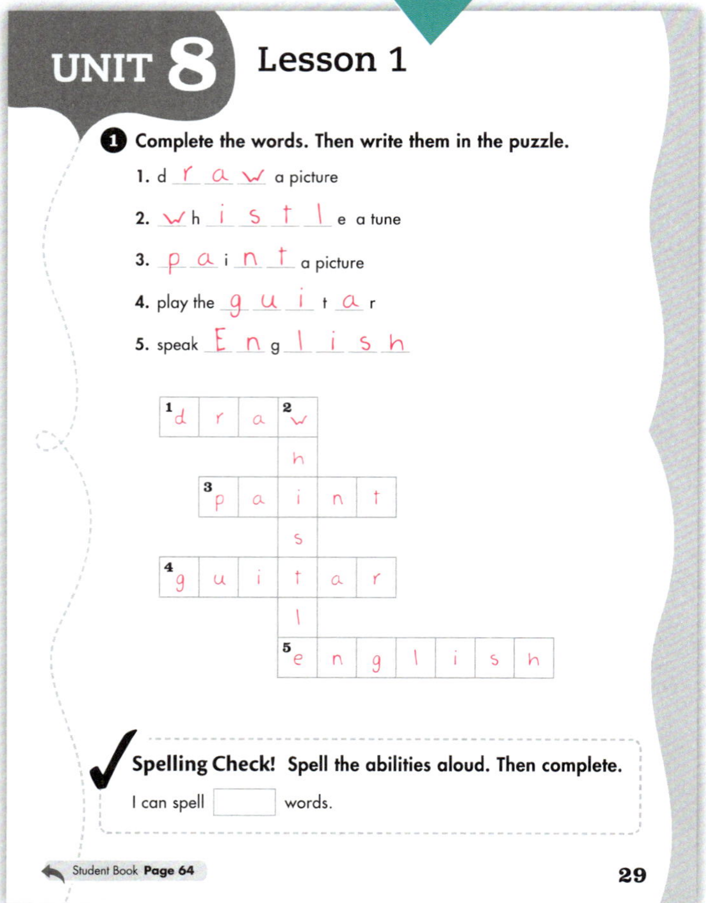
UNIT 8 Lesson 1

1 Complete the words. Then write them in the puzzle.

1. d r a w a picture

2. w h i s t l e a tune

3. p a i n t a picture

4. play the g u i t a r

5. speak E n g l i s h

| | | | | | | | |
|---|---|---|---|---|---|---|---|
| 1 d | r | a | 2 w | | | | |
| | | | h | | | | |
| | 3 p | a | i | n | t | | |
| | | | s | | | | |
| 4 g | u | i | t | a | r | | |
| | | | l | | | | |
| | | | 5 e | n | g | l | i | s | h |

Spelling Check! Spell the abilities aloud. Then complete.

I can spell ______ words.

Student Book Page 64

29

# Lesson 1

This may also be completed for homework.

# Lesson 1 Vocabulary

**Lesson Objective:** Identify activities and abilities.
**New Vocabulary:** draw, hop, paint, play the guitar, play the drums, jump rope, speak English, whistle
**Materials:** Audio **Tracks 46 and 47**, music

## Start the Class

5 min

Have students look at **Pages 64 and 65** and predict what the lesson is about. Write *abilities* on the board. Tell them an example of an unusual ability you or someone well-known has. Elicit some unusual abilities students have and write them on the board.

### 1 46 Listen. Then echo.

10 min

Explain that they are going to listen and point to the different abilities. Play **Track 46** and have students listen and point to the pictures as they hear them mentioned. Point out that *hop* is usually on one leg, while *jump* is on both legs. Hop and jump to demonstrate the meanings.

Play **Track 46** again and have students echo the phrases.

### 2 47 Listen and complete. Then number.

15 min

Have students look at the pictures of the children on **Pages 64 and 65**. Ask *What's he/she doing?* Explain to the class that they are going to listen to a song and point to the corresponding pictures as they listen. Play **Track 47**.

Tell students you are going to play the song again for them to complete the sentences for the first verse of the song on **Page 65**. Pause when an answer is given to give students time to write. Then check answers as a class. Explain that they are going to listen again, and this time they are going to number the check boxes to indicate the order of the song. Play **Track 47** and check answers with the class.

**Try This!**

5 min

Elicit some special abilities students have (play soccer, swim, dance, etc.) and write them on the board, along with some of the abilities in Activity 1. Tell students to choose an ability they can do well and write it on a piece of paper. Play some music. Have students stand up and walk around the classroom, showing one another their pieces of paper. Explain that you will stop the music and they must get together in groups based on their abilities. Have groups say their abilities aloud.

### 3 Page 29 The Language Lodge

10 min

Have students flip to The Language Lodge **Page 29**.

**1 Complete the words. Then write them in the puzzle.**

Have a volunteer read the directions. Explain to students that they will complete the words in the clues, and then complete the puzzle. Have students compare their answers with a partner.

**Spelling Check! Spell the abilities aloud. Then complete.**

Have students close their books. Tell them that they will take turns saying and spelling the abilities with a partner. Then tell students to write the number of words they can spell correctly.

## Finish the Class

5 min

Tell students they are going to listen to the song again, but this time they are going to act out the activities when they hear them. Play **Track 47**.

Use the **Presentation Kit** for interactive activities in this lesson.

Have students use the **Happy Campers app** for additional practice with the new vocabulary.

**The Language Lodge Page 29** may also be completed for homework.

# Lesson 2 Grammar

**Lesson Objective:** Ask and answer questions about abilities.
**New Grammar:** I can play the guitar. I can't whistle.
**Vocabulary Review:** draw, hop, paint, play the guitar, play the drums, jump rope, speak English, whistle
**Materials:** Audio **Track 47**

## Start the Class

5 min

Ask students how many words and phrases they remember from Lesson 1. Allow students two minutes to open their books and see how well they remembered.

### ① 47 Sing: All Day Long!

5 min

Tell students they are going to listen to the song again and read as they listen. Play **Track 47**. Tell the class to sing along and have them wag their fingers when they hear the word *can't*. Play **Track 47** again.

### ② Match.

10 min

Have the class read the Grammar Snapshot! together. Explain to students that we use *can* for affirmative statements and *can't* for negative statements. Mime an activity you cannot do and elicit *I can't*. Then mine an activity you can do and elicit *I can*.

Tell students that they will listen carefully and indicate when they hear *I can* by raising their right hands, and raising their left hands when they hear *I can't*. Say *I can / I can't / I can't / I can* and have students raise their hands.

Tell students to look at the sentences and pictures in the activity and match them. Have them compare their answers with a partner before checking as a class.

### ③ Talk to a friend.

5 min

Have volunteers read the sentences aloud. Tell students that they will talk with a partner about things they can or can't do. Have volunteers share their sentences with the class.

**Try This!** 5 min

Divide the class into several groups and have each group form a circle. The first student says something he or she can do, such as: *I can jump rope*. The second student repeats the first sentence and adds a sentence. Continue until a student makes a mistake, then begin a new chain of words with the next student.

### ④ Page 30 The Language Lodge

10 min

Have students flip to The Language Lodge **Page 30**. Have volunteers read the Grammar Snapshot! aloud.

**1 Check (✓) or cross (✗) the things you can or can't do. Then write sentences.**

Explain to the class that they will look at the abilities and write a check mark for the things they can do and a cross for the things they cannot do. Students then write sentences about their abilities. Have volunteers share sentences with the class.

**2 Complete the sentences. Write what you can and can't do.**

Explain to students that they need to write true sentences about themselves. Have volunteers share their sentences with the class.

## Finish the Class

10 min

Write the following on the board: *spell my name backward, draw a cat, whistle "Happy Birthday," hop five times,* and *say the names of five classmates.* Tell the class that they are going to take turns naming the activities and doing them with a partner. If they make a mistake or can't do it, they say *I can't (spell my name backward)*.

Use the **Presentation Kit** for interactive activities in this lesson.

**The Language Lodge Page 30** may also be completed for homework.

For the next lesson, use **Skills Book Pages 46 and 47** (Picture Talk). Go to Teacher's Edition **Page T 181** for teacher notes.

UNIT 8

**Lesson 1**

1 46 Listen. Then echo.

draw
hop
paint
play the guitar
play the drums
jump rope
speak English
whistle

2 47 Listen and complete. Then number.

play the guitar
play the drums

3 Page 29 The Language Lodge

**Lesson 2**

1 47 Sing: All Day Long!

**All Day Long!**

I can ______
All day long!
I can ______
And sing this song.
But I can't whistle
All day long.
I can't whistle and sing
this song.

jump rope

*Grammar Snapshot!*

I can play the guitar.
I can't whistle.

2 Match.

1. I can draw.
2. I can't draw.

3 Talk to a friend.

I can't play the drums.
I can speak English.

4 Page 30 The Language Lodge

64 65

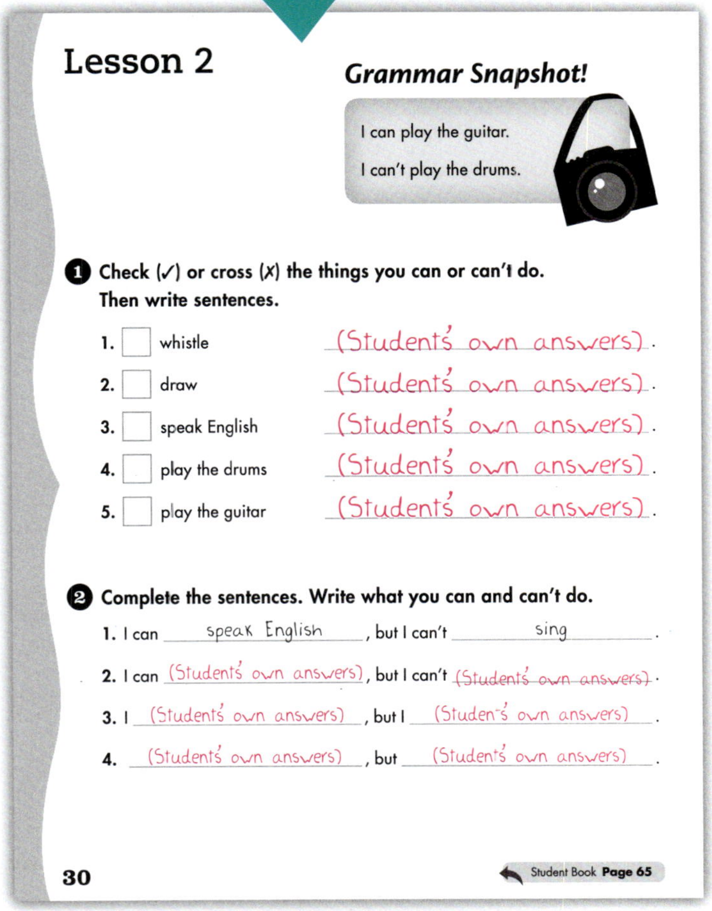

**Lesson 2**

*Grammar Snapshot!*

I can play the guitar.
I can't play the drums.

1 Check (✓) or cross (✗) the things you can or can't do. Then write sentences.

1. ☐ whistle (Students' own answers).
2. ☐ draw (Students' own answers).
3. ☐ speak English (Students' own answers).
4. ☐ play the drums (Students' own answers).
5. ☐ play the guitar (Students' own answers).

2 Complete the sentences. Write what you can and can't do.

1. I can speak English, but I can't sing.
2. I can (Students' own answers), but I can't (Students' own answers).
3. I (Students' own answers), but I (Studen's own answers).
4. (Students' own answers), but (Students' own answers).

30

Student Book Page 65

# Lesson 2

This may also be completed for homework.

# Lesson 3

**Shutterbugs**

1. **Can Lisa ride a skateboard?**
2. 48 **Read and listen.**

3. 49 **Dictation! Listen and write. Then say.**

1. climb trees
2. whistle
3. play the guitar
4. draw
5. paint
6. speak English

4. Page 31 **The Language Lodge**



# Lesson 4

1. 48 **Listen again to Shutterbugs.**

2. ***Grammar Snapshot!*** **Answer for Lisa.**

1. Can you play the guitar? __________.
2. Can you jump rope? __________.
3. Can you ride a skateboard? __________.

3. 50 **Listen and cheer!**

Yeah, yeah! Can you draw? Yes, I can. I can draw.
Hey, hey! Can you paint? No, I can't. I can't paint.

CHEER BOX!

4. Page 32 **The Language Lodge**



# Lesson 3

1 **Unscramble. Then match.**

1. oph hop
2. rwda draw
3. pmuj rpeo jump rope
4. gisn sing
5. inatp paint
6. htiwsle whistle
7. encda dance
8. paesk ghislnE speak English

✓ **Spelling Check! Spell the activities aloud. Then complete.**

I can spell ____ words.

Student Book Page 66



# Lesson 3

This may also be completed for homework.

# Lesson 3 Vocabulary in Context

**Lesson Objective:** Identify characters and their abilities.
**Vocabulary Review:** climb trees, whistle, play the guitar, draw, paint, speak English
**Materials:** Audio **Tracks 47, 48, and 49**

## Start the Class

5 min

Divide the class into three groups and assign each group a verse from "All Day Long!" Tell them they will sing their verse and mime an action for it. Play **Track 47** again and have students sing along while miming the actions.

### 1 Can Lisa ride a skateboard?

5 min

Have a volunteer read the question aloud. Have students point to the appropriate picture and say the answer: *No, she can't.* Remind students that *can* or *can't* are used to talk about abilities.

### 2 48 Read and listen.

10 min

Remind students that they will read the comic strip as they listen. Play **Track 48**. Point to the scenes in the story and ask questions about the activities Lisa can do: *Can Lisa climb trees? Yes. Can Lisa ride a skateboard? No.* Point out that Sam uses the expression *I bet you can't* to say that he thinks Lisa can't ride a skateboard.

**Try This!** 5 min

Divide the class into groups of four. Explain to students that they will each read a part from the comic strip: Lisa, Clare, Tom, or Sam. Have students read their parts aloud. If there is enough time, have them switch roles and reread the story.

### 3 49 Dictation! Listen and write. Then say.

10 min

Have a volunteer read the directions on **Page 66**. Play **Track 49** and pause for students to write the phrases. Play **Track 49** again and then have students check their answers with a partner. Have volunteers write the answers on the board.

Tell students they are going to listen again and will repeat what they hear. Play **Track 49**.

*Audio script* ***Track 49***
*1. climb trees 2. whistle 3. play the guitar 4. draw 5. paint 6. speak English*

### 4 Page 31 The Language Lodge

10 min

Have students flip to The Language Lodge **Page 31**.

**1 Unscramble. Then match.**

Have a volunteer read the directions aloud. Explain to students that they are going to unscramble the words for the abilities and then match each word to the corresponding picture. Review the answers as a class. Have volunteers write the words on the board.

**Spelling Check! Spell the activities aloud. Then complete.**

Have students close their books. Tell them that they will take turns saying and spelling the activities with a partner. Then tell students to write the number of words they can spell correctly.

## Finish the Class

5 min

Write the following words in a list on the board: *play, jump, speak, ride, climb, play, build,* and *fly.* Have students copy the words in their notebooks. Then write the following words in different places around the board: *a skateboard, volleyball, the guitar, a kite, trees, English, a sandcastle,* and *rope.* Explain to students that they will complete the words or phrases using the verbs in the list. Circulate around the class and provide help as needed. Have volunteers share their complete phrases with the class.

Use the **Presentation Kit** for interactive activities in this lesson.

Have students use the **Happy Campers app** for additional practice with the new vocabulary.

**The Language Lodge Page 31** may also be completed for homework.

# Lesson 4 Grammar in Context

**Lesson Objective:** Ask and answer questions about abilities.
**New Grammar:** Can you whistle? Yes, I can.
**Vocabulary Review:** draw, hop, paint, play the guitar, play the drums, jump rope, speak English, whistle
**Materials:** Audio **Tracks 48 and 50**

## Start the Class

5 min

Play Simon Says. Tell students that if you say *Simon says* before an action, they mime the action. If you don't say *Simon says*, they don't mime it. Students who mime the actions at the wrong time sit down. Use a variety of actions they have learned throughout the school year, such as *ride a bike, play basketball, talk on the phone, eat ice cream, eat cake, drink lemonade, dance*, and *play the drums*. Continue playing until there is only one student standing.

### ① 48 Listen again to Shutterbugs.

5 min

Tell the class that they will read and listen again to the comic strip. Play **Track 48**.

### ② *Grammar Snapshot!* Answer for Lisa.

10 min

Tell students to look at the comic strip and find questions beginning with *Can you*. Have students underline the four questions in the comic strip and draw a circle around Lisa's answers.

Explain to the class that they will write Lisa's answers next to the questions. Tell students to work individually, and then have them compare their answers with a partner. Then have volunteers share their answers with the class.

**Try This!** 5 min

Write five of the abilities from Lesson 1 on the board. Explain to students that they will ask questions about those abilities, for example, *Can you (draw)?* Then divide the class into pairs of students sitting next to each other. Have them take turns asking and answering the questions in their pairs.

### ③ 50 Listen and cheer!

10 min

Tell the class they will listen to a cheer and read the words as they listen. Play **Track 50**. Explain to the class that you will play the cheer again and this time they will do the cheer with the track. Play **Track 50** again. Divide the class into two groups. Have one group say the questions and the other group say the answers. Switch roles.

### ④ Page 32 The Language Lodge

10 min

Have students flip to The Language Lodge **Page 32**. Have volunteers read the Grammar Snapshot!

**1 Complete.**
Tell the class that they will complete the questions and the answers. Have students compare their answers with a partner. Check answers as a class.

**2 Answer for you.**
Tell students they will answer questions about themselves. Have volunteers read the questions for other volunteers to answer.

## Finish the Class

5 min

Have students work in groups of three to make a new grammar cheer. Tell them to change the activity words in the grammar cheer for other activities. Remind them to include clapping and finger snapping for rhythm. Have volunteers say their cheers for the class.

Use the **Presentation Kit** for interactive activities in this lesson.

**The Language Lodge Page 32** may also be completed for homework.

For the next lesson, use **Skills Book Pages 48 and 49** (Happy Reader). Go to Teacher's Edition **Page T 182** for teacher notes.

# Lesson 3

## Shutterbugs

1 Can Lisa ride a skateboard?

2 48 Read and listen.

3 49 Dictation! Listen and write. Then say.

1. ______ 2. ______
3. ______ 4. ______
5. ______ 6. ______

4 Page 31 The Language Lodge



# Lesson 4

1 48 Listen again to Shutterbugs.

2 *Grammar Snapshot!* Answer for Lisa.

1. Can you play the guitar? Yes, I can.
2. Can you jump rope? Yes, I can.
3. Can you ride a skateboard? No, I can't.

3 50 Listen and cheer!

Yeah, yeah! Can you draw? Yes, I can. I can draw.
Hey, hey! Can you paint? No, I can't. I can't paint.

CHEER BOX!

4 Page 32 The Language Lodge



# Lesson 4

This may also be completed for homework.

## Lesson 4

### *Grammar Snapshot!*

Can you whistle?
Yes, I can.
No, I can't.

1 Complete.

1. Can you swim? Yes, I can.
2. Can you play golf? No, I can't.
3. Can you jump rope? Yes, I can.
4. Can you play the guitar? No, I can't.

2 Answer for you.

1. Can you play soccer? (Student's own answers).
2. Can you run? (Student's own answers).
3. Can you whistle? (Student's own answers).
4. Can you bake a cake? (Student's own answers).
5. Can you ride a bike? (Student's own answers).
6. Can you swim? (Student's own answers).
7. Can you play baseball? (Student's own answers).



Student Book Page 67

# Lesson 5

**1** **Circle what the family is making.**

**a.** a tree house   **b.** a table

**2** 51 **Read and listen.**

## I Can Help, Too!

It's Saturday. Daniel, Tina, and their dog Bruno are very happy. Mom and Dad are building a tree house.
"I can help, Mom!" Tina says.
"I can help, too, Dad!" Daniel says.

Daniel can help. There are so many things that he can do!
Daniel can climb trees. He can help paint the tree house.
Daniel can also ride a bike. He can go to the store.

Tina wants to help, too. She can't climb trees.
She can't ride a bike to the store.
But she can draw. She can make decorations.
She can make sandwiches for the family.

What can Bruno do?
Look! He can help, too!
He can eat the sandwiches!

# Lesson 5 Fiction Reading

**Lesson Objective:** Read a text to understand the main ideas and details.
**Vocabulary Review:** make decorations, eat sandwiches
**Grammar Review:** She's making decorations. Mom and Dad are building a tree house.
**Materials:** Audio **Track 51**, strips of paper with cut-up sentences

## Start the Class

10 min

Prepare sets of cut-up sentences on strips of paper: *I can / play / the guitar / .; I can't / whistle / .; Can / you / play / the guitar / ?; Yes, / I can / .; No, / I can't /* . Divide students into groups of four and give each group a set of cut-up sentences. Explain that they have four sentences and are going to put the words in each sentence in order. Remind them that they have to put the correct punctuation at the end of each one. Check the answers with the class by asking different groups to read the different sentences aloud.

### 1 Circle what the family is making.

5 min

Tell students to open their books to **Page 68**. Have a volunteer read the title of the story. In pairs, have them name as many things as they can in the first picture. Circulate around the class to monitor students and provide help as needed. Then have them read the directions and circle the correct answer: *a tree house*. Ask students if any of them or their friends have a tree house and what it's like.

### 2 51 Read and listen.

15 min

In pairs, have students look at the remaining pictures and predict what happens in the story. Play **Track 51**. Students listen to the track and follow the words in their books with their fingers as they listen. Students say if their predictions are correct. Ask them to point to and name the characters in the story: *Mom, Dad, Daniel, Tina*, and *Bruno*. Then have students look for words in the text that show what Daniel can do: *climb trees, paint the tree house, ride a bike*, and *go to the store*.

Divide the class into groups and tell students that they are going to read the text again in their group. Explain that they will take turns reading a part of the text aloud. Remind them to read clearly so everyone can understand; the rest of the group will follow the words in their books as they listen. Circulate among the groups to check intonation and rhythm, and provide help as needed.

**Try This!** 10 min

Explain to students that they are going to read a sentence pyramid. Write the following words and phrases on the board, each one on a line below the previous one, in the form of a pyramid: *Daniel / Daniel can / Daniel can ride / Daniel can ride a bike / Daniel can ride a bike to the store.* Read each line aloud, beginning with the top line, and have students repeat until the entire sentence is read out. Divide the class into pairs. Write the following sentence on the board: *Tina can make sandwiches for the family.* Explain that they are going to make their own sentence pyramids and take turns reading them in the same way. Circulate around the classroom, correcting pronunciation and providing help as needed.

## Finish the Class

10 min

Draw a line down the middle of the board and ask students to stand in a straight line in front of it. Write *Yes, I can* to the left of the line and *No, I can't* to the right. Ask *can* questions using actions from the story: *Can you ride a bike? Can you go to the store?* Students stand to the left or the right of the line depending on what their answers are. Play several times. If you want to, add other activities to make the game more challenging.

Use the **Presentation Kit** for interactive activities in this lesson.

# Lesson 6 Reading Comprehension / Writing

**Lesson Objective:** Recall the main idea and details from a text.
**Vocabulary Review:** climb trees, paint the tree house, ride a bike, go to the store, draw, make decorations, make sandwiches
**Grammar Review:** Daniel can climb trees. She can't climb trees.
**Materials:** Audio **Track 51**

## Start the Class

5 min

Write the following words on the board: *hop, play jump, whistle, the, rope,* and *bike*. Explain that there is a hidden phrase and students have to copy the words and color the ones that make the hidden phrase: *jump rope*. Write several other hidden phrases on the board for students to find and color.

### ① 51 Listen again to I Can Help, Too!

5 min

Listen to the story again and remind students to follow the text in their books as they listen. Play **Track 51**. Ask comprehension questions such as *What can Daniel do? What's the dog's name? What can the dog do?*

### ② Read and circle Tina's answers.

10 min

Ask students to point to Tina on **Page 69**. Have volunteers read the four questions aloud. Explain that they will work individually to decide if Tina can do those things or not. Remind them that they can look at the story on **Page 68** to help them. Allow students time to complete the activity, and then have them share their answers with a partner.

Tell students they will listen to the story again to check their answers. Play **Track 51** again and pause when appropriate to give students time to check the activities. Have volunteers read the sentences while the class says Tina's answers: *Yes, I can* or *No, I can't.*

Draw four squares on the board. Label the left column *Daniel* and label the right column *Tina*. Tell students to copy the chart in their notebooks. Explain that they will work with a partner to list the things Daniel and Tina *can* do in the top two squares, and the things they *can't* do in the bottom two squares. Have volunteers write their ideas in the chart on the board and then read them aloud.

**Try This!** 5 min

Have students sit in groups of four and say as much as they can from memory about the story "I Can Help, Too!" Walk around and monitor groups as they work. Allow them to refer back to the book if necessary.

### ③ Say Cheese! Draw your family building a tree house.

10 min

Write the following sentences on the board: *What is Daniel's family doing? They're building a tree house.* Have students describe the tree house Daniel's family is building. Explain to students that they will draw pictures of themselves and their families building a tree house. Circulate around the class to monitor students' drawings and provide help as needed. Ask students questions about their pictures: *What are you doing? Can you ride a bike? Can you make sandwiches?* Have students show their drawings to a partner and say what they can do.

### ④ Writing Time! Write about your picture.

10 min

Explain to the class that they will complete the sentences about the picture they drew in Activity 3. Circulate around the class and provide help as needed. Have them read their sentences to a partner. Have volunteers share their writing with the class.

## Finish the Class

5 min

Divide the class into small groups. Explain that one student mimes an action for the group to guess. The first student to guess correctly repeats the word for the action, then chooses and mimes the next word. Continue until all students have mimed at least one word.

Use the **Presentation Kit** for interactive activities in this lesson.

For the next lesson, use **Skills Book Pages 50 and 51** (Word Work). Go to Teacher's Edition **Page T 183** for teacher notes.

# Lesson 6

## Lesson 6

**1** 51 **Listen again to I Can Help, Too!**

**2 Read and circle Tina's answers.**

**1.** Can you climb trees? Yes, I can. (No, I can't.)

**2.** Can you draw pictures? (Yes, I can.) No, I can't.

**3.** Can you make sandwiches? (Yes, I can.) No, I can't.

**4.** Can you ride a bike? Yes, I can. (No, I can't.)

**3 Say Cheese! Draw your family building a tree house.**

(Students' own answers.)

**4 Writing Time! Write about your picture.**

It's Saturday. (Students' own answers) ______, ______,
and I are very happy. ______ and ______ are building
a tree house. I can ______. I can't ______.

# Lesson 7

Lesson 7

## Team Up!

**1** **Think about four activities you can and can't do. Make a list.**

| I can | I can't |
| --- | --- |
| | |

**2** **Share your ideas.**

Can you play the drums?

No, I can't.

**3** **Team up and make an Abilities Chart.**

We can all whistle.

Leo and Ann can't play tennis.

# Lesson 7 Creative, Collaborative, and Critical Thinking Activity

**Lesson Objective:** Talk about activities students can and can't do.
**Vocabulary Review:** draw, hop, paint, play the guitar, play the drums, jump rope, speak English, whistle
**Grammar Review:** I can play the guitar. I can't whistle. Daniel can climb trees. She can't climb trees.
**Materials:** construction paper; colored pencils, markers, or crayons

## Start the Class

10 min

Distribute sheets of paper. Write different abilities on the board, such as *ride a bike, climb a tree, jump rope, hop, play the drums, play soccer, play the guitar, play tennis, fly a kite, build a sandcastle, swim, whistle*, and *sing*. Have students fold a sheet of paper so it has four squares, cut it, and write an ability on each square. Explain that they are going to walk around and ask one another questions, such as *Can you ride a bike?* If his or her partner has *ride a bike*, the student asking the question collects the square. Make sure they take turns asking and answering. Stop the activity after eight minutes and see who has collected the most abilities.

### 1 Think about four activities you can and can't do. Make a list.

5 min

Tell students to look at **Page 70** and have a volunteer read the directions aloud. Explain that they are going to work individually to write a list of things they can and can't do. Circulate around the classroom and provide help as needed.

**Try This!**

5 min

Students stand in a circle. Explain that they are going to spell words, letter by letter, and then say the word. Give them a word from Unit 8 to spell; the first student says the first letter, the next student says the second letter, and so on. After the last letter, the next student says the word again. Then give them another word and repeat the procedure again.

### 2 Share your ideas.

5 min

Ask two volunteers to read the sample dialogue on the page.

Tell students that they are going to work in pairs and share the activities they can and can't do that they wrote down in Activity 1. Circulate around the classroom, correct pronunciation, and provide help as needed.

### 3 Team up and make an Abilities Chart.

20 min

Put two pairs together. Explain that they will make an illustrated Abilities Chart showing who can and who can't do different activities. Ask groups to make one *can* chart with four activities, and one *can't* chart with four activities.

Have teams share their charts with the class. Be sure each member of the team speaks at least once. Display the charts in the classroom.

## Finish the Class

5 min

Have students write down their three favorite abilities. Have them stand up and form two teams. Have each team form a circle, one on the inside, and one on the outside of the other. Play some music while they walk around in opposite directions. Stop the music. Have students turn and face a person in the opposite circle and tell them to share their favorite abilities. Repeat several times so they tell different classmates.

Use the **Presentation Kit** for interactive activities in this lesson.

Use the **Assessment Pack** to carry out the Unit 8 Teamwork Assessment during this lesson.

# Lesson 8 Review

**Lesson Objective:** Review vocabulary and grammar from Unit 8.
**Vocabulary Review:** draw, hop, paint, play the guitar, play the drums, jump rope, speak English, whistle, climb trees, ride a skateboard
**Grammar Review:** I can play the guitar. I can't whistle. Can you whistle? Yes, I can.
**Materials:** 8–12 pairs of cards with matching pictures and ability vocabulary words from this unit

## Start the Class

10 min

Have students stand in a circle. Explain that you are going to call out a topic, for example, *abilities*, and students go around the circle naming abilities. After students have said five or six phrases, change the topic and continue. Change the topic often to review different vocabulary sets students have learned throughout the year. As students become comfortable with the game, you may choose to have a volunteer call the category.

### ① Spelling! Unscramble.

5 min

Point to the scrambled words and explain to students that they are going to unscramble them. Circulate around the class to monitor students and provide help as needed. Tell students to compare their answers with a partner. Review the answers by having volunteers write the words on the board.

**Try This!**

5 min

Explain to the class that they are going to stand up and do a *This is the way we …* demonstration. You will call out an ability, for example, *hop*. They will respond *This is the way we hop* while they all mime the activity. Make sure all students are miming the activity at the same time, even though they may be miming it in different ways. Repeat with different activities from this unit. You may also choose to have volunteers lead a round.

### ② Find and circle the activities.

5 min

Have a volunteer read the directions aloud. Explain to students that they will first identify the abilities in the pictures and then find the words in the word search. Circulate among the class and provide help as needed. Have students say the words they circled.

### ③ Word Play! Find and circle the words from Unit 8 on Page 72.

15 min

Have students turn to **Page 72** and tell them to find and circle the ability vocabulary words from Unit 8. Then have students check the words they found with a partner.

## Finish the Class

10 min

Make a set of 8 to 12 cards with matching pictures and words from this unit. Randomly write a number on the back of each and put them up on the board so the number side faces students. Divide the class into two teams and have them take turns choosing two numbers. Turn over the cards; if they are a pair, students have to say the activity aloud so they can claim both cards. If they guess incorrectly, the next team plays. Continue in this manner until all the pairs of cards have been found. The team with the most cards wins.

Use the **Presentation Kit** for interactive activities in this lesson.

For the next lesson, use Unit 8 Language Assessment from the **Assessment Pack** or create your own test using the **Test Generator** on the **Teacher's Resource Center**.

# Lesson 8

## Lesson 8

## Round Up!

**1 Spelling! Unscramble.**

1. hiltwse w h i s t l e
2. iptna p a i n t
3. skape Eihgnls s p e a k E n g l i s h
4. ypal het rmdsu p l a y t h e d r u m s

**2 Find and circle the activities.**

| | | | | | | | | | | | |
|---|---|---|---|---|---|---|---|---|---|---|---|
| S | A | K | H | O | P | A | E | I | M | W | O |
| W | P | B | V | Y | U | F | B | A | T | H | W |
| I | Y | A | R | L | C | S | I | N | G | I | H |
| M | D | T | A | T | A | E | Y | Q | M | S | S |
| R | I | D | E | A | B | I | K | E | D | T | Z |
| A | V | U | F | H | Z | X | G | N | B | L | D |
| Z | L | L | P | A | I | N | T | G | C | E | A |
| W | B | V | A | I | J | P | I | M | H | U | N |
| Q | Y | X | I | H | B | R | G | W | I | R | C |
| P | L | A | Y | G | U | I | T | A | R | X | E |

**3 Word Play! Find and circle the words from Unit 8 on Page 72.**

# Unit 1

## Skills Book Picture Talk

**Lesson Objective:** Ask and answer questions about a picture.
**Materials:** Audio **Track 05**

### Start the Class

Organize students into teams and have the teams form circles. Give students vocabulary words from Unit 1 to spell. The first student in each circle says the first letter, the second student says the second letter, and so on until the complete words are spelled out.

### ① Look at the picture. Find and match. Then write.

Have students find the people on **Page 4** in the picture on **Page 5**. Tell students to draw a line to match each person's picture to his or her name. Then have students write how old each person is. Have volunteers write the correct answers on the board.

### ② Ask and answer.

Have students read the example dialogue on **Page 5**. Then have students work in pairs to take turns asking and answering questions about the people in the picture. For example, the first student asks *How old is James Smith?* The second student responds *He's eight.*

### Finish the Class

Divide students into three groups and explain that they will sing the song "Young and Old!" again. Each group will sing one verse. Play **Track 05** and sing along. Then have the groups switch the verses they sing so that each group sings each verse once.

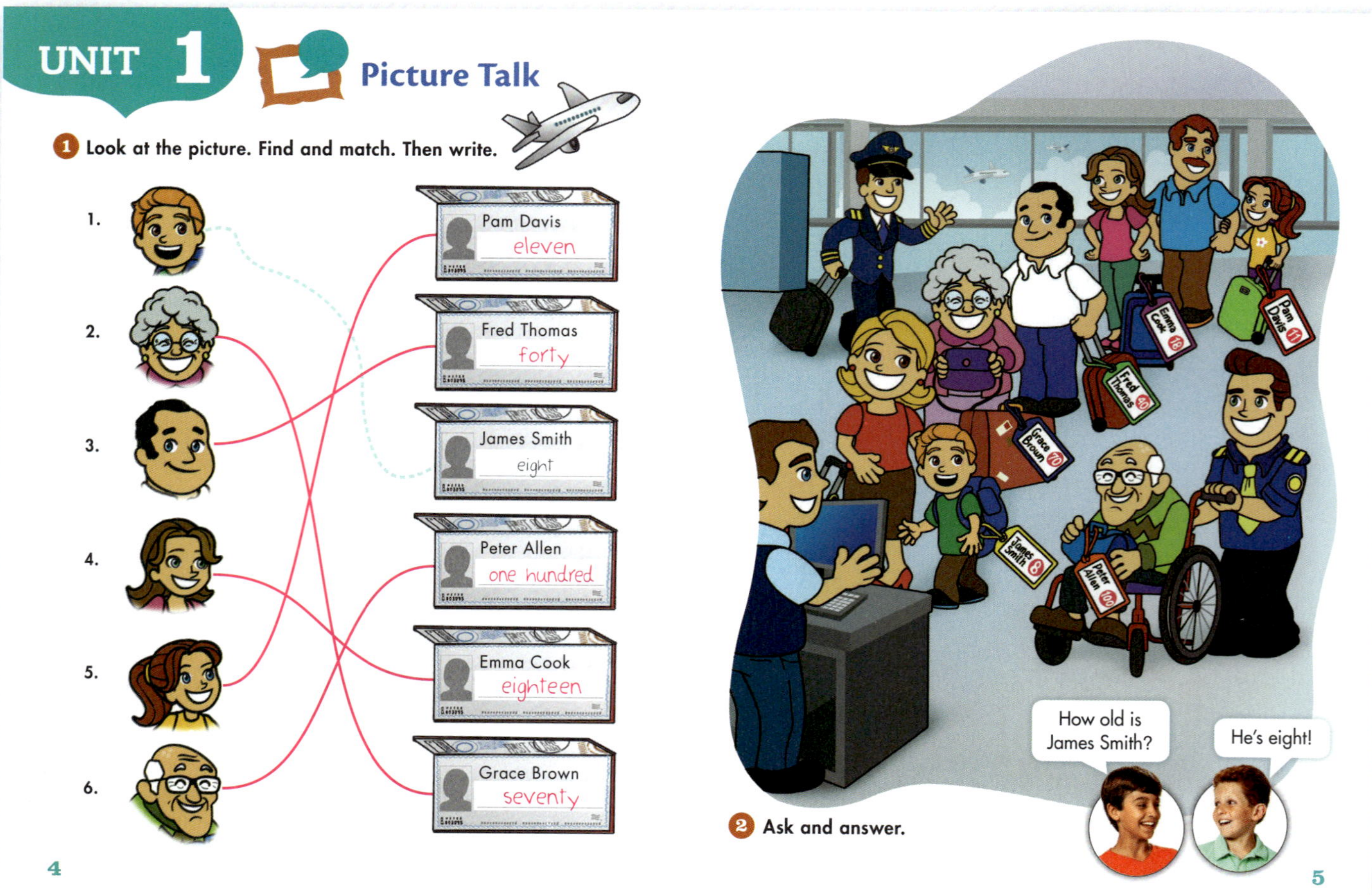

# Skills Book Happy Reader

**Lesson Objectives:** Identify characters in a fiction text.
Summarize the story.
**Materials:** Audio **Track 52**

## Start the Class
5 min

Point to the different family members on **Pages 6 and 7**. Have students guess which members of the family the characters might be.

### 1 52 Read and listen.
20 min

Have students look at the illustrations on **Pages 6 and 7** and have a volunteer read the title of the story. Play **Track 52**. Elicit from students what is unique about Anna's family: the family members have very similar names. Allow students to answer in L1.

### 2 Write the names.
10 min

Have a volunteer read the directions. Tell students that they will write the correct name under each picture. Have volunteers write their answers on the board.

### Page 52 Happy Writer
10 min

Tell students to complete the blanks with the family member words from the story. Do the first two answers as a class. When students have completed the activity, read the paragraph aloud and have the class chorally say their answers.

## Finish the Class
5 min

Have students line up in alphabetical order by first name. Remind them that if several students have a name beginning with the same letter, they must use the second, or even third, letters of their names. When students have lined up, have them call out their names in order.

**Page 52** sister; aunt; grandma; dad; uncle; grandpa; cousins

### Happy Reader

1 52 **Read and listen.**

## The Family Picnic

1
**Anna:** Hi, Daisy! Today is my family picnic!
**Mom:** Hello, girls. The food is ready!
**Anna:** This is my mom. Her name is Ann. And this is my sister, Annabel.
**Daisy:** Wow! They look just like you!

2
**Anna:** That's my Aunt Annie and my grandma, Anita. She likes dancing!
**Daisy:** How old is she?
**Anna:** She's eighty-eight!

3
**Dad:** Lunch is ready!
**Daisy:** Who's that?
**Anna:** He's my dad. His name is James. That's my Uncle Jimmy and my grandpa, Jim.

**Daisy:** Who are they?
**Anna:** They're my three cousins. They're Pat, Rick, and Patrick. They're thirteen, fourteen, and fifteen years old. Come on! Let's eat!
**Daisy:** Wait! Your names! You're Anna, and there is Ann, Annabel, Annie, and Anita! Then there's James, Jimmy, and Jim! And your cousins are Pat, Rick, and Patrick!
**Anna:** That's right!

**2 Write the names.**

1.  Annabel
2.  Ann
3.  Annie
4.  Anita

Happy Writer Page 52

# Skills Book Word Work

**Lesson Objectives:** Identify and produce word endings. Recognize spelling patterns. Categorize words. Read clues to identify words.

## Start the Class

10 min

Write numbers on the board, such *16*, *42*, or *85*. Point to the numbers and have the class say them aloud.

### ① Complete.

5 min

Have students look at the numbers at the top of the activity and say them aloud. Tell students to complete the words below with the correct endings: *-ty* or *-teen*. Have volunteers write their answers on the board.

### ② Unscramble. Then check (✓).

10 min

Elicit the numbers on the birthday cards in Item 1. Tell the class to unscramble the number word and check the correct card. Have students complete the activity and then write the unscrambled words on the board.

### ③ Color the word that's different. Then match.

7 min

Explain that one word in each pie chart is different from the other two words. Have students read the sentences on the right. Tell students to identify each word that's different and match it to the correct reason.

### ④ Answer Ricky's Riddle!

8 min

Write seven lines on the board. Have a volunteer read the first sentence and write the first letter on the board. Then have volunteers read the clues and complete the word on the board.

## Finish the Class

10 min

Have students write riddles with a partner about a unit word. Have pairs exchange their riddles to solve.

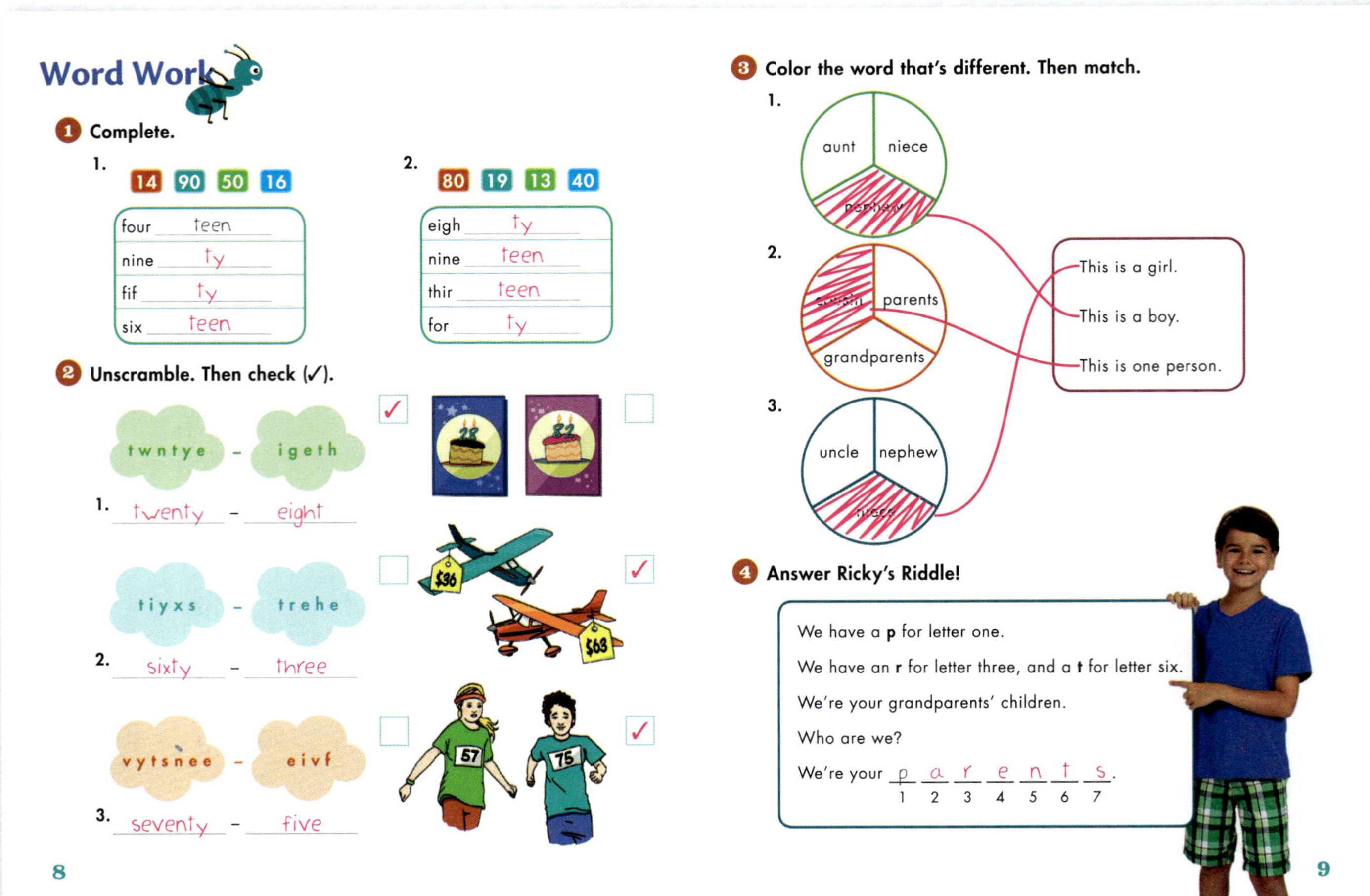

Word Work

1 Complete.

1. 14 90 50 16

four teen
nine ty
fif ty
six teen

2. 80 19 13 40

eigh ty
nine teen
thir teen
for ty

2 Unscramble. Then check (✓).

twntye - igeth
1. twenty - eight

tiyxs - trehe
2. sixty - three

vytsnee - eivf
3. seventy - five

3 Color the word that's different. Then match.

1. aunt, niece, nephew
2. cousin, parents, grandparents
3. uncle, nephew, niece

This is a girl.
This is a boy.
This is one person.

4 Answer Ricky's Riddle!

We have a **p** for letter one.
We have an **r** for letter three, and a **t** for letter six.
We're your grandparents' children.
Who are we?
We're your p a r e n t s.

8 9

Skills Book

## Picture Talk

**Lesson Objective:** Ask and answer questions about a picture.

# Unit 2

## Start the Class

10 min

Have students play Find Someone Who Has the Same Birthday Month. Students walk around the room and ask one another *When's your birthday?* When students find someone with the same birthday month, they sit down together.

### 1 Look at the picture. Unscramble. Then find and complete.

20 min

Have students look at the example for Item 1. Then for each item number, have students unscramble the month, look at the calendar on **Page 11**, and write the name of the person with a birthday in that month. Tell students to complete the activity with a partner, and review the answers as a class.

### 2 Ask and answer.

10 min

Tell each student to work with a partner. Student A chooses a child from **Page 10**, and Student B asks *When's your birthday?* to guess the child. Then have them switch roles. Walk around the classroom and provide help as needed.

## Finish the Class

10 min

Have students study the calendar on **Page 11** for two minutes and then close their books. Ask students *When's Nick's birthday?* Students respond from memory: *It's in October*. Repeat with the other birthdays on the calendar. If time allows, have different students lead the activity.

UNIT 2 Picture Talk

1 Look at the picture. Unscramble. Then find and complete.

1. aaryJnu — My birthday's in January. My name is John.
2. bctOero — My birthday's in October. My name is Nick.
3. ayM — My birthday's in May. My name is Monica.
4. Fbrueyra — My birthday's in February. My name is Angela.
5. tugAsu — My birthday's in August. My name is Mike.
6. merbNove — My birthday's in November. My name is Julie.



2 Ask and answer.

10

11

# Skills Book Happy Reader

**Lesson Objectives:** Recall details in a fiction text. Give opinions.
**Materials:** Audio **Track 53**

## Start the Class (10 min)

Write ten key words from this unit on the board with a few letters missing in each word. Have students complete the words in their notebooks.

### 1 53 Read and listen. (15 min)

Have students look at the illustrations on **Pages 12 and 13**. Explain that Field Day is a day when there are no classes, and there are games, competitions, and food. Tell the class they will read the story as they listen. Play **Track 53**.

Have students explain what happened to Mike. They may answer in L1.

### 2 Answer the question. (5 min)

Tell students that they will look for the answer in the story. Have students work individually, and then play **Track 53** again. Pause the track for students to check their answers.

### Page 52 Happy Writer (10 min)

Ask students what they liked about the story. Then have them complete the sentence about their favorite parts of the story. Have students draw the corresponding scenes and then share their work with a partner.

## Finish the Class (10 min)

Divide the class into groups of four. Explain that each group is going to design a cheer for the sack race that includes gestures and words. Walk around the classroom and provide help as needed. Then have each group take turns acting out their cheer.

Page 52 (Students' own answers)

## Happy Reader

1 53 Read and listen.

# Field Day

1
Today is April 18th. It's Field Day! It's Mike's favorite day at school. He doesn't have math, science, English, or geography today!

There are a lot of great games on Field Day. Mike is in the sack race. Mike, Sarah, and Ben stand up in the sacks. "Go!" Miss May shouts. They hop across the field.

2
Oh, no! Mike is on the ground!

3
Wait! He's up again! He can't see his friends. "I'm first! Wow!" Mike thinks. He hops to the white line in the sack. He's very fast!

4
Mike's feet touch the white line.
"Hooray! I'm the winner!" Mike says.
"No, Mike! Ben is first. Look, this is the start line!" Miss May says.
"Oh, no!" Mike says.

Ben is first in the race. Sarah is second, and Mike is third. Good job, everybody!

2 Answer the question.

When's Field Day?

It's on April 18th.

Happy Writer Page 52

# Skills Book Word Work

**Lesson Objectives:** Identify multi-syllable words.
Identify abbreviations for ordinal numbers.
Read clues to identify words.

## Start the Class

10 min

Divide the class into two lines. Explain that the first student from the first line will say *The (ninth) month is …* , and the first student from the second line will complete the sentence with the month. Then they will each go to the back of the line. Switch roles when each student has been at the front of the line.

### ① Match.

10 min

Explain that each word is divided into three syllables and students will match the syllables to complete the words. Do Item 1 as a class.

### ② Answer Ricky's Riddle!

10 min

Write eight lines on the board. Have a volunteer read the first sentence and write the fourth letter on the board. Then have volunteers read the clues and complete the word on the board.

### ③ Complete.

10 min

Have students look at the numbers at the top of the activity and say them aloud. Tell students to complete the words below. Have volunteers say their answers.

### ④ Read the clues. Then choose and write.

Have a volunteer read the clue for Item 1 and elicit *June*. Then have students complete the activity in pairs.

## Finish the Class

10 min

Have students form pairs to write riddles about a word on **Page 15**. Have pairs exchange their riddles and solve them.

## Word Work

**1 Match.**

| | | | |
|---|---|---|---|
| 1. | Sep | cem | ber |
| 2. | Oc | to | ber |
| 3. | No | tem | ber |
| 4. | De | vem | ber |

**2 Answer Ricky's Riddle!**

My fourth letter is in **ten** and in **red**.
My sixth letter is in **bat** but not in **hat**.
My last letter is in **art** but not in **at**.
I'm next to December.
What am I?
I'm N o v e m b e r.
1 2 3 4 5 6 7 8



**3 Complete.**

1. 1st 2nd 3rd
fir st
seco nd
thi rd

2. 4th 5th 6th
four th
fif th
six th

**4 Read the clues. Then choose and write.**

1. 

It's the sixth month.
June

2. 

It has 31 days.
August

3. 

It's the third month.
March

4. 

It's before May.
April

**Lesson Objective:** Make statements about a picture and respond.

## Start the Class

10 min

Tell students that they will do a time sequence. Explain that you will say a time and the next person will say the hour that follows. Say *It's noon*. The next student says *It's one o'clock*. The next student continues *It's two o'clock*. When students get to midnight, they will start again.

## ① Look at the pictures. Find and check (✓).

20 min

Tell students to look at the clocks in the pictures on **Page 17** and work in pairs to ask and answer *What time is it?* Have a volunteer read the directions on **Page 16**. Explain to the class that they will look for the matching clocks on **Page 17** and check the correct answers on **Page 16**. Have volunteers write the correct answers on the board.

## ② Say and answer.

10 min

Explain to students that they will work in pairs to take turns describing and identifying the pictures. For example, Student A says *It's 11:30 at night*, and Student B says *Picture F*. Walk around the classroom and provide help as needed.

## Finish the Class

10 min

Play What Time Is It, Mr. Fox? Have students stand in a circle with a volunteer in the middle. Explain that this person is Mr. Fox and the class has to ask *What time is it?* Mr. Fox will say a time and the students in the circle will take steps to the right according to the time. Demonstrate by saying *It's nine o'clock*, and have students in the circle take nine steps to the right. Have several volunteers take turns standing in the center.

UNIT 3 Picture Talk

**1** Look at the pictures. Find and check (✓).

1. It's — in the morning. ☐ / in the evening. ✓
2. It's — in the afternoon. ✓ / in the morning. ☐
3. It's — It's early. ✓ / It's late. ☐
4. It's — in the morning. ✓ / at night. ☐
5. It's — at night. ✓ / in the morning. ☐
6. It's — It's early. ☐ / It's late. ✓

16

**2** Say and answer.

17

# Skills Book Happy Reader

**Lesson Objectives:** Identify the sequence of events in a fiction text. Summarize the story.
**Materials:** Audio **Track 54**

## Start the Class

10 min

Ask several students *What time do you go to bed?* Then have students line up in chronological order according to the time they go to bed. Ask *Is it sunny when you go to bed?*

### ① 54 Read and listen.

15 min

Have students read the title and look at the illustrations on **Pages 18 and 19**. Play **Track 54**. Ask *Can you see the sun or the moon when they go to bed?* Explain that in many parts of Alaska it is light during most of the night during summer.

### ② Number the pictures in order.

10 min

Have students work individually to number the pictures from the story in order. Then play **Track 54** again, pausing for students to check their answers.

### Page 53 Happy Writer

10 min

Have students identify Benny and Sammy's relationship. Elicit *cousins* and have students complete the first blank. Then have students complete the paragraph. Have volunteers read the completed sentences aloud.

## Finish the Class

5 min

Write a scrambled sentence from the story on the board, such as *movie / they / go / the / afternoon / to / the / In / theater /* . with nine blanks below it. Have a volunteer choose a word and write it on the blank where it belongs in the sentence. Continue until the sentence is written correctly.

Page 53 Alaska; 7 o'clock; 12:00; go to bed

## Happy Reader

**① 54 Read and listen.**

## Summer in Alaska

1
It's summer. Benny is in Alaska with his cousin Sammy.
It's cold in the summer here, but Benny likes Alaska very much.

"What time do you get up?" Benny asks.
"I get up at 7 o'clock," Sammy says.
"Me, too!"

Benny and Sammy eat breakfast.
"Do you have school today?" Benny asks.
"No! It's summer. I play at home every day," Sammy says.
"Me, too!"

2
Benny and Sammy go outside to play soccer.
"What time do you eat lunch?" Benny asks.
"At 12:00," Sammy says.
"Me, too!"

3
Benny and Sammy eat lunch.
"I like hamburgers and French fries," Sammy says.
"Me, too!"

4
In the afternoon they go to the movie theater. Then they eat dinner in the evening.

It's 10:30 at night. Benny and Sammy go to bed.
"Do you have night in Alaska?" Benny asks.
"Yes. But it's summer in Alaska. It's sunny late at night!"

**② Number the pictures in order.**

2 3 1 4

Happy Writer Page 53

18 19

# Skills Book Word Work

**Lesson Objectives:** Identify correct prepositions for time phrases. Categorize words. Read clues to identify words.

## Start the Class

10 min

Line the class up in pairs. Say a word from the unit for each pair. The students in each pair take turns writing the letters for the word on the board.

### ① Write. Then number the pictures in order.

10 min

Have students look at the pictures and say the times of day using *a.m.* and *p.m.* as guides. Tell students to write the phrases and number the pictures in order. Have volunteers share their answers with the class.

### ② Color the word that's different. Then match.

10 min

Explain that one word in each pie chart is different from the other two words. Have students read the sentences below. Then tell students to identify each word that's different and match it to the correct reason.

### ③ Answer Ricky's Riddle!

10 min

Write nine lines on the board. Have a volunteer read the first sentence and write the first letter on the board. Then have volunteers read the clues and complete the word on the board.

## Finish the Class

10 min

Have students write riddles about a word on **Page 21** with a partner. Have pairs exchange their riddles and solve them.

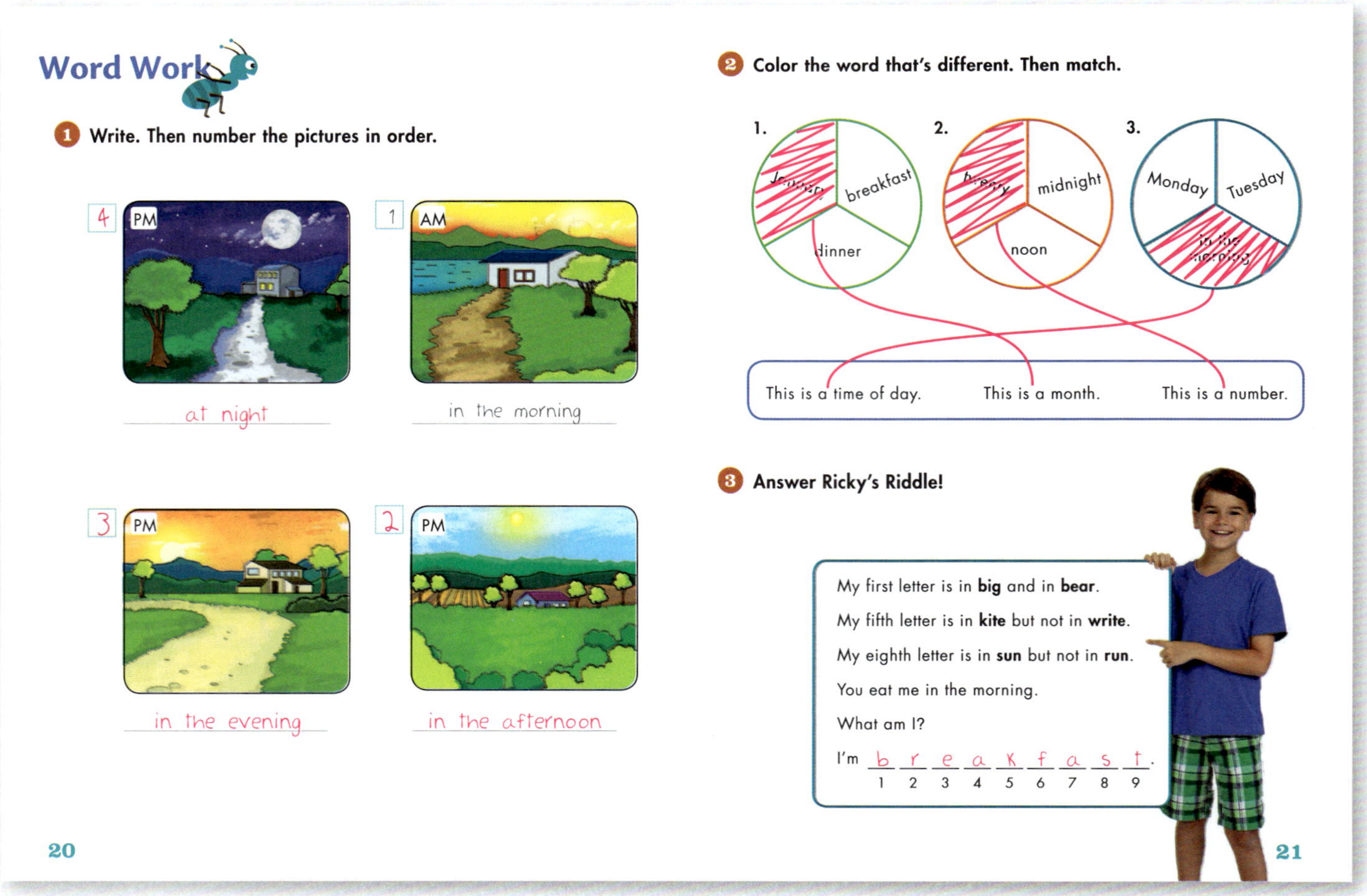

**Lesson Objective:** Talk about the differences between two pictures.

## Start the Class

10 min

Divide the class into two teams and have each team line up in pairs (so there are four lines of students). Say a word from the unit, and tell the first pair in each team to go to the board and take turns writing the word. The first student writes the first letter, the second student writes the second letter, the first student writes the third letter, and so on. The first pair to correctly spell the word wins a point for the team.

### ① Look at the pictures. Find and write.

15 min

Explain that students will find the differences between what the children are playing in Picture A and Picture B on **Page 23**. Refer students to the examples. Have volunteers share their answers with the class.

### ② Say what's different.

15 min

Tell students they will work with a partner and take turns talking about the pictures. Explain that one student will talk about what the children are doing in Picture A and the other will talk about those same children in Picture B. Walk around the classroom and provide help as needed. Have volunteers share their dialogues with the class.

## Finish the Class

10 min

Have students stand up. Call out different sports and then have students repeat the sports aloud and mime them in place. If time allows, have different students lead the activity.

UNIT 4 Picture Talk

❶ Look at the pictures. Find and write.

Main Street Park

| Picture A | Picture B |
|---|---|
| 1. soccer | golf |
| 2. volleyball | tennis |
| 3. basketball | ping pong |
| 4. football | baseball |

❷ Say what's different.

22 23

**Lesson Objectives:** Recall details in a nonfiction text. Personalize the text.
**Materials:** Audio **Track 55**

## Start the Class

5 min

Do a dictation activity with the second set of vocabulary from Unit 4: *listen to music*, *watch TV*, *do homework*, *talk on the phone*, *work on the computer*, and *take pictures*. Then check answers as a class.

## 1 55 Read and listen.

15 min

Have students look at the photos on **Pages 24 and 25**. Ask *What's the weather like?* Elicit *It's rainy*. Have a volunteer read the title of the text. Remind students to read along as they listen. Play **Track 55**.

## 2 Complete.

15 min

Tell students that they will write what each person does on the rainy day. Have students look at the example. Tell students to complete the chart individually. Then play **Track 55** for students to confirm their answers. Check answers as a class.

## Page 53 Happy Writer

10 min

Have students write what they do on rainy days at the top of the idea web. Then have students write their family members' names and what they do on rainy days. Tell students to share their ideas with a partner. Then have volunteers share their ideas with the class.

## Finish the Class

5 min

Have students draw what they do on rainy days and then share their drawings with a partner.

Page 53 (Students' own answers)

Happy Reader

1 55 Read and listen.

### Rainy Days

1
My name is Lily. It's a rainy day, and I'm at home with my family. There are many things to do inside on rainy days.

I'm listening to music. I'm not watching TV. I don't have a TV in my bedroom. My brother and sister are watching TV in the living room.

I really like soccer. When it's raining, I play soccer on the computer. I do my homework on the computer, too, but not today. It's Saturday!

Sometimes I take pictures of my family. Look at Dad! He's reading a book. My mom is working on the computer.

2
Hey! It isn't raining now. They're playing outside. I want to play, too! Rainy days are fun!

2 Complete.

| Family Member | Activity |
|---|---|
| Lily | listening to music |
| Dad | reading a book |
| brother and sister | watching TV |
| Mom | working on the computer |

Happy Writer Page 53

24 25

# Skills Book Word Work

**Lesson Objectives:** Read clues to identify words. Identify multi-syllable words.
**Materials:** strips of paper

## Start the Class

10 min

Write parts of vocabulary phrases on strips of paper. Give one to each student. Tell students to walk around the class to find the other parts of the phrases. Have each group say their phrase at the end.

### ① Read the clues. Then choose and write.

10 min

Have a volunteer read the clue for Item 1. Elicit *golf* from the class. Have students complete the activity in pairs. Check answers as a class.

### ② Match.

10 min

Tell students to match the syllables to complete the words. Do Item 1 as a class. Then have volunteers write the words on the board for the class to confirm their answers.

### ③ Answer Ricky's Riddle!

10 min

Write six lines on the board. Have a volunteer read the first sentence and write the first letter on the board. Then have volunteers read the clues and complete the word on the board.

## Finish the Class

10 min

Tell students that they will do what you do, but only if the sentence you say matches your actions. For example, say *We're playing golf,* but mime playing soccer. Explain that students should not repeat the action. Repeat with different sentences and actions. When students are comfortable with the game, have volunteers lead it.

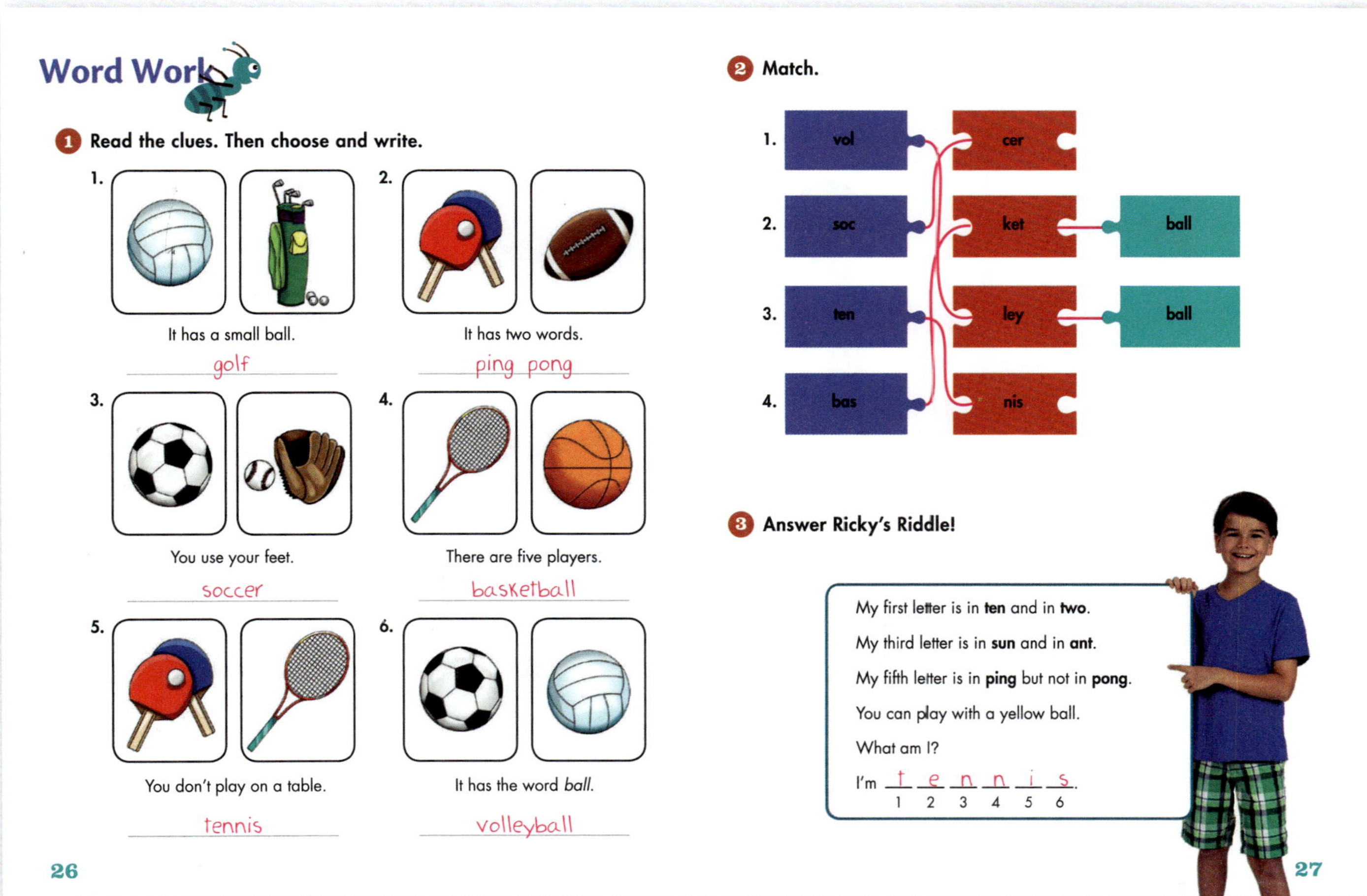
Word Work

1 Read the clues. Then choose and write.

1. It has a small ball. golf
2. It has two words. ping pong
3. You use your feet. soccer
4. There are five players. basketball
5. You don't play on a table. tennis
6. It has the word *ball*. volleyball

2 Match.

1. vol — cer
2. soc — ket — ball
3. ten — ley — ball
4. bas — nis

3 Answer Ricky's Riddle!

My first letter is in **ten** and in **two**.
My third letter is in **sun** and in **ant**.
My fifth letter is in **ping** but not in **pong**.
You can play with a yellow ball.
What am I?
I'm t e n n i s.
1 2 3 4 5 6

26 27

# Unit 5 Skills Book Picture Talk

**Lesson Objective:** Ask and answer questions about a picture.

## Start the Class

10 min

Draw a line down the center of the board. Label the left side *Correct* and the right side *Incorrect*. Say *She's taking a walk*. Since the sentence is correct, students will point to the *Correct* side of the board. Say *She are taking a walk*. Since the sentence is incorrect, they will point to the *Incorrect* side of the board. Repeat with other sentences.

### ① Look at the picture. Find and match.

15 min

Have a volunteer read the directions on **Page 28**. Tell the class that these are images from **Page 29**. Explain that they will match the pictures from the first column to the actions in the second column, and then to the children in the third column. Have students compare their answers with a partner.

### ② Ask and answer. Then find and point.

15 min

Have students work in pairs. Tell them to take turns pretending to be a child on **Page 29**. The first student will mime an action and the second will point to the correct child in the picture. Have volunteers read the speech bubbles. Explain to the class that they will ask and answer questions about the actions as they mime them.

## Finish the Class

10 min

Have students stand up to play Spelling Aerobics. Explain that you will say a word and they will spell out the word by raising their hands over their heads for letters that extend up (*b, d, f, h, k, l, t*), putting their hands on their hips for middle letters (*a, c, e, i, m, n, o, r, s, u, v, w, x, z*), and stretching their hands down for letters that fall below the lines when written (*g, j, p, q, y*).

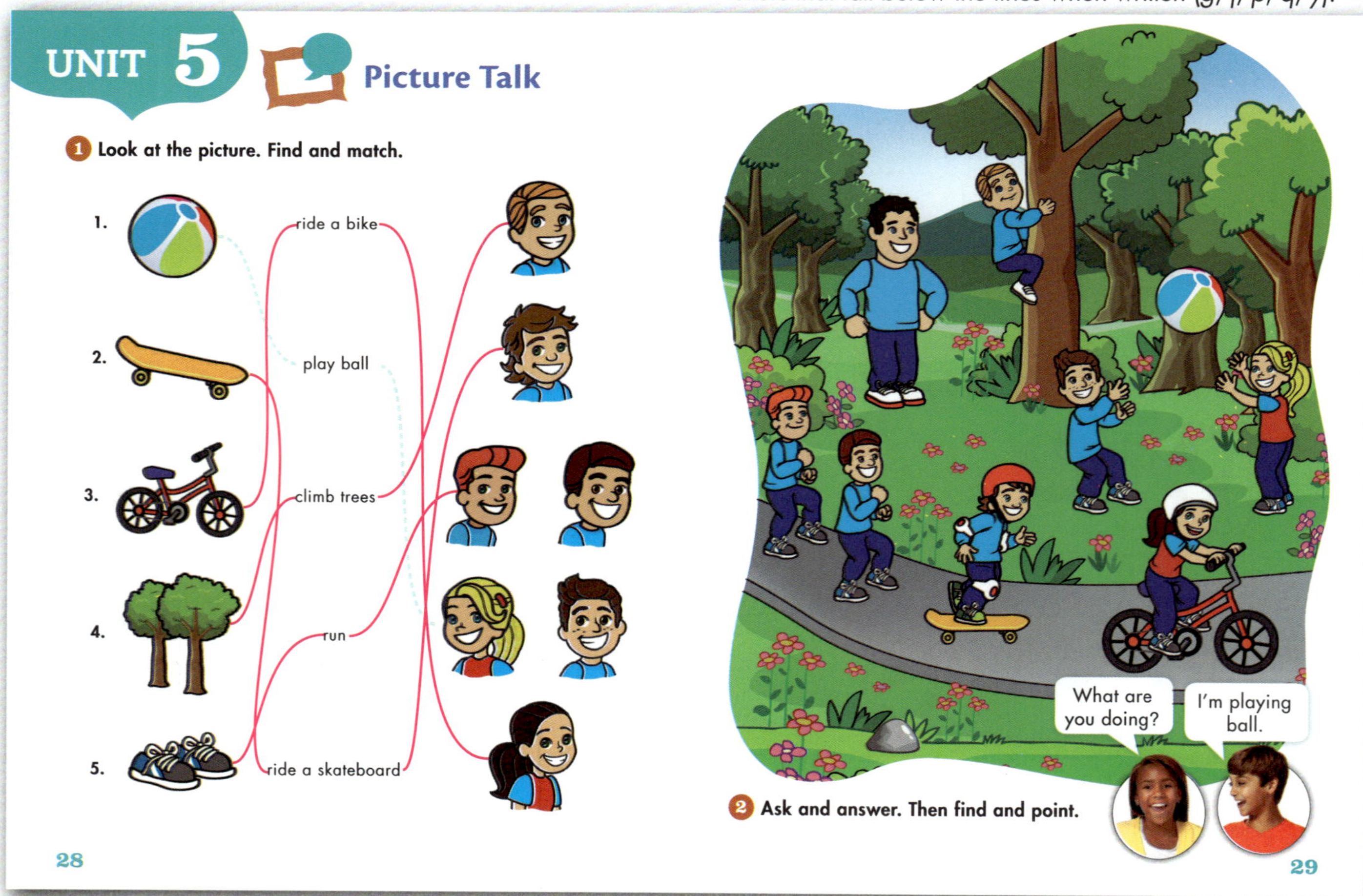
UNIT 5 Picture Talk

1 Look at the picture. Find and match.

1.
2.
3.
4.
5.

ride a bike
play ball
climb trees
run
ride a skateboard



2 Ask and answer. Then find and point.

28

29

# Skills Book Happy Reader

**Lesson Objectives:** Recall details in a nonfiction text. Personalize the text.
**Materials:** Audio **Track 56**

## Start the Class

5 min

Organize the class into two lines. Write some letters on the board. Explain that the student at the front of each line will write a word beginning with one of the letters on the board. Then the next students in each line will write words beginning with other letters on the board, and so on.

## 1 56 Read and listen.

20 min

Have students look at the photos on **Pages 30 and 31** and identify them. Play **Track 56**.

## 2 Check (✓) the things they do for Mother's Day.

10 min

Tell students to check all the activities in the chart that the family does for Mother's Day. Have students compare their answers with a partner.

## Page 54 Happy Writer

10 min

Ask students when they celebrate Mother's Day and what they do for their own mothers on Mother's Day. Tell students to write sentences about what they do on Mother's Day. Have volunteers share their sentences with the class.

## Finish the Class

5 min

Write a scrambled sentence from the text on the board. Below it, write a blank for each word. Have volunteers write the words in the correct order.

Page 54 (Students' own answers)

### Happy Reader

1 56 Read and listen.

## Mother's Day

1
Mother's Day is a day to celebrate our moms. They do many things to help us. In the morning, they help us get up and get ready to go to school. They help us do our homework, and they make yummy dinners for us. On Mother's Day I like to do things for my mom.

Today is Mother's Day. This is our mom. We love her very much. Every Mother's Day we get up early and make a big breakfast for her. She likes to eat breakfast in bed as a special treat.

2
When we get home from school, we make a snack for her. Mom likes cookies and milk. Then we all take a walk before dinner.

Today we're eating a delicious dinner. It's Mom's favorite. After dinner Mom watches TV. I'm washing the dishes, and my brother is taking out the trash. My mom has a great day on Mother's Day. And we do, too!



2 Check (✓) the things they do for Mother's Day.

| | | | |
|---|---|---|---|
| ✓ | make breakfast | ✓ | take out the trash |
| ✓ | make a snack | ✓ | eat dinner |
| | ride a bike | ✓ | wash the dishes |

Happy Writer Page 54

30 31

# Skills Book Word Work

**Lesson Objectives:** Recognize spelling patterns. Identify letter-sound relationships. Read clues to identify words.
**Materials:** park activity and chore flashcards from Unit 5

## Start the Class

10 min

Mime different park activities and chores for students to guess aloud as a class. If time allows, have different students lead the activity.

### ① Unscramble. Then check (✓).

10 min

Have a volunteer read the example. Tell students to unscramble the word and check the picture that matches the sentence. Have students complete the rest of the activity and then check the answers as a class.

### ② Use the letters to complete the words.

10 min

Explain to the class that they will use the letters on the cat's bowl to fill in the blanks for each phrase. Have students chorally pronounce the sounds on the bowl. Have a volunteer read the example. Tell students to work in pairs to complete the activity. Have volunteers write their answers on the board. Then have the class chorally say the words.

### ③ Answer Ricky's Riddle!

10 min

Write six lines on the board. Have a volunteer read the first sentence and write the first letter on the board. Then have volunteers read the clues and complete the word on the board.

## Finish the Class

10 min

Display park activity and chore flashcards from Unit 5 on the board. Organize the class into teams. Say a sentence about a park activity or chore and have a student from each team touch the corresponding flashcard on the board.

---

## Word Work

**1 Unscramble. Then check (✓).**

1. She's riding a skateboard.

r s d t e b k a a o

2. They're playing ball.

l l b a

3. He's washing the dishes.

s h s d e i

4. He's taking out the trash.

r s t h a

**2 Use the letters to complete the words.**

1. f e e d the pets
2. m a k e a snack
3. t a k e a walk
4. take out the tra s h
5. wa s h the dishes
6. ride a b i k e
7. r i d e a skateboard
8. sw e e p the floor

**3 Answer Ricky's Riddle!**

My first letter is in **ride** and in **cold**.
My second letter is in **sit** but not in **set**.
My fourth letter is in **she** but not in **see**.
You wash me in the kitchen.
What am I?
I'm d i s h e s
1 2 3 4 5 6

**Lesson Objective:** Ask and answer questions about a picture.
**Materials:** clothes flashcards from Unit 6

## Start the Class

10 min

Display the clothes flashcards from Unit 6 on the board: *T-shirt, pants, cap, shorts, jeans, swimsuit, sandals,* and *sneakers.* Point to the different clothes and have students chorally say them aloud.

## ① Look at the picture. Find and write.

15 min

Point to the different children on **Page 35** and ask *What's he/she wearing?* Have the class answer chorally: *He's/She's wearing (a T-shirt, shorts, and sandals).* Point to each clothing item for students to say aloud.

Have a volunteer read the directions on **Page 34**, and tell students that they will write what each model is wearing under his or her picture. Remind students to look at the picture on **Page 35** to see what each model is wearing. Tell students to work individually and then have them compare their answers with a partner. Check answers as a class.

## ② Point, ask, and answer.

15 min

Have two volunteers read the dialogue. Have a student stand up. Ask *What's he/she wearing?* Then have a volunteer answer. Continue with several more students.

Tell students they will work in pairs to take turns pointing to the models on **Page 35** and asking and answering questions about the models' clothes.

## Finish the Class

10 min

Say the clothes words and have the class spell them out chorally. Then play the Shark Game with a few clothes words; have volunteers from the class guess the letters.

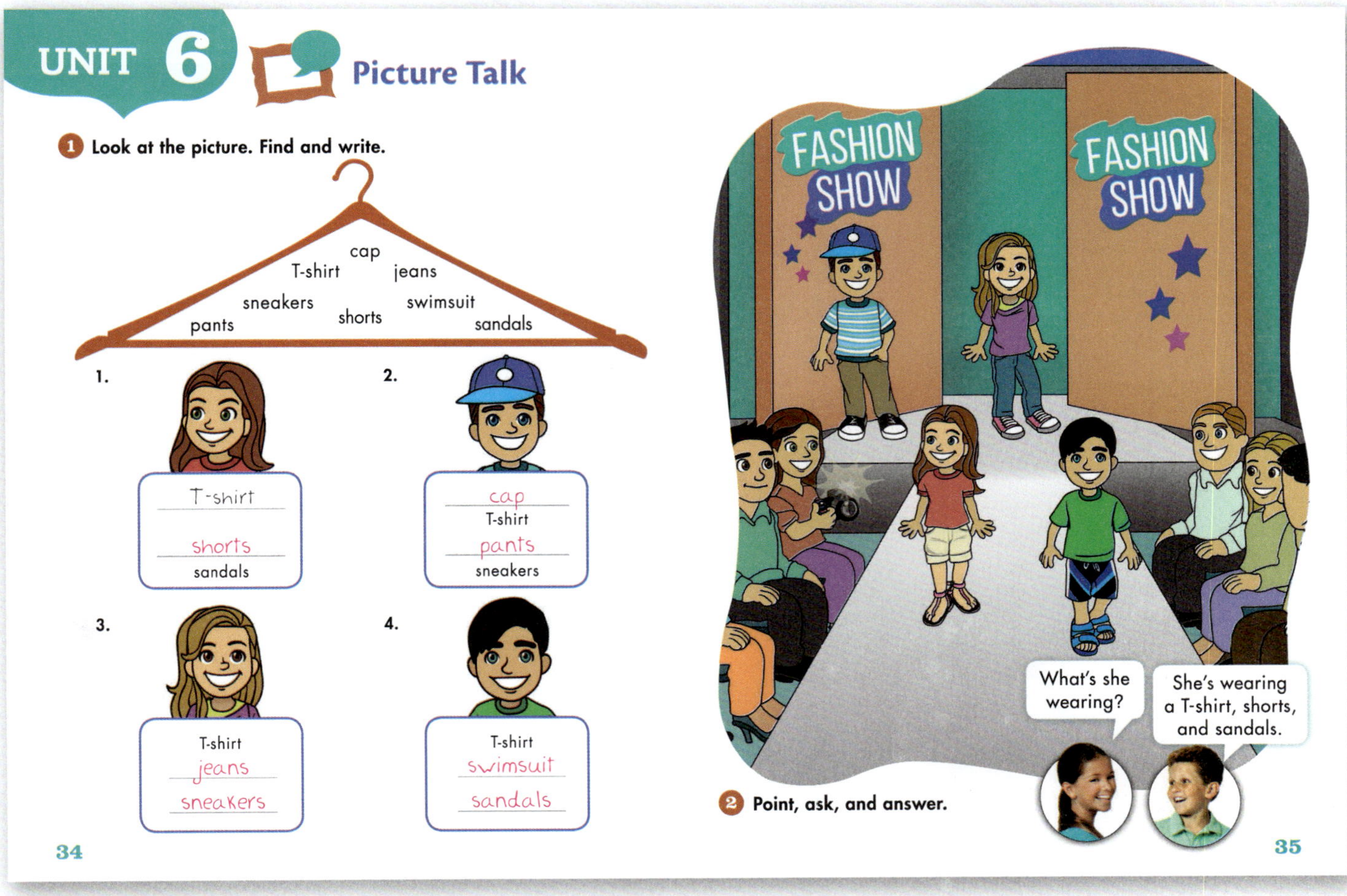

UNIT 6 Picture Talk

① Look at the picture. Find and write.

cap
T-shirt
jeans
sneakers
swimsuit
pants
shorts
sandals

1. T-shirt / shorts / sandals

2. cap / T-shirt / pants / sneakers

3. T-shirt / jeans / sneakers

4. T-shirt / swimsuit / sandals



② Point, ask, and answer.

34

35

# Skills Book Happy Reader

**Lesson Objectives:** Recall details in a nonfiction text. Summarize the text.
**Materials:** Audio **Track 57**

## Start the Class

10 min

Have students look at the photos on **Pages 36 and 37**. Ask *Is this nonfiction or fiction?* Elicit *nonfiction*.

Ask students questions about the scene to review vocabulary and grammar: *Where is the boy? What's he doing? Is it winter or summer? What's the weather like? What animals do you see?*

## 1 57 Read and listen.

10 min

Have a volunteer read the title of the text. Remind the class to read along as they listen. Play **Track 57**.

## 2 Check (✓) the things that are in the sandcastles.

10 min

Tell students to check the things that are in the sandcastles. Have them compare their answers with a partner and identify the items they did *not* check.

## Page 54 Happy Writer

10 min

Tell students to look at the photos and complete the sentences about sandcastle contests. Have volunteers share their sentences with the class.

## Finish the Class

10 min

Write a base-form verb in each Tic-Tac-Toe square in a grid on the board. In teams, have students take turns spelling the *-ing* forms of the verbs. The team wins the square if they correctly spell the verb.

Page 54 beach; hot; sunny; (Students' own answers)

Happy Reader

1 57 Read and listen.

Sandcastles

1
Every summer there are sandcastle contests at the beach in my town. It's always very hot and sunny. This year people are building very big sandcastles. Sandcastles aren't just for kids. Adults like to build things with sand, too. It's a great day for the whole family!

Artists use sand and water to make the sandcastles. They walk to the ocean to get water. Then they use the water to make the sand hard. Artists use tools to draw in the sand. They are very careful.

2
Look at the dragon. Is he sleeping? Yes, he is.

There is also a sandcastle with an elephant, and one with a shark. It takes a long time to build these beautiful sandcastles.

2 Check (✓) the things that are in the sandcastles.

☐ crocodile ☑ elephant ☐ boat ☑ shark

36

Happy Writer Page 54

37

## Skills Book Word Work

**Lesson Objectives:** Read clues to identify words. Recognize spelling patterns. Categorize words.
**Materials:** card stock

### Start the Class
5 min

Have students play Memory with a set of cards with matching pictures and words for unit vocabulary.

### ① Read the clues. Then choose and write.
10 min

Have a volunteer read the clue for Item 1. Have the class identify each item. Then elicit the answer: *T-shirt*. Tell students to complete the activity in pairs.

### ② Answer Ricky's Riddle!
10 min

Write five lines on the board. Have a volunteer read the first sentence and write the second letter on the board: *a*. Then have volunteers read the clues and complete the word on the board.

### ③ Complete.
5 min

Tell students that they will write letters in the boxes to complete phrases about beach activities.

### ④ Color the word that's different. Then match.
10 min

Explain that one word in each pie chart is different from the other two words. Have students read the sentences on the right. Then have students identify each word that's different and match it to the correct reason.

### Finish the Class
10 min

Tell the class that they will write a riddle with a partner about another word on **Page 39**. Then have pairs exchange their riddles to solve.

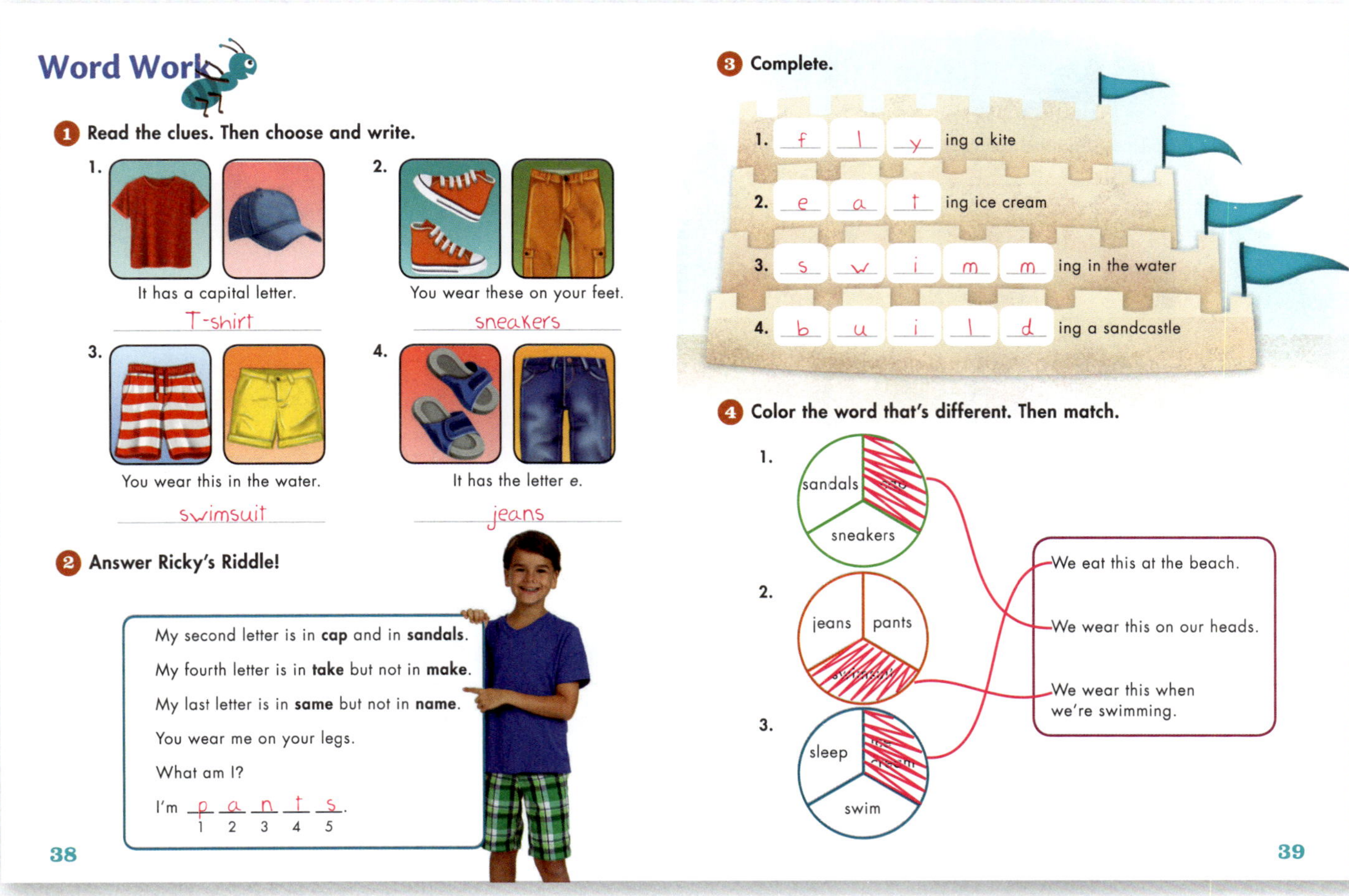
Word Work

1 Read the clues. Then choose and write.

1. It has a capital letter. T-shirt
2. You wear these on your feet. sneakers
3. You wear this in the water. swimsuit
4. It has the letter *e*. jeans

2 Answer Ricky's Riddle!

My second letter is in **cap** and in **sandals**.
My fourth letter is in **take** but not in **make**.
My last letter is in **same** but not in **name**.
You wear me on your legs.
What am I?
I'm p a n t s.
1 2 3 4 5

38

3 Complete.

1. f l y ing a kite
2. e a t ing ice cream
3. s w i m m ing in the water
4. b u i l d ing a sandcastle

4 Color the word that's different. Then match.



39

# Skills Book
# Picture Talk

**Lesson Objective:** Ask and answer questions about a picture.
**Materials:** party food flashcards from Unit 7

## Start the Class (10 min)

Draw a Tic-Tac-Toe grid on the board and put a party food flashcard from Unit 7 face down in each square. Divide the class into two teams: X and O. Explain to students that they will take turns turning over one of the flashcards. If their team correctly spells the party food word pictured, they will remove the flashcard and draw their symbol in the square. The first team to get three squares in a row (vertically, horizontally, or diagonally) wins.

### ① Look at the picture. Find and count. Then complete. (15 min)

Have students look at the picture on **Page 41** and identify where the children are. Elicit what each child is eating and/or drinking.

Have a volunteer read the directions on **Page 40**. Tell students that they will count each party food in the picture on **Page 41** and write the numbers in the squares on **Page 40**. Then they will complete the sentences below with the party food words. Tell students to work individually and then compare their answers with a partner. Have volunteers share their answers with the class.

### ② Ask and answer. (15 min)

Have volunteers read the dialogue on **Page 41**. Tell students they will take turns asking and answering questions about the food/drinks the children in the picture are eating/drinking. Have volunteer pairs share their dialogues with the class.

## Finish the Class (10 min)

Tell students to draw what you say: *The girl is at a party. She's eating cake. The boy is at a party. He's eating popcorn.* Have them compare their pictures with a partner.

---

UNIT 7 Picture Talk

**1** Look at the picture. Find and count. Then complete.

| | | |
|---|---|---|
| 1 soda | 2 popcorn | 3 candy |
| 3 juice | 1 chips | 2 lemonade |

1. Lucy is eating chips.
2. Sam is drinking soda.
3. Sue and Sam are eating popcorn.
4. Jim and Wendy are drinking lemonade.
5. Sarah, Ann, and Bill are eating candy.
6. Lucy, Sue, and Ann are drinking juice.

**2** Ask and answer.

# Skills Book Happy Reader

**Lesson Objectives:** Identify the sequence of events in a fiction text. Draw conclusions.
**Materials:** Audio **Track 58**, strips of paper

## Start the Class

10 min

Have students stand in a circle. Say a topic such as *party foods*. The first student will say a party food, and each student will say another word to make a chain. Change the topic after five or six words.

## 1 58 Read and listen.

10 min

Play **Track 58**. Ask students comprehension questions: *Is Danny happy or sad at the beginning of the story? What do Kyle and Kevin have?*

## 2 Number the sentences in order.

10 min

Explain to students that they will number the sentences in the order of the story. Play **Track 58** for students to check their answers.

## Page 55 Happy Writer

10 min

Tell students to think about what happens next in the story after Danny returns the kite. Explain that each student will draw a picture of his or her idea and write a sentence about it. Walk around the class and provide help as needed. Have volunteers share their ideas with the class.

## Finish the Class

10 min

Write sentences from the text on strips of paper. Cut them up so that each student gets one word or phrase, such as *I / want to / play / with / my old friends*. Tell students to find the rest of their sentences. Have the groups read their sentences aloud.

Page 55 (Students' own answers)

### Happy Reader

1 58 Read and listen.

## New Friends

1

Danny's family has a house in a new town. Danny's new house is great, but Danny misses his friends.

**Danny:** I want to go home. I want to play with my old friends.

**Dad:** It's OK, Danny. There are lots of new friends at your new school. Let's see your new bedroom! It's really big!

Danny is in his bedroom. He sees a birthday party outside in the park.

**Danny:** Are they eating ice cream, Dad?

**Dad:** Yes. They're dancing and singing, too. Let's go say hello!

**Danny:** No, I don't want to.

2

Two boys are flying a kite in the park. The kite is up high. It's flying in Danny's window!

**Danny:** Uh-oh! Now the boys don't have the kite.

**Dad:** They're Kyle and Kevin! They live next door. Run to the park and give the kite back!

3

**Kyle:** Thank you! What's your name?

**Danny:** I'm Danny!

**Kevin:** Come play with us, Danny!

2 Number the sentences in order.

4 Come play with us, Danny!

1 I want to play with my old friends.

2 They're dancing and singing, too.

3 Now the boys don't have the kite.

Happy Writer Page 55

# Skills Book Word Work

**Lesson Objectives:** Recognize spelling patterns. Identify multi-syllable words. Read clues to identify words.

## Start the Class

5 min

Have students stand in a circle. Explain that they will spell words, letter by letter. Say a word from the unit. The first student says the first letter, the next says the second letter, and so on until the word is spelled out completely. Repeat with other words.

### ① Unscramble the two party foods. Then number.

15 min

Have students look at the example. Then ask students to unscramble two party food words for each item number and number the corresponding pair of pictures below. Have volunteers write the unscrambled pairs of words on the board.

### ② Match.

10 min

Explain to students that each word is divided into two or three syllables. They will match the syllables to complete the words. Do Item 1 as a class. Then have students complete the activity individually. Have students write their answers on the board.

### ③ Answer Ricky's Riddle!

10 min

Write ten lines on the board. Have a volunteer read the first sentence and write the first letter on the board. Then have volunteers read the clues and complete the word on the board.

## Finish the Class

10 min

Tell the class that they will write a riddle with a partner about another word on **Page 45**. Then have pairs exchange their riddles to solve.

## Word Work

**1 Unscramble the two party foods. Then number.**

1. elcmedeoakna — a. cake b. lemonade
2. dcuayincje — a. candy b. juice
3. poichoprnpcs — a. popcorn b. chips
4. esasnsddwoiach — a. soda b. sandwiches

44

**2 Match.**

1. so — dy
2. sand — wich — es
3. lem — on — ade
4. can — da

**3 Answer Ricky's Riddle!**

My first letter is in **T-shirt** but not in **shorts**.
My third letter is in **vet** but not in **pet**.
My eighth letter is in **bike** but not in **bake**.
You send me to friends for a party.
What am I?
I'm an i n v i t a t i o n.
1 2 3 4 5 6 7 8 9 10

45

**Lesson Objective:** Talk about the differences between two pictures.

## Start the Class

10 min

Mime the abilities (*whistle, jump, paint,* etc.) and have the class say them chorally. If time allows, have different students lead the activity.

### ① Look at the pictures. Find, write, and check (✓) or cross (✗).

15 min

Have a volunteer read the directions on **Page 46**. Explain to students that they will look for each child on **Page 47** and identify the activity he or she is doing. They will write the activity in the first column on **Page 46**. They will put a check in the box for the picture in which the child *can* do the activity, and they will put a cross in the box for the picture in which the child *can't* do the activity. Tell students to work individually. Then have volunteers share their answers with the class.

### ② Say what's different.

15 min

Tell students they will each work with a partner and take turns talking about the activities the children in the two pictures can or can't do. Walk around the classroom and provide help as needed.

## Finish the Class

10 min

Write several activities on the board; include one that few students can do and one that most students can do. Have students stand up. Say one of the activities aloud and tell students to sit down if they can't do it. Continue by listing more and more activities until only one student remains standing.

UNIT 8 Picture Talk

❶ Look at the pictures. Find, write, and check (✓) or (✗).

| Name | Activity | Picture A | Picture B |
|---|---|---|---|
| 1. Pat | play the drums | ✓ | ✗ |
| 2. Sally | whistle | ✗ | ✓ |
| 3. Bill | paint | ✗ | ✓ |
| 4. May | jump rope | ✓ | ✗ |

❷ Say what's different.

46 47

# Skills Book
# Happy Reader

**Lesson Objectives:** Compare and contrast information in a nonfiction text. Write a descriptive text.
**Materials:** Audio **Track 59**

## Start the Class
5 min

Say animal names and have students say what the animals can and can't do.

### 1 59 Read and listen.
10 min

Have students look at the photos on **Pages 48 and 49**. Have a volunteer read the title. Ask *Can you name the animals in the pictures?*

Remind the class to read along as they listen to the text. Play **Track 59**. Tell students to read the text again and underline each animal's abilities. Have volunteers share their ideas with the class.

### 2 Complete.
15 min

Explain to students that they will complete the chart showing the abilities animals have. Remind students to look at the text they underlined to help them complete the activity. Then check answers as a class.

### Page 55 Happy Writer
10 min

Explain to the class that they will choose one of the animals pictured and complete the sentence about it. Then they will write sentences about what it can and can't do. Have volunteers share their writing with the class.

## Finish the Class
10 min

Choose an animal from the text and have the class ask questions to guess what it is: *Can it swim? Can it fly? Is it fast? Is it slow? Is it big? Is it small?* If time allows, have different students lead the activity with other animals.

Page 55 (Students' own answers)

Happy Reader

1 59 Read and listen.

Amazing Animals

1 Bats aren't birds, but they have wings and they can fly. They sleep upside down. They don't sleep at night. They wake up at night and eat. They use their ears to find food.

2 Elephants are very big animals, and they live in big families. Elephants can run very fast, and they can swim, too! They can live to be seventy years old.

3 Sloths like trees. They can climb trees, but they are very slow. Sloths can swim, too. They have big arms. Sloths can sleep for 20 hours in one day!

4 Crocodiles have big mouths with many teeth. They open their mouths when they're hot. Then they can be cool. Can crocodiles run? Yes, they can. They can swim, too. They swim with their tails. Some crocodiles can swim under the water for two hours!

Animals are amazing!

2 Complete.

| Ability | Animals |
|---|---|
| swim | elephants, sloths, and crocodiles |
| fly | bats |
| run | elephants and crocodiles |
| climb trees | sloths |

Happy Writer Page 55

48 49

Skills Book Word Work

**Lesson Objectives:** Categorize words. Identify letter-sound relationships. Read clues to identify words.

## Start the Class

10 min

Have students write as many vocabulary words from the level as they can and check them with a partner.

### ① Color the word that's different. Then match.

10 min

Explain that one word in each pie chart is different from the other two words. Have students read the sentences on the right. Then have students identify each word that's different and match it to the correct reason.

### ② Answer Ricky's Riddle!

10 min

Write six lines on the board. Have a volunteer read the first sentence and write the first letter on the board. Then have volunteers read the clues and complete the word on the board.

### ③ Complete. Then number.

10 min

Tell students that each word matches an activity a child on the sailboat is doing. Have students complete each word and number the corresponding child. Have volunteers write the words on the board. Then point to the children on the sailboat and have the class chorally say the numbers they wrote.

### ④ Read the clues. Then choose and write.

Have a volunteer read the clue for Item 1. Ask the class which activity has two words—*speak English* or *play the drums*. Elicit *speak English*. Then have students complete the activity in pairs.

## Finish the Class

10 min

Tell the class that they will write a riddle with a partner about another word on **Page 51**. Then have two pairs take turns solving each other's riddles.

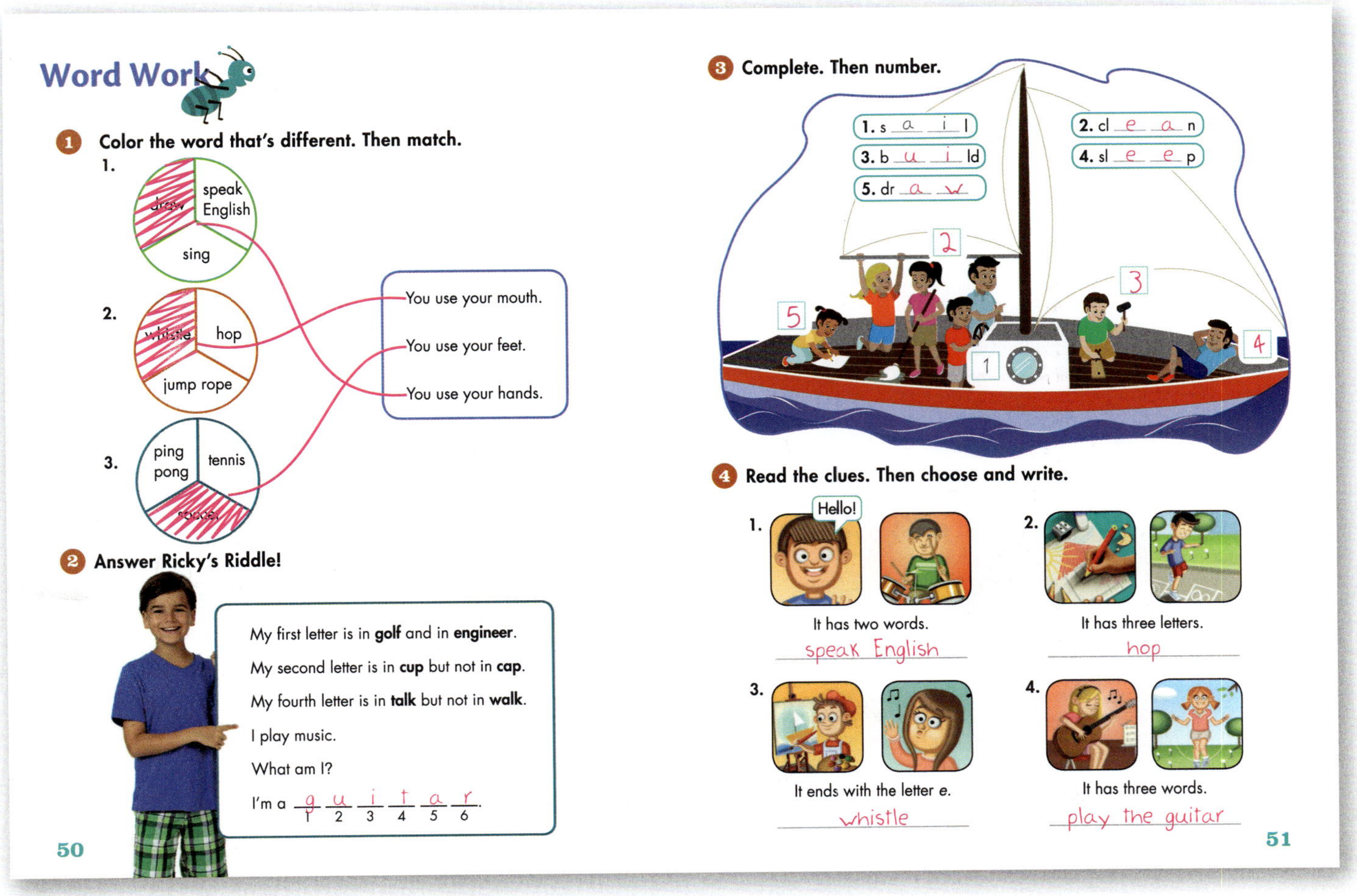
Word Work

1 Color the word that's different. Then match.

1. drew / speak English / sing
2. whistle / hop / jump rope
3. ping pong / tennis / soccer

You use your mouth.
You use your feet.
You use your hands.

2 Answer Ricky's Riddle!

My first letter is in **golf** and in **engineer**.
My second letter is in **cup** but not in **cap**.
My fourth letter is in **talk** but not in **walk**.
I play music.
What am I?
I'm a g u i t a r
1 2 3 4 5 6

50

3 Complete. Then number.

1. s a i l
2. cl e a n
3. b u i ld
4. sl e e p
5. dr a w

4 Read the clues. Then choose and write.

1. Hello!
It has two words.
speak English

2. It has three letters.
hop

3. It ends with the letter *e*.
whistle

4. It has three words.
play the guitar

51

Macmillan Education
4 Crinan Street
London N1 9XW
A division of Macmillan Publishers Limited

Companies and representatives throughout the world

ISBN 978-85-511-0156-8



First published 2015



**Teacher's Edition Credits:**
Original design by Nancy Ortega Cruz
Page make-up by Erika González Guzmán
Cover design by Roberto Martínez
Cover illustration by Scott Burroughs
Cover photograph by © Alamy/Big Cheese Photo LLC
Picture research by Penelope Bowden, Proudfoot Pictures and Tessa Hammond (cover photo)

The author and publishers would like to thank the following for permission to reproduce their photographs: Alamy/Big Cheese Photo LLC (p. iii), Alberto Padrón (pp. T 35, T 89), Juan Jose Palacio (pp. T 53, T 107), Ilse Valle-Jones (pp. T 17, T 71, T 125, T 143)

Commissioned photographs by George Contorakes, pp. ii, iii, v, T 16, T 34, T 52, T 70, T 88, T 106, T 124, T 142

**Student Book Credits:**
Text, design and illustration © Macmillan Publishers Limited 2015
Written by Patricia Acosta and Angela Padrón
The authors have asserted their rights to be identified as the authors of this work in accordance with the Copyright, Designs and Patents Act 1988.

Designed by Pronk Media Inc.
Student Book pages illustrated by: Russ Daff (stories: pp. 20, 36, 44–45, 52–53, 68–69); Scott Burroughs (comic strips: pp. 6–7, 10–11, 18–19, 26–27, 34–35, 42–43, 50–51, 58–59, 66–67); Valentina Mendicino (vocabulary art: pp. 10, 16, 23, 24–25, 26, 32, 34, 39, 40, 42, 48, 50, 55, 56, 58, 64, 66, 71); Pronk Media Inc. (pp. 8–9, 13, 14, 17, 18, 22, 25, 30, 31, 33, 38–39, 46, 47, 54, 58, 62–63, 65, 70, 72)
The Language Lodge pages illustrated by: Valentina Mendicino (pp. 2–3, 4, 11, 12–13, 15, 16–17, 18–19, 21, 23, 25, 26, 28, 31); Pronk Media Inc. (pp. 2, 6, 9, 10, 14, 20, 22, 24, 27)
Cover design and illustration by Roberto Martínez
Cover photograph by George Contorakes
Picture research by Penelope Bowden, Proudfoot Pictures

The authors and publishers would like to thank the following for permission to reproduce their photographs: **Alamy**/BSIP Sa p. 28(br), Alamy/Go Go Images corporation p. 33(tr), Alamy/David J. Green – Lifestyle p. 9(tr), Alamy/Image Source p. 64(t), Alamy/Juice Images p. 65, Alamy/MBI p. 40(br), Alamy/STOCKCHILDREN p. 40(tl), Alamy/Tetra Images p. 28(tl); **Bananastock** p. 9(br); **Corbis**/Monalyn Gracia p. 40(tr); **Getty Images**/Alistair Berg p. 33(tl), Getty Images/George Doyle p. 64(b), Getty Images/Fuse p. 8(r), Getty Images/Tom Grill p. 28(tr), Getty Images/Jack Hollingsworth p. 12(l), Getty Images/Lucy Lambriex p. 9(bl), Getty Images/Purestock p. 29, Getty Images/Gandee Vasan pp. 12(r), 13; **Glow Images**/Corbis p. 60(tl), Glow Images/Jamie Grill p. 60(tr); **Stockbyte** p. 33(br,bl); **Superstock**/Blend Images p. 40(bl), Superstock/Blue Jean Images p. 17(t), Superstock/Antoine Juliette/Oredia Eurl p. 28(bl), Superstock/Mint Images p. 60(br), Superstock/Stockbroker p. 12(t); **Thinkstock**/Goodshoot/Jupiterimages p. 60(bl), Thinkstock/iStock/Katarzyna Bialasiewicz p. 61(t), Thinkstock/iStock/Jani Bryson pp. 9(tl), 16, Thinkstock/iStock/julief514 p. 8(l), Thinkstock/iStock/tetmc p. 17(b)

Commissioned photographs by George Contorakes, pp. 5, 14, 22, 24, 30, 38, 46, 48–49, 54, 56–57, 62, 70

The authors and publishers wish to thank the following for their help with the photo shoot: Karen Greer Models, LLC; Anaiya; Angela; Evan; and Sam

Props for commissioned photographs by Luise Johnson-Dailey, Bluwave Creative

**Skills Book Credits:**
Text, design and illustration © Macmillan Publishers Limited 2015
Written by Katie Foufouti
The author has asserted her right to be identified as the author of this work in accordance with the Copyright, Designs and Patents Act 1988.

Original design by Pronk Media Inc.
Page make-up by Victory Productions Inc.
Illustrated by Pronk Media Inc. (icons throughout);
Victory Productions Inc. (pp. 4–14, 16–31, 33–37, 39–43, 45–50, 51(t), 52–55)
Cover design and illustration by Roberto Martínez
Picture research by Penelope Bowden, Proudfoot Pictures

The author and publishers would like to thank the following for permission to reproduce their photographs: **Alamy**/Andrew Buckin pp. 37(tr), 54(m), Alamy/Esa Hiltula pp. 37(tl), 54(b), Alamy/Jamie Roach p. 37(bl); **Comstock Images** p. 31(tl); **Corbis**/Tim Hall/cultura p. 25(tl), Corbis/Mika p. 31(br), Corbis/Onoky p. 24(b); **FLPA**/THOMAS HAUPT/Imagebroker pp. 49(tl), 55(tr), FLPA/Jelger Herder, Buiten-beeld/Minden Pictures pp. 49(cr), 55(br); **Getty Images**/Ulf Amundsen pp. 48, 49(background), Getty Images/Robert Daly/OJO Images p. 25(tr), Getty Images/Odilon Dimier pp. 36, 37(bottom background), Getty Images/itsabreeze photography p. 36(tc), Getty Images/Richard Newstead/Moment pp. 36, 37(top background), Getty Images/John Rensten p. 30(bl); **iStockphoto** p. 31(tr); **Thinkstock**/belchonock pp. 24, 25(background), Thinkstock/cowboy5437 pp. 48(tr), 55(tl), Thinkstock/Creatas Images p. 25(ml), Thinkstock/Dean Pictures/Fuse pp. 31(ml), 54(t), Thinkstock/Liang Zhang p. 30(br), Thinkstock/Zokru pp. 48(bl), 55(bl)

Commissioned photographs by George Contorakes, pp. 5, 9, 11, 14, 17, 21, 23, 27, 29, 33, 35, 38, 41, 45, 47, 50

The author and publishers wish to thank the following for their help with the photo shoot: Karen Greer Models, LLC; World of Kids Inc.; Anaiya; Angela; Charlie; Evan; and Sam



Printed and bound in Thailand

2019 2018 2017 2016 2015
10 9 8 7 6 5 4 3 2